The Causes of
The War of 1812

The Causes of
The War of 1812

by

Reginald Horsman

OCTAGON BOOKS

A DIVISION OF FARRAR, STRAUS AND GIROUX

New York   1979

OCTAGON BOOKS
A DIVISION OF FARRAR, STRAUS & GIROUX, INC.
19 Union Square West
New York, N.Y. 10003

Library of Congress Cataloging in Publication Data

Horsman, Reginald.
    The causes of the War of 1812.

    Bibliography: p.
    1. U.S.—History—War of 1812—Causes. I. Title.
[E357.H72   1972]   973.5′21   75-120632
ISBN 0-374-93960-8

Manufactured by Braun-Brumfield, Inc.
Ann Arbor, Michigan
Printed in the United States of America

To my

MOTHER and FATHER

Acknowledgments

Professor John D. Barnhart of Indiana University has given me constant encouragement in the preparation of this book, and I have gained immeasurably from his careful scholarship. I have also received invaluable help and advice from Professor John A. Hawgood of the University of Birmingham, England. Two other Indiana University professors—Robert H. Ferrell and Leo F. Solt—have given me most perceptive criticism, and I am very grateful to them.

I should also like to thank the many librarians who have helped me in my research, and the editors of the *Mississippi Valley Historical Review* and the *Indiana Magazine of History* for giving me permission to use material from my articles which originally appeared in those journals.

My wife and son have made the task of research and writing an exceedingly pleasant one.

University of Wisconsin—Milwaukee
April, 1961   REGINALD HORSMAN

Contents

The Causes of
The War of 1812

I *Background of Conflict*

REGENCY ENGLAND had a surfeit of foreign news in the summer of 1812. Her mighty adversary, Napoleon, had decided to humble the Tzar, and in the warmth of late June the French host began its triumphal progress into Russia. As the summer passed, England learned of the Corsican's relentless thrust into the heart of that vast country. By September Napoleon commanded Moscow, and seemingly Russia had followed Austria and Prussia into vassalage. It was not until November that England learned that the French invader had been forced to abandon the wasted Russian capital, and was fleeing westward in the snow and ice of a Russian winter. While Napoleon was seeking world dominion in the east, England had essayed modest gains in the Peninsula. The victory at Salamanca in July had allowed Wellington to take Madrid in August, and had brought at least some compensation for the disastrous news from the east. Yet Wellington's small army could not hold its hard-won gains, and by October he was forced to yield the Spanish capital and retreat towards Portugal.

It was at the end of July, as Napoleon advanced in Russia and Wellington in the Peninsula, that the news reached England of the American declaration of war on June 18. Though it came into an England satiated by European events, it carried a surprising impact. For more than a year, while England had been wracked by economic distress, a growing body of opinion had called for friendship with America in the hope of producing a renewal of commercial intercourse and an easing of the depression. One positive result of this agitation had been the removal in June of the British Orders in Council restricting American trade, and England had confidently expected a renewal of friendly commercial intercourse with the United States as a result of this measure. It was thus with a feeling of profound shock that England received the news that her concessions had been too late, and that the United States was at war. At a time when the fate of Europe hung in the balance, England was obliged to face a new adversary. The editor of the provincial Tory *Leicester Journal* bubbled with exasperation as he printed President James Madison's war message and commented that it was "the most laboured, peevish, canting, petulant, querulous, and weak effusion, that ever issued from a man assuming the character of a statesman and the President, or elective quadrennial King, of a professedly Republican country."[1]

England was indeed shocked in the summer of 1812 that the United States could have thrown her forces on the side of Napoleonic tyranny, for throughout the spring and early summer it had been prophesied that there would be no war.[2] Actually what is really surprising is not that America declared war on England in 1812, but that she had not done so several years earlier. In many ways it is easier to show why America should have gone to war in 1807 or 1809 rather than in 1812. In 1812 America had been independent of England for less than thirty years. Relations between a nation and its ex-colonists are never a simple matter, and after the achievement of American independence in 1783 there was no love lost between England and the United States. In the years preceding the War of 1812, when America had ample reason for declaring war on both France and England, but discretion made it necessary to choose only one adversary, the traditions of the Revolution cannot be ignored as a factor influencing the American decision. It was no accident that the young War Hawks of 1811 and 1812 spoke so often of following the example of their fathers, and urged the young Americans of 1812 to cherish the independence that had been bequeathed to them. The fact that France was an old ally, and England the old adversary, was of no small importance in influencing American policy in the years before 1812. Strong anti-French feeling arose as a result of the obvious threat of Napoleon to American interests, but it was hardly possible for France to injure America sufficiently to persuade the majority of Americans that France and not England was the main enemy. "I scarcely know of an injury that France could do us, short of an actual invasion of our Territory," wrote Henry Clay in August, 1810, "that would induce me to go to War with her, whilst the injuries we have received from Great Britain remain unredressed."[3] England was distrusted in America after 1783—it was to take far longer than one generation for the two nations to discover that they had so much in common. Apart from a pro-British Federalist minority, the traditions of the War of Independence were enough to embitter American feeling against England far into the nineteenth century, and the feeling did not entirely disappear in the twentieth.

In England, too, the traditions of the Revolution were of importance. The prevailing sentiment was one of dislike of the ex-colonists, though, as in America, there were certain minority groups that viewed the country across the Atlantic with friendliness. The English manufacturing classes who had a lucrative export trade to the United States were the counterpart of the commercial New Englanders who had their financial center in London. It was in the interest of both groups to cultivate a policy of amity between the two countries. Another group in England that looked with favor upon the experiment on the other side of the Atlantic was the doctrinaire Whigs originally centered around Charles James Fox, but the most prominent sentiment was one of animosity. There was a natural resentment at a new country which had been formed at the expense of Great Britain, and every opportunity was taken to cast scorn upon the American way of life. This dislike extended into all classes of English life, and prompted the pro-American *Monthly Review* in March, 1808, to agree with an anonymous pamphleteer that "hatred of America seems a prevailing sentiment in this country."[4] In England, as in America, dislike and distrust were common sentiments. It was too much to expect within thirty years of the War of Independence—thirty years filled with problems in Anglo-American relations—that a sound friendship could be established between the two countries. There was still too much unforgotten, and too many of the generation that had fought in the Revolution still alive, to expect a close understanding. As misunderstanding grew in the years before 1812, this latent resentment became more and more obvious.

The problems in Anglo-American relations after 1783 were, however, far more than a mere legacy of hostility—there were exceedingly acute practical difficulties. The fact that England retained colonies bordering the United States was in itself the source of some of the greatest problems in British-American relations. Canada on the north meant not only boundary difficulties, which were an irritant until well into the nineteenth century, but also a struggle for the fur trade south and west of the Great Lakes, and an acrimonious controversy concerning the suspected British backing of the Indians in the Northwest. In the years from 1783 to 1795 these difficulties were particularly acute. The British retention of the Northwest posts, and the encouragement given to Indian resistance, met with vigorous American protests. It was not until Wayne's defeat of the Indians at Fallen Timbers in August, 1794, and the Treaty of Greenville in the following year, that peace was attained in the Old Northwest, and feeling against the British allowed to diminish. From 1795 to 1807 comparative peace existed in the

Northwest. The British officials neglected the Indians, and the Indians themselves recuperated from their 1794 defeat, preparing for their next stand along the Indiana frontier. Though the Northwest was temporarily quiet, the potential British-American clash in the area was not removed. It was quite obvious that it was only a matter of time before the American pressure would force the Indians to renew hostilities. When this occurred, England's position and interests in the Northwest ensured that the Americans would trace a guilty connection between British agent and Indian warrior. In addition, the British officials would once again be obliged to meet the temptation of whether or not to give aid to the Indians. The peace that reigned on the Northwest frontier after 1795 was only a truce. The Indians had for the moment been defeated, and then assuaged by the granting of a definite boundary at Greenville, but once the American frontiersmen started to advance beyond that boundary further Indian resistance was inevitable, and a testing time could be expected in Anglo-American relations.[5]

It was not only on the frontier that problems were left in 1783. The American colonies had long been an integral part of the British colonial system, both as a market for British manufactures and as the chief source of provisions for the British West Indies. In 1783 England faced the problem of discovering and formulating a new commercial relationship with her ex-colonists. The year following American independence had brought a bitter dispute in England between the groups favoring a liberal policy and the granting of commercial privileges, and groups which favored the maintenance of the British Navigation System and the exclusion of the United States. Those favoring a liberal commercial policy, mainly a small group led by young William Pitt and Lord Shelburne, had endeavored to establish a free commercial intercourse between the two countries. They had, however, been frustrated by a considerable body of opinion in favor of a rigid maintenance of England's Navigation System.

Most influential in this group had been the shipping interest, which was struggling to preserve its maritime monopoly. The problem had been complicated by the West India interest, which generally gave the shipping interest its wholehearted support in defense of the Navigation System, but which on this occasion was anxious to permit American vessels to supply the West Indies. Though the West India group opposed the extreme views of Pitt and his supporters, they clearly realized that the British West Indies were dependent upon these American supplies.[6]

The victory of the protagonists of Britain's established system in 1783 and 1784 meant that in the years immediately following independence the United States was placed strictly on the footing of any other foreign nation. Instead of prospering within the same system, and achieving a sound basis of friendly commercial relations, the United States and England became commercial rivals in the years after 1783. An opportunity for friendly relations was lost, and by the beginning of the nineteenth century considerable resentment was felt in Great Britain at the commercial prosperity of the United States.

Yet in spite of all the problems left in 1783—and there were a host of minor difficulties which were to have an important cumulative influence when more bitter arguments separated the two countries—America managed to weather the decade after independence without engaging in actual conflict with Great Britain. In fact, it was not the achievement of independence but the outbreak of war between England and France in 1793 that ultimately was to lead to the War of 1812. Here special problems were created which lay at the core of the causes of that war. America as a great commercial neutral could not avoid difficulties concerning neutral rights and trade. In her desire to reap benefits from the European war, and to engage, with as much freedom as possible, in trade with both belligerents, she discovered that war could produce great profits for the enter-

prising neutral, but that there were also corresponding difficulties. The United States discovered in the years before 1812
that England had no desire to see France reap the benefits of an
extensive neutral trade. France, fully cognizant of the power of
the British navy, opened the trade between the French West
India colonies and France to United States shipping shortly after
the outbreak of war. England in turn invoked the so-called Rule
of 1756, by which a trade closed to a neutral in time of peace
could not be opened in time of war. America's answer was to
inaugurate the system of the "broken voyage," by which produce eventually destined for France was first taken to the United
States. Britain, though aggravating the Americans by extreme
commercial Orders in Council in the months immediately
following the outbreak of war, acquiesced in this American device for most of the first phase of her wars with France. The
West India interest, which was likely to lose most by this neutral
competition in European markets, was enjoying, until almost
the end of the century, a considerable prosperity, and was far
less concerned by competition than it was to be in the years
after 1800.[7]

Moreover, the warfare between England and France had not
assumed the markedly commercial character that was to come
at a later date. When the war developed into a struggle of
blockade and counter-blockade, American trade was to assume
a vital importance. The first phase of the British wars with
France, from 1793 to 1801, did not attain the bitterness and
desperation of the later Napoleonic phase from 1803 to 1815.
England could far more afford to act with reason in her policy
towards America in the 1790's than she could after the renewal
of the war in 1803. England's moderation in the 1790's meant
that America could take advantage of the new commercial
opportunities. American trade prospered on the profits of
neutrality. The war undoubtedly came as a great boon to the
commerce of the neutral United States, and the Americans took

full advantage of their opportunities. America's large and rapidly expanding marine, and her proximity to the enemy colonies in the West Indies, ensured her a most powerful commercial position in this time of war. Apart from her profits from engaging in trade between France and her colonies, America also found that the British West Indies were unable to do without American supplies in time of war. Temporary British acts enabled the Americans to become the regular suppliers of the British West Indies, and added to the prosperity of American commerce.[8]

There were many disadvantages as well as advantages to the American position as a neutral; eventually the former were far to outweigh the latter. America had to face a whole series of difficulties connected with the term "neutral rights." The American and British opinions on these questions were obviously radically different. America discovered that England was prepared to dispute her right to trade freely in time of war. She tried to maintain that "free ships make free goods," but Great Britain flouted this doctrine, which would have permitted French-owned goods to travel unmolested on American ships. There was also a constant dispute concerning the articles that constituted contraband. America desired to limit the list to those articles which would directly help the French war effort, and England wished to make it as broad as possible—in particular she argued that American provisions intended for France could legitimately be prevented from reaching their destination by the British. The question of what constituted a proper blockade also arose to plague Anglo-American relations. America maintained that the only legal blockade was that which stationed ships directly off the port or coast involved. England on the other hand issued "paper blockades," which covered large stretches of coast, and she felt free to capture ships that were far out at sea and presumed to be heading for a forbidden destination. The process of stopping and searching ships itself brought grave difficulties. Great Britain interpreted the right of visit and search as the right to search a ship rigorously from top to bottom, whereas the Americans would have liked to restrict the right to that of merely examining the ship's papers. The war at sea produced innumerable difficulties of this type.

Yet of all the maritime difficulties that arose to pester Anglo-American relations, none was so persistent as that of impressment. Conditions in the British navy at that time were such that many seamen had taken the opportunity to desert and find employment on American ships. England, who maintained the doctrine of inalienable allegiance, claimed the right to take British seamen from American merchant ships wherever they might be found on the high seas. Naturalization was not recognized by the British, and indeed the ease with which naturalization papers could be obtained in the United States gave the British captains ample reason for their distrust of these documents. The British exercise of the right of impressment produced constant difficulties in Anglo-American relations. There was always the problem that the English language as spoken in America and in England could, on occasions, be practically the same, and mistakes could and were frequently made. It is quite obvious that not all of these mistakes were accidental. Though the impressing of Americans was frowned upon by the British government, there was more than one British sea captain of this period prepared to turn a blind eye to regulations. The mortality rate at sea was high, and a British captain short of seamen to fight the French did not draw too fine a distinction between Briton and American. Any protest that ensued would probably take a year or more to reach him. At times American ships were left with hardly enough seamen to navigate back to port. No solution was ever found for the impressment controversy, and while England was at war it was a constant irritant in Anglo-American relations.[9]

The years immediately after the start of the European war in

1793 produced a crisis in the relations between England and America. British policy at sea combined with the difficulties on the Northwest frontier created a definite possibility of war in 1794. This possible conflict eventually was avoided by a combination of the timely compromise of Jay's Treaty, the relaxation of British maritime policy, and Wayne's victory over the Indians at Fallen Timbers. The signing of Jay's Treaty on November 19, 1794, inaugurated a decade of much improved Anglo-American relations. It would be a mistake, however, to suppose that potential difficulty between the two countries had been removed. The accommodation was made possible by the fact that England did not use her full maritime power against American commerce in the late 1790's. The improvement in relations was also aided by the negative factor of American difficulties with France at that time, which culminated in the quasi-war of 1798 to 1800. Once America and France settled their difficulties the likelihood of a British-American clash increased immensely. The conditions necessary for an acute increase of difficulties between England and America had been created by the outbreak of war between England and France in 1793. If ever England decided to wage all-out war at sea, America, as a commercial nation desiring to reap the advantages of neutrality, would be obliged to face the problem of how to cope with British depredations upon her commerce. In 1794 and 1795 a crisis in Anglo-American relations was solved, but the continuation of good relations depended upon the willingness of Great Britain to wage limited maritime warfare.

If the Peace of Amiens between England and France, of which the preliminary articles were signed in 1801, could have lasted, there seems little reason to suppose that America would have gone to war with Great Britain in 1812. Certainly, while there were two years of peace in Europe, British-American relations were in a very satisfactory state.[10] The inevitable renewal of American difficulties with the Indians in the Northwest would probably have once again produced acrimony in Anglo-American relations, but it seems very unlikely that this alone would have produced warfare between the two countries. Though the period from 1783 to 1795 had been one of constant Indian problems for the Americans, and they had repeatedly connected Indian warfare with British activities on the frontier, it was only when the major complications of a European war and British actions at sea arose that British-American animosity reached a crisis. Moreover, chances of serious clashes in that area were considerably reduced when England, by Jay's Treaty, agreed to hand over the Northwest posts.

While there was peace in Europe, as there was between 1801 and 1803, England and America faced no great danger of going to war—in fact they could view each other with something approaching friendship. But when war was renewed, as it was in 1803, everything was once again thrown into the balance. If England was content to wage the more limited maritime war of the period before 1801, all could still be well, but if England felt compelled to wage total maritime war a deterioration in Anglo-American relations was inevitable. The question of whether there was to be peace or war between England and America was decided in the years between 1803 and 1812. It was decided by the manner in which England determined to wage her war against France.

2 *The Threat of Invasion*

THE RENEWAL of war between England and France in May, 1803, was of vital importance to the course of Anglo-American relations. For England the war immediately assumed an intensity far beyond that of the years before 1801. Napoleon was determined to defeat England on her own soil, and never again until the summer of 1940 was England so near invasion and defeat. Inevitably, British policy towards the United States in these years was governed to a great extent by European affairs. The all-important task was the defeat of Napoleon, and other considerations were sacrificed to this end. In the years from 1803 to 1812, as from 1914 to 1917 and from 1939 to 1941, the United States found herself involved inextricably in the affairs of Europe. Isolation, unless in the form of Jefferson's masochistic Embargo, proved as impossible in the early nineteenth as in the twentieth century. From 1793 to 1801 the United States had been treated comparatively gently by Great Britain—the only belligerent with the maritime power to harm her. Under the stress of the years after 1803, this moderation proved impossible.

From at least 1803 to 1805 England considered herself in imminent danger of invasion. This fear was apparent even before the actual renewal of the war, and by the summer and the fall of 1803 had become acute. In August there were discussions in

Parliament as to whether or not London should be fortified, and by December plans had been completed for the evacuation of the royal family from London in the event of invasion. So real was the fear that it was proposed that if the French landed in Essex the King would move to Chelmsford, and if in Kent he would travel to Dartford. Meanwhile the Queen was to travel north to Worcester, as were some thirty wagons of royal treasure that was to be deposited in Worcester Cathedral on the banks of the Severn.[1] Though such an emergency did not come to pass, England was kept in the same state of apprehension throughout 1804, and in July of that year James Maury, the American consul in Liverpool, informed Secretary of State James Madison that invasion "is pretty generally expected."[2] Even in June, 1805, over two years after the renewal of the war, the speaker of the House, Charles Abbot, was lamenting that Parliament was debating inconsequential matters at a time when "hourly invasion is threatened." The year 1805 was a glorious one for England's heritage, but it ended in tragedy rather than triumph. Nelson, inspired by England and by Emma, smashed the French fleet at Trafalgar in October, but the victory was irreparably marred by his death. In December England's ally, Russia, was overthrown by the French at Austerlitz, and once again there was fear at the Admiralty that Napoleon might renew his designs on Great Britain.[3]

Britain's policy towards America in these years after 1803 must be considered against this background of total war. When England declared war on France on May 18, 1803, the British government, fortunately for the United States, was in the hands of Henry Addington, who had been chosen by George III after Pitt's resignation in February, 1801, and served until April, 1804. The weak, vacillating Addington, known because of his father's profession as "the Doctor," was no war minister, and his administration depended upon the support of Pitt. From the very start of the war Addington and his friends underwent considerable attack. His Whig opponent, Thomas Creevey, only four days after the renewal of the war expressed his horror at "the wretched destiny of mankind in being placed in the hands of such pitiful, squirting politicians as this accursed Apothecary and his family and friends."[4] Not all of his critics were quite that scathing, but Addington received little praise. Indeed, this peaceful first minister did not possess the personality needed to lead the country in a time of imminent danger. He had neither the ability nor the energy to undertake a forceful prosecution of the war. Yet England's misfortune was America's advantage. America was to suffer greatest only when England decided on an energetic prosecution of the war at all costs. Addington's lack of forceful measures was a comparative boon to the United States.

In one respect, however, America could hope for no respite even from the weak Doctor and his friends. The renewal of war immediately produced a lack of seamen in England. From 1803 to 1805 England needed sailors as a last, and only, line of defense against the all-conquering armies of Napoleon. Even when the immediate fear of invasion passed there was no respite. After 1805 the war in Europe rapidly assumed the character of a commercial struggle. Napoleon controlled the land and England controlled the sea. More and more ships, and more and more sailors, were needed to patrol the huge Napoleonic coastline. It was increasingly maddening to the British that, at a time when their need for sailors was becoming greater and greater, the United States should continue to harbor large numbers of British deserters. Attracted by the higher pay and better living conditions in the American merchant service, British sailors frequently deserted to the United States. Even the British ship which took the new British minister, Anthony Merry, to the United States in the fall of 1803 lost fourteen men by desertion.[5] It was such occurrences that made the British Admiralty adamant in its refusal to renounce the right of impressing British

seamen found on board American merchantmen. If British seamen could desert with impunity, how could England man her
ships? Shortly before the renewal of the war in 1803 the First
Lord of the Admiralty, Earl St. Vincent, assured the Foreign
Secretary, Lord Hawkesbury, that England could not give up
this basic right. He stated that the most that could be conceded
was that "whenever British Seamen are found on board an
American ship at sea, care shall be taken that the officer who
demands them shall either leave or supply as many men as may
be absolutely necessary for the navigation of the ship to her
destined port."[6]

In the years after 1803 the problem of impressment became
acute, not because Britain was maintaining any new principle,
but because owing to her need for sailors she was searching for
her deserters with far more care and energy. In proportion as
England's difficulties in Europe increased and her need for seamen grew greater, problems regarding impressment became
more and more acute in Anglo-American relations. Before 1801
impressment had not been the same corroding force that it became after 1803. The reason for this was simply that England
in those earlier years, particularly after 1797, had not felt the
same desperate need for seamen that she was to experience in the
dark days following the renewal of the war in 1803. The conclusion of a definite peace in 1802 had brought rapid disarma-
ment, and England discharged some 40,000 sailors within a few
months. When war was renewed, England faced the problem
not only of bringing her depleted forces to full strength but also
of increasing them to face the danger of invasion. It is not surprising that more men were impressed from American ships in
the years from 1803 to 1806 than in the entire period of the
Revolutionary and Napoleonic Wars to that date.[7]

Moreover, the prosecution of a more vigorous policy in regard to her deserted seamen, as well as to the war in general,
undoubtedly received a great impetus from the fall of Adding-

ton and the return of Pitt to power in the spring of 1804. At the end of April Pitt decided he could no longer support the weak Addington, and he turned against him in the House of Commons. This was more than enough to doom the weak Doctor and his friends. The thought of Pitt "thundering over poor little Addington" was still haunting Augustus Foster in Washington after Pitt's death in 1806.[8] Pitt hoped to form a new administration on a broad basis to prosecute the war, but the King would not accept the leader of the Whig opposition, Charles James Fox, into the government. This meant that Pitt lost still more support, for Lord Grenville and his followers, who had split off from the Tory party in 1801 in opposition to the peace with France, refused to take office without Fox. Pitt was thus obliged to form an administration with his own personal followers, helped by some members of the late Addington administration. All this placed even Pitt in a somewhat precarious position. Some of his old followers were now grouped around Addington, others around Grenville. His problem was a standard one for English political leaders of this period—party lines were fluid and personal allegiance was of great importance. Fox estimated in the summer of 1805 that Pitt and Addington could each command only sixty followers in the House, that some 150 were in opposition, and that another 180 always gave their votes to any government that was in power. At the close of 1804 Pitt attempted to make his position more stable by negotiating the entry of Addington into his government to gain the voting support of his followers. This succeeded in January, 1805, when Addington came in as Viscount Sidmouth, but in July of the same year he once again resigned.[9]

From the point of view of America this meant that from May, 1804, until Pitt's death in January, 1806, a group of the more ardent Tories were led by Pitt in a more vigorous prosecution of the war against France. It was during this period that the first definite signs of an Anglo-American break became apparent. It was somewhat ironic that this should occur while England was led by Pitt. William Pitt, son of the equally famous Chatham, had been only twenty-four when he had assumed the leadership of England in 1784. For seventeen years, in peace and war, he had governed England. Though the burdens of office, ill-health, and a surfeit of port had prematurely aged him, he was not likely to indulge in concession to America. Though in his youth he had looked with friendship upon the possibilities of extended American trade, he now gave all his energies to defeating France—all else was sacrificed to this end.

It could hardly be expected that the right of impressment, which had been maintained vigorously even by Addington, would be given up by the new energetic administration of Pitt. In fact, the inevitable happened and the problem became worse. Henry Dundas, who had become Viscount Melville in 1802, entered the administration as First Lord of the Admiralty, and immediately infused a new energy throughout that department. After he was forced to resign in April, 1805, owing to charges of corruption, Melville was succeeded by Sir Charles Middleton, a naval veteran of the American Revolution. Though called "a superannuated Methodist" by one critic, he continued the energetic work of his predecessor.[10]

This energy that infused the Admiralty was obviously not lacking in the individual British sea captains. In the summer of 1804 British ships acted with considerable aggression around the port of New York. The original visit of the two British ships, *Cambrian* and *Driver,* had been to watch two French ships within the port, but during the period from June to November they and the *Leander,* which arrived later, inflicted considerable injury on American commerce and caused sharp resentment within the United States. A midshipman on board the *Leander,* Basil Hall, later wrote vividly of his experiences off New York. He told how each morning the British vessel would force dozens of ships to heave to and submit to search; making many lose tide, fair wind, and their market.[11] Such actions, which occured again and again in the years before 1812, were a constant source of bitterness to the United States. It was impossible for the United States to view British control of American ports with equanimity. America had fought a revolution, but now seemed to be suffering worse indignities than before 1775. America could not submit passively, but neither could England give up the right to fight France in her own way.

In the early winter of 1804 Pitt's Foreign Secretary, Lord Harrowby, who was shortly to resign for the somewhat novel reason of falling downstairs, had summarized in no uncertain terms England's attitude on the question of impressment. Writing to the British minister in Washington, Anthony Merry, he informed him that "the Pretension advanced by Mr. Madison that the American Flag should protect every Individual sailing under it on board of a Merchant Ship is too extravagant to require any serious Refutation." In spite of all American representations and protests, England did not materially alter this attitude in these years before the War of 1812. She could not afford to allow her seamen to desert to America with impunity. Only three months before the American declaration of war in 1812, the Tory *Quarterly Review* stated that "it would be little short of madness . . ., and an act of political suicide, to give up our right of search for British seamen, and to admit the American flag to protect all those sailing under it." England was prepared to fight the United States rather than yield on the question of impressment.[12]

The more vigorous prosecution of the war, which came with the formation of the Pitt administration, also brought with it new and important changes in the commercial relations of England and the United States. On the renewal of war between Great Britain and France in 1803, the latter immediately reopened the ports of her West India colonies to neutral vessels. The United States was thus given the opportunity to re-establish and augment her extensive carrying trade between these colonies and Europe. The attitude of England presented no immediate problem, for by an Order in Council of June 24, 1803, Britain made it evident that her attitude in regard to this trade was to be essentially the same as during the Revolutionary Wars with France. The main modification was that enemy colonial produce could be brought to England only in British ships; previously neutrals had been allowed into this traffic. Yet American commerce could still prosper in the trade to Europe. The "broken voyage," by which the Americans carried commodities between the enemy colonies and Europe by way of their own ports, once again became the foundation of the American trade. American commerce was allowed to prosper by the Addington administration. Two months after Addington's fall, the American minister in London, James Monroe, was able to state in a letter to James Madison that "our commerce never enjoyed in any war, as much freedom, and indeed favour from this govt. as it now does." He had reason for his optimism. American commerce was indeed reaping great benefits from the European wars. To take one example, American exports to Europe of sugar and coffee, which in 1792 had amounted to 1,122,000 and 2,136,742 lbs., had risen to 74,000,00 and 48,000,000 lbs. respectively in 1804. Monroe could well speak happily of American commercial prosperity in the summer of 1804.[13]

Yet as Monroe was writing in such confidence to Madison, certain groups in England were engaged in energetically chipping away at the pedestal on which American commerce so proudly stood. A definite move was afoot to end the abundant freedom that was being given to American commerce. This movement stemmed, on one hand, from British patriots anxious to eliminate the aid that America was giving to the French, and, on the other, from British shipping interests jealous of the growing commercial power of the United States. This distinction was complicated by the fact that the shipping interests themselves used patriotic arguments to support their demand for restrictions upon American shipping, and made it difficult to know where patriotism ceased and self-interest began. Two facets of the American trade brought particular protests from the British. The first was the American participation in the carrying trade between the French West India colonies and Europe, and the second was the American trade with the British West Indies. The latter trade had proved essential since the outbreak of war in 1793, for it had been found impossible to do without American supplies in the British colonies. Temporary orders had been issued suspending the Navigation Acts, and allowing the Americans to take part in this trade. The governors of the British West India islands were empowered to suspend the Navigation Acts in order to permit the entry of goods in American ships, and acts of indemnity were annually passed in their favor. American shippers found extensive employment carrying produce from the French colonies to Europe, from America to the British West Indies, and returning with goods and produce in exchange.[14]

This situation, which could bring radiant smiles to the austere cheeks of Puritan New Englanders, brought little joy in England. To the many Englishmen who desired to uphold Britain's Navigation System and her maritime supremacy, America appeared as the main commercial threat. In particular, the shipping interest had watched the wartime relaxations of the British Navigation System with great uneasiness, and when peace came in 1801 the first moves were made in an effort to restore England's maritime monopoly. In order to understand the unyielding firmness of the British government in commercial matters in the years immediately preceding the war of 1812, it is necessary to consider the thought that lay behind the creation of this policy in the years from 1803 to 1807.

The main sections of British opinion that were concerned with the problems of American commercial encroachments were the shipping and West India interests, but concern extended far beyond these pressure groups. All believers in the theory that England's maritime prosperity, and thus her greatness, depended upon a firm adherence to the Navigation Laws naturally looked with great disfavor on any concession that might aid the growth of American shipping. Moreover, it could not be denied that the American trade between the French West Indies and Europe was aiding the war effort of England's enemy. Disinterested patriots as well as self-interested shipowners were concerned about the prospering American commerce. The significance of the shipping and West India interests was that they were in the best position to influence government through organized pressure.

The shipping interest was composed of the shipowners, shipbuilders, and a group of allied trades that included rope-makers, sail-makers, blacksmiths, coppersmiths, biscuit-makers, and mast-makers.[15] It was an exceedingly powerful group, for it could use the argument, obviously persuasive at a time of great danger, that England's greatness and safety depended upon the prosperity of her shipping, and that any injury it suffered was automatically an injury to the whole country. The shipping interest dreaded any breakdown in the Navigation Laws, which it thought were essential to its continued prosperity, and in 1783 it had been particularly influential in resisting the efforts of the Pitt-Shelburne group to establish a liberal commercial intercourse between the United States and Great Britain. Its attitude had not changed in the intervening years.

The West India interest, which was composed of West Indian planters, agents, and British merchants interested in the West Indian trade, exhibited two fronts on this problem of American commerce. In general, the West India interest was enthusiastically in favor of the preservation of the British Navigation Laws, and was also anxious to restrict the extensive American trade between the French West Indies and Europe, but in the

2

matter of the American trade with the British West Indies it was on the side of the liberals, and opposed to the views of its natural ally the shipping interest. The reason for this was that in the years before the American Revolution the British West Indies had depended upon the American colonies for supplies. In 1783 they had been unsuccessful in their efforts to secure this trade, but their prosperity after that date, in spite of more expensive supplies, had kept them comparatively quiet. It was with the decline in its prosperity from the beginning of the nineteenth century that the West India interest gained a new and vital interest in cheap American supplies.[16] This desire of the British West Indies for American produce was of immediate benefit to the United States. The efforts of the West India interest were for a time devoted to securing a permanent supply of produce from America, and the interest was thus diverted from joining its full energies in an alliance with the shipping interest to bring an end to the American carrying trade between the French West Indies and Europe. Until 1806 the shipping and the West India interests clashed over this question of the American trade to the British West Indies, and only after the West India interest attained some of its objects in 1806 could the two interests join their forces in an attack on the American carrying trade to Europe.

The shipping interest, which had so uneasily watched the concessions in the British Navigation Laws introduced after 1793, quickly took advantage of the opportunity presented by the preliminary peace with France in 1801 to oppose such concessions. In that year an anonymous writer published a short pamphlet dedicated to the shipping interest of Great Britain, and entitled *Observations on the Importance of a Strict Adherence to the Navigation Laws of Great Britain*. The gist of his argument was that the events of the war had shown that certain nations were looking with jealousy at British maritime supremacy, and were prepared to use every effort to rival her on her native element.

In order to protect the shipping interest, to retain British sea-men, and to "preserve our Country from falling even below the level of surrounding nations," the author advocated that the British shipowners should form an association to resist the re-laxations of the Navigation Laws.[17]

This appeal did not pass unnoticed—the pamphlet itself being only the external expression of a desire to unite—and on May 6, 1802, at the London Tavern, the Society of Shipowners of Great Britain came into being, "in order more effectually at this alarm-ing crisis to promote and protect the shipping interest of Great Britain, and to endeavour *to prevent any further infringement of the navigation laws.*" It was said in March, 1804, that the principal object of the Society was "to give effect to the *old maritime principles* of the country, and *the establishments* which have arisen out of them."[18] Needless to say the chief power en-gaged in undermining Britain's *"old maritime principles"* was the United States. After 1802, when the Society of Shipowners began its task of opposing any further relaxations of the Naviga-tion Laws, and securing their more rigorous enforcement, the United States bore the brunt of its attack.

The shipowners were convinced that their interests were being neglected. Immediately after the foundation of their Society, they conducted an enquiry with the object of proving that the British shipping industry was in a depressed state, produced by the suspensions of the Navigation Laws.[19] The shipping interest wanted immediate action against American commerce, and a convenient first point of attack was the trade between the United States and the British West Indies. In 1803 an anonymous pam-phlet made a direct attack on the concessions granted to the United States,[20] but it was that pillar of England's maritime supremacy, Lord Sheffield, who provided the main arguments for the supporters of England's Navigation Laws. John Baker Holroyd, first Earl of Sheffield, had long striven for the main-tenance of England's Navigation Laws. His most famous work had been his *Observations on the Commerce of the American States,* published in 1783. By 1791 the pamphlet had gone through some six editions, and was the most influential work opposing concession to the United States. It had done much to resist the attempts of those who desired liberal commercial intercourse with the United States. With his beloved institutions once again in danger, Sheffield in 1804 again took up his pen to point out the dangers of American competition, and published a most significant pamphlet in support of the Navigation System.[21]

Sheffield first attacked the extensive intercourse between the British West Indies and the United States. He thought that it was enabling the Americans to make grave encroachments on the British carrying trade. More significant, however, in view of subsequent British legislation, were the warnings he gave of the growth of the general commercial prosperity of the United States. He pointed out that in the years from 1789 British shipping had declined as American profits had increased. "Shall it, then, any longer be said," wrote Sheffield, "that Britain has not cherished the thriving branch of American prosperity at the expense of her own welfare." His remedy for all this was a firm and unconciliatory policy on the part of Great Britain.[22]

The return of Pitt to power in the spring of 1804 brought new hope to the shipping interest and its friends, who had been disappointed by the inaction of Addington. In the summer of 1804 interviews were obtained both at the Board of Trade and with Pitt himself. The shipowners were pleased to hear Pitt express the conviction that some remedy would have to be found for the relaxations that had been permitted in Britain's Navigation System.[23] The West India interest, however, was striving to counteract these arguments for a stricter enforcement of the Navigation Laws. In 1804 it campaigned vigorously for the opening of a regular commercial intercourse between the United States and the West Indies, and the pamphleteers of the group expounded this West Indian point of view.[24] Yet the arguments of the upholders of England's maritime system carried more weight with the Tories of Pitt's administration, anxiously waging war on France and awaiting French invasion. In the fall the first efforts were made to curb American trade to the British West Indies. Instructions were sent to the governors of the West India islands ordering them not to open their ports to American goods *"except in cases of real and very great necessity."*[25]

In the West Indies these instructions had rapid effect. On November 21, 1804, Lieutenant-Governor Nugent of Jamaica issued a resolution stating that in six months permission to import lumber and provisions, previously granted to neutrals, would be revoked. Within the island, reaction to this step came almost immediately. The governor received representations from the Assembly asking him to withdraw the resolution, but he would not act on his own responsibility and he advised them to address the King. They did this in less than a month after the governor's proclamation, stressing the fact that they depended upon the United States for their supply of provisions, and emphasizing that the British North American colonies were incapable of supplying their needs. In England, the cause of the West India planters was taken up by the colonial agents. The agent for Jamaica, Edmund P. Lyon, wrote to the Secretary for War and the Colonies on March 7, 1805, telling him of the alarm of the Jamaican planters at Governor Nugent's proclamation.[26]

Adverse reaction to this decision to restrict American-West Indian trade was not confined to England and the British West Indies. In the United States the governor's November proclamation produced considerable consternation when the British consul-general in New York, Thomas Barclay, indiscreetly published it without official permission. The adverse reaction, both from the West India planters and from the United States, induced the British Foreign Secretary, Lord Mulgrave, who had succeeded Lord Harrowby, to inform the British minister in Washington that he could assure the United States that there

had been no change in the wartime policy. He was given permission to state that the West India governors still had the discretion of admitting American ships in violation of the Navigation Laws. It would seem that Mulgrave was influenced more by
the protests of the influential West India planters than by
American concern at this stricter policy. On May 20, 1805, the
day before neutral ships were to be excluded from the island
by his November proclamation, Governor Nugent extended for
six months the permission to import timber and grain in neutral
ships.[27]

In this matter of American intercourse with the British West
Indies, where the welfare of an important British interest was at
stake, the Americans were allowed certain concessions. The
American carrying trade between the French West Indies and
Europe did not, however, enjoy the advantage of being beneficial to an important segment of British opinion. Instead, this
trade was directly helping the enemy at a time when England
feared immediate invasion. How long could England continue
to ignore an American carrying trade that was nullifying British
control of the seas? It was of little use to sweep the French from
the seas if the Americans could immediately take their place. The
American trade was aiding the enemy, and it was also arousing
jealousy among the British shipowners who saw the United
States shipping industry waxing rich on wartime profits. As the
struggle in Europe became increasingly involved, it became obvious that it was only a matter of time before some action would
be taken to curb the vast American trade to the Continent.

Pitt's administration had been in office for just a year when,
in May, 1805, the Lords Commissioners of Appeals handed down
the decision in the case of the *Essex* which sharply checked the
system of the "broken voyage." The Court of Appeals decided
that the mere importation of goods into a neutral country was
not enough to neutralize these goods unless a *bona fide* import
duty was paid.[28] The *Essex* decision, which has attracted so

much attention in works on this period, was the logical outcome of the all-out war effort inaugurated by the second Pitt administration, and the rapidly arising jealousy of American commercial prosperity in England. The decision was an important step in the deterioration of Anglo-American relations. England was now interfering with an exceedingly large and profitable American trade which, though never legally sanctioned by England, had at least been given the important sanction of custom for several years.

The manner in which England gave force to her new decision added insult to injury. America was given ample cause for complaint. Before any official notification of the change in policy had been given, or before the Americans had even received unofficial warnings of the new decree, numerous American ships had been seized. In the summer and autumn of 1805 American shippers suffered extensive losses in the Caribbean region, and only a few weeks after the decision, before even the American minister in Great Britain, James Monroe, had any clear idea of the new development in British policy, many ships were being seized in the Channel and the North Sea.[29] In the months following the judgment in the case of the *Essex,* the decision was enforced in a manner which left no doubt of the attitude of Pitt's administration towards American trade. The first step had now been taken toward the Orders in Council of November, 1807. America was now to learn the real difficulties of neutrality.

In October, 1805, the famous pamphlet *War in Disguise; or, the Frauds of the Neutral Flags,* by James Stephen, was presented to the English public. Stephen was a lawyer who had practiced in the West Indies from 1783 to 1794, and had then worked at the prize appeal court of the Privy Council. Significantly, he was a friend of Spencer Perceval who became Prime Minister in 1809, and who as Chancellor of the Exchequer bore chief responsibility for the Orders in Council of 1807. Stephen himself was to enter Parliament in 1808, and his pamphlet is of far more than usual interest. It is valuable as perhaps the best contemporary expression of the philosophy which lay behind England's commercial policy towards the United States in the years before the War of 1812. Before publication Stephen had submitted the manuscript to Sir William Scott, judge of the High Court of Admiralty, who had shown it to Pitt. Scott advised Stephen to issue it privately as a pamphlet well designed to educate the public. Also the government would be committed less by the private appearance of a pamphlet than by any more official communication.[30] The pamphlet when issued ran to more than two hundred pages, and explained not only the type of thinking which lay behind the *Essex* decision, but also foreshadowed the theory of the later Orders in Council.

In this extremely well-reasoned work, Stephen considered in detail the origins and extent of the American carrying trade between the enemy colonies and Europe, its effect on Britain, the British policy that should be adopted towards it, and the effect this new policy would have on Anglo-American relations. He first dealt with the origins of the Rule of 1756, and emphasized the fact that though it had for some time been left in abeyance, its principle had never been abandoned. He contended that from the outbreak of war between France and England in 1793 the United States had taken advantage of every British concession to build an extensive commerce. Using his previous experience as a lawyer in the West Indies, Stephen treated in detail and with conviction the history of the system of the "broken voyage" and its many abuses. With considerable skill he depicted all the injuries suffered by England as a result of this trade. In turn, he sketched the harm sustained by the British West India and shipping interests, the great aid given by the United States to Napoleon, and the long-term commercial advantages gained by the United States to the detriment of British power and prosperity. He attributed the distress of the

British West India colonies to the fact that the produce of the enemy colonies, carried under neutral flags, was underselling the British West Indian produce in the European markets. As if this was not enough, he then pointed out that this trade was helping to sustain Napoleonic power, and was increasing American maritime strength to the point where it was a danger to the maritime supremacy of Great Britain. The remedy he proposed for all this is not difficult to imagine; he wanted a total prohibition of the American carrying trade. "The neutral powers can subsist without this newly acquired commerce; but Great Britain cannot long exist as a nation, if bereft of her ancient means of offensive maritime war."[31]

Stephen finally considered the very important question of the effect a prohibition of this American trade would have on Anglo-American relations. Here Stephen used the same reasoning, and made the same mistakes, as did the British government in its relations with the United States from this time until the outbreak of war in 1812. Stephen was convinced that the United States would not support her pretensions to the extent of going to war against England. The Americans could not fail to see, he argued, "that the subjugation of England, would be fatal to the last hope of liberty in Europe," and that even the Atlantic would be unable to protect them if England should fall.[32] Stephen, like so many Englishmen of his period, had fallen into the mistake of assuming that America would correlate England with liberty and Napoleon with tyranny, and would quite clearly see that a victory for Napoleon would eventually be disastrous for the United States and all that she stood for in the early nineteenth century. Unfortunately for Anglo-American relations, the majority of England's late colonists still distrusted England, feared her maritime power, and were more concerned with present than future evils. Americans have always been loath to admit that their future fortunes might depend on the result of a European struggle. Even as late as 1940 many Americans could not be convinced that a victory for Hitlerism would be disastrous to their future safety. It could hardly be expected in the first decade of the nineteenth century, so soon after fighting for independence, that they would view defeat for England as a tragedy for America. Yet, Stephen and so many like him could not envisage America fighting on the side of Napoleon.

Stephen's doubts as to whether America would ever actually declare war on England became even greater when he considered the weakness of the American position. He reasoned that no war would be so destructive to the prosperity of the United States as a war with Great Britain, and that no American in his right mind would countenance it. American economic retaliation he thought was equally impossible—a nonimportation measure would injure only the United States, and a nonexportation act would be openly evaded. Significantly, however, in the midst of his arguments that America would not find it in her interest to resist, Stephen put forward the view that if at the last instant it should become a question of fighting the United States or of sacrificing any of Britain's maritime rights, the latter would be infinitely the worse.[33] The idea that America would not fight, and that if she did it would be preferable to any concession, guided the Tory party in these years before the War of 1812.

The year 1805, with the *Essex* decision and the theories of *War in Disguise,* marked a definite stage in the steady movement in opposition to American commerce. British opinion was crystallizing in favor of a stricter policy towards neutrals. Coinciding with Stephen's pamphlet, in October, 1805, came Nelson's victory at Trafalgar, which only added to this feeling that there was no need to conciliate America at sea. At the end of 1805 the complete proscription of American commerce, which was to come in the Orders in Council of November, 1807, seemed very near. That it did not come about for almost two years was due primarily to a change in the internal politics of Great Britain.

The joy, marred by the sorrow at Nelson's death, which suffused England after the victory at Trafalgar, was quickly shattered by the Continental events of December, 1805. The crushing victory of Napoleon over the Russians at Austerlitz in that month threw England into gloom, and dealt the death blow to Pitt. His third coalition smashed beyond repair, Pitt had no heart left in him. On January 23, 1806, he died with the "Austerlitz look" on his face. All England mourned its loss. His great political rival, Charles James Fox, felt "as if there was something missing in the world—a chasm, a blank that cannot be supplied."[34] Yet for America the death of Pitt promised a respite. This event opened the way to the formation of a Whig ministry with sentiments far more favorable towards the United States than those of the Tory government of Pitt.

3 *American Indecision*

WHILE ENGLAND was steadily tightening her hold upon American commerce, the policy of the United States was undergoing somewhat remarkable fluctuations. Thomas Jefferson, who had become the American President in 1801, had from the outset of his administration enjoyed remarkably good luck in his relations with England. Within seven months of his accession to office in March, 1801, England and France had signed preliminary articles of peace. The conclusion of peace in Europe meant that the improvement in Anglo-American relations that had occurred since Jay's Treaty in 1795 could continue without the problems of European war. Only a month before Jefferson's inauguration the peaceful Henry Addington had assumed power in England. Never since the American Revolution had signs been so auspicious for a period of co-operation and amity in the relations of the two countries.

Diplomatic events on the Continent in these years served to increase the community of interest between the United States and England. On October 1, 1800, at San Ildefonso, Spain agreed to retrocede Louisiana to France. The prospect of the transfer of that area, vital to the welfare of the western United States, from weak and moribund Spain to all-powerful Napoleon, inevitably produced anxiety in the United States. By June, 1801, rumors of the cession had reached America, but it was not until November, 1801, that the American minister in Great Britain, Rufus King, transmitted the definite news of the treaty to the United States. The shock in America, particularly in the western country, was very great. So much so that in April, 1802, Jefferson wrote his famous letter to the American minister in France, Robert Livingston, stating that "the day that France takes possession of N. Orleans fixes the sentence which is to restrain her forever within her low water mark. It seals the union of two nations who in conjunction can maintain exclusive possession of the ocean. From that moment we must marry ourselves to the British fleet and nation."[1] In November of the same year, when news reached Washington that Spain had withdrawn the right of deposit at New Orleans, a clash between the Americans and the French became increasingly likely, and the prospects for Anglo-American relations had never seemed fairer. Edmund Thornton, the British chargé d'affaires in Washington, suddenly found himself treated with great friendship by the American government. At a Cabinet meeting in early April, 1803, a majority of members agreed that should the attempt at the purchase of Louisiana from France fail, negotiations could be begun for an alliance with England. Secretary of State James Madison's instructions to Robert Livingston and James Monroe, who were being empowered to negotiate with France for the purchase of the territory, also gave them power to negotiate for an alliance with England should the discussions with France fail.[2] In the spring of 1803, when America's purchase of Louisiana hung in the balance, no one would have prophesied that within less than a decade the United States would have been at war with England.

Apart from the negative advantage of America's alienation from France over the transfer of Louisiana, several positive gains in Anglo-American relations had been made in this period of peace in Europe. At long last in January, 1802, Rufus King had negotiated a convention settling the long and acrimonious dispute over the debts owed to British merchants from before the American Revolution. England agreed that the United States should pay only the very moderate sum of £600,000. Moreover, in May, 1803, Rufus King also negotiated a partial settlement of the contentious Canadian-American boundary problem, which drew the boundary between the Lake of the Woods and the Mississippi River, and of the islands in Passamaquoddy Bay. Unfortunately, by the time this convention came before the United States Senate, other developments made its full ratification impossible.[3]

Early in May, 1803, Napoleon had agreed to sell the whole of Louisiana to the United States. By this sale the pressure which had forced America into the hands of England was removed. It has been argued that the Louisiana Purchase was the first step towards the War of 1812.[4] To the extent that certain external factors propelling America into an alliance with England were removed, this view is correct. Yet it is also evident that the removal of the threat of war with France did not automatically mean that America would have to go to war against England. The fact still remained that America could be forced into war only by a British policy consistently hostile to American interests. Such a policy did not exist in 1803, and it would seem that this was more influential than the American dispute with France in producing comparatively friendly Anglo-American relations. The winter of 1802-03 was not the last time that Jefferson was to talk of an Anglo-American alliance—he was to suggest it even more forcibly in the summer and fall of 1805 at the time of the controversy with Spain over the Floridas.

The purchase of Louisiana did, however, have at least one immediate effect on relations between the United States and England. When Jefferson, in October, 1803, submitted to the Senate the boundary convention which had been signed in England in May, that body refused to ratify Article V, which fixed the boundary from the Lake of the Woods to the Mississippi.

The Senate feared that by ratifying this article it ran the risk of losing the northern part of the territory obtained from Napoleon. On its part, the British government refused to accept the emasculated convention, and the good work of Rufus King came to nought.[5]

The signing of the treaty for the purchase of Louisiana was followed within a few weeks, on May 18, 1803, by the rupture of the Peace of Amiens, and the recent Anglo-American cordiality now had to stand the strains of a European war. To this renewal of the European war, far more than to the purchase of Louisiana, can be traced the roots of Anglo-American difficulties in the following years. Wartime difficulties at sea were soon to break open the old scars of the Revolution that had temporarily healed in the period since 1795.

The British, who had been without a fully accredited minister in the United States since the departure of Robert Liston at the end of 1800, now finally decided in 1803 to send the mediocre Anthony Merry to represent them in the United States. One can well doubt the wisdom of sending a man who had spent some twenty years as consul general and chargé d'affaires in ceremony-laden Spain into the informal atmosphere of early Washington. Merry, who was described by one Washington lady as "plain in his appearance, and called rather inferior in understanding," arrived in Washington in November, 1803, and as might have been expected immediately involved himself in a controversy concerning etiquette and diplomatic protocol. Unused to the easy informality of the Virginian Jefferson, Merry was convinced that the President was determined on a consistent policy of hostility to Great Britain through insults to Mrs. Merry and himself. The various incidents, made famous by Henry Adams in his brilliant account of this period, of Merry being received by Jefferson in carpet slippers, and of Merry and his wife scrambling for a place at table, serve better to illustrate the difficulties of conducting Anglo-American relations at this period rather than any specific hostility on the part of the American President.[6]

The fact was that Jefferson had no desire to observe the European formality of the early nineteenth century. Another British diplomat wrote from Washington in 1805 telling how "an ambassador from Tunis arrived here with the most splendid dress I ever saw, and the President receives him in yarn stockings and torn slippers, as he does us all." Jefferson was not trying to insult England through Merry, he was merely being Jefferson. Madison, in February, 1804, wrote a special letter to James Monroe in London, asking him to make every effort to counteract the impression that difficulties with Merry over questions of etiquette were any part of a hostile design against Great Britain : "The Govt. of the U.S. is sincerely and anxiously disposed to cultivate harmony between the two Nations." Jefferson himself wrote to Monroe telling him the same thing.[7]

In this period before the War of 1812 it is surprising to what extent both England and America increased their difficulties through thoughtless behavior and minor quarrels. At a time when careful negotiation and skillful diplomacy were essential, both sides frequently blundered over minor points. On this occasion Jefferson alienated Merry not because of any studied design, but because he did not realize or care what effect that behavior, natural to himself, might have upon a foreign country. Merry, on his part, failed to make any allowance for the different customs of the country to which he was accredited. Perhaps the difficulty was that which has often plagued Anglo-American relations—the fact that the countries are and were similar in so many ways has meant that there has been far less toleration and understanding of differences than one would expect. The Americans and British have so often failed to exhibit the tolerance toward each other that they would use automatically in dealing with countries less like their own. The difficulty that Merry experienced was by no means unique in this period.

Augustus Foster, who was to hold the post of British minister in the United States in the vital period immediately preceding the War of 1812, made some striking observations about the Americans during his first visit to the country as Secretary of Legation in 1804. President Jefferson made much the same impression on Foster as he had on Merry : "he is dressed and looks extremely like a plain farmer, and wears his slippers down at the heels." He thought there were about five persons in Congress who were like gentlemen—the rest attended in "the filthiest dresses." Washington he regarded as a "demi-city demi-wilderness." American women he thought of as "in general a spying, inquisitive, vulgar, and most ignorant race." In short, his conclusion regarding America was that "from the Province of Maine to the borders of Florida you would not find 30 men of Truth, Honour, or Integrity. Corruption, Immorality, Irreligion, and above all, self-interest, have corroded the very pillars on which their Liberty rests." A little more understanding on either side would have done wonders in this period before the War of 1812.[8]

The most serious problem that faced the American government with the renewal of the European war in 1803 was undoubtedly that of impressment. Rufus King, realizing that war was imminent, had made a last effort to solve this problem before his departure for the United States in the spring of 1803. King tried to persuade the British to agree to the principle that no person should be impressed upon the high seas by either country. For a time it seemed that he was making progress, but as might have been expected Britain would not agree to the proposal.[9] Impressment constantly offended American opinion in this period. Yet when the problem existed without the additional complication of the extensive restriction of American trade, as it did in these years of 1803 and 1804, it never seemed likely that it would drive America as far as open conflict. It was its continuation over many years, combined with restrictions on trade, that proved of basic importance in producing the War of 1812.

By the end of 1803 the increase in the practice of impressment that followed the renewal of the European war had persuaded America to press once again for a solution of the problem. The situation in the waters around America was particularly irritating to the American government, even though James Monroe, who succeeded Rufus King as minister to England, was reporting that violations of American maritime rights were not as severe as in the former war. In January, 1804, Madison sent Monroe the draft of another convention designed particularly to end impressment, and also to deal with the problems of blockade, contraband, and the enlargement of American trade with the enemy colonies.[10] American feeling against impressment was undoubtedly growing at this time, and in the same month that Madison wrote to Monroe a bill was reported in Congress that would have given the President the power to prohibit by proclamation the giving of provisions to any vessel which had been engaged in impressing seamen from American ships. On February 29 action on this bill was postponed until the first Monday in December.[11] It is apparent that though American opinion was irritated by impressment, it was as yet nowhere near the breaking point. In London, the British government was in no hurry to proceed on this subject, and when James Monroe left on a mission to Spain in October, 1804, no action had been taken.[12]

Though the American government thought that the impressment controversy merited negotiation and an attempt at solution in 1803 and 1804, there as yet seemed no desire to wage war over this issue. The United States still hoped that by a policy of moderation she could persuade England to come around to her way of thinking. Though in January, 1804, Madison had informed Monroe that a convention was necessary to solve the problem of impressment, he was able to say in a letter of March 8 that "the present administration in Great Britain appears more liberal and cordial towards the United States than any preceding one."[13] By the summer and fall of 1804, the American government had far more reason to be bitter towards the British, for it was at this time that the British ships *Cambrian* and *Leander* were investing the port of New York, stopping and searching ships.[14] Yet Madison's opinion of March was still echoed in the American administration. On September 16 Jefferson stated in a letter to the Attorney General, Levi Lincoln, that "the new administration in England is entirely cordial. There has never been a time when our flag was so little molested by them in the European seas, or irregularities there so readily and respectfully corrected." He connected the recent actions off New York to the previous administration of Addington rather than to the new ministry of Pitt.[15] Anxious to keep the peace, and ill-prepared to wage war, the American government was always ready to believe the best in the years before 1812. It was a constant hope that by a policy of moderation and repeated negotiation England would be persuaded to recognize American rights.

Thus, though Madison was disappointed at British delays in 1804 on the subject of a convention, he wrote to Monroe commending him for winking at British procrastinations, and leaving the way open for a friendly settlement on his return from Madrid.[16] Congress, however, influenced by the incidents off New York in the previous year, was less cordial in these early months of 1805. In March an act was introduced into the Senate to empower the President to prevent the ship of any officer who had interfered with American ships from coming into American waters.[17] Resentment was growing in the United States, but the time was still far distant when the country decided that the accumulation of grievances merited the risk of war. This was shown quite clearly by the developments in American foreign policy in the summer and fall of 1805.

An important factor in the reluctance of America to involve herself in a bitter controversy with England in 1804 and 1805 was the American desire for Spanish territory in the New World. Since the acquisition of Louisiana in 1803, Jefferson had grown most covetous of Spanish territory east of the Mississippi River. In February, 1804, Congress authorized the President to create a separate customs district for Mobile. The wording of the act clearly implied American control over West Florida, and brought immediate protests from Spain. Jefferson, however, decided to push his claims for West Florida, and at the same time to press for the satisfaction of all other claims against Spain, which were mainly seizures of American ships by the Spanish, and by French action in Spanish waters after 1796. In April, 1804, Madison informed Monroe in England that if the situation there was satisfactory, he should join the American minister Charles Pinckney in Madrid in an effort to obtain satisfaction from Spain. They were to endeavor to obtain the Spanish territory east of the Mississippi, and arbitration on the American claims. Monroe finally left London in October, 1804, and was absent from his post until the following summer. His negotiations at the court of Spain were a failure.[18] Spain, who was at war against England from December, 1804, took courage from the fact that she now had the support of France, and she was no longer plagued by the fear of war with the United States.

The failure of the American designs on Spanish land, and the backing given to Spain by France, now had the effect of once again turning America towards the possibility of an English alliance. As early as July, 1805, Madison had suggested the possibility that American disputes with Spain might involve France, and thus throw the United States into the British scale.[19] This possibility became much more likely at the end of July when the official news of the failure of Monroe's mission reached the United States.[20] In spite of the increasing rigor of the British in the matter of impressment from 1803, and in spite of the Louisiana purchase in the same year, the American government was still thinking seriously in 1805 of an alliance with England.

On August 4 Jefferson informed Madison that they "should take into consideration whether we ought not immediately to propose to England an eventual treaty of alliance, to come into force whenever (within   years) a war shall take place with Spain or France."[21] By August 17 Jefferson was becoming anxious. He thought that the "cavalier conduct" of Spain plainly showed that France was to settle with America for her, and that if she could keep America isolated until peace had been made with England, she could enforce her will by force of arms. Jefferson was anxious to obtain the opinion of the cabinet members at the earliest possible moment, for if they should decide on negotiations with England, it was necessary to commence them immediately. "I am strongly impressed with a belief of hostile and treacherous intentions against us on the part of France," wrote Jefferson, "and that we should lose no time in securing something more than a neutral friendship from England."[22]

Madison was less sanguine than Jefferson over the chances of securing this alliance with England. He argued, with good reason, that England would not commit herself to an alliance to gain Spanish territory without binding America in return. Jefferson, on the other hand, hoped that England would agree to a provisional treaty, which would come into force only in the event of the United States being engaged, during the European war, in a conflict with either France or Spain. Moreover, he considered that England would stipulate not to make peace until America had secured her objectives, which were to be the "rightful boundaries of Louisiana," and indemnification for American spoliation claims. For the latter he thought that the United States should be allowed to make reprisal on the Floridas and retain them. America's co-operation in the war, he thought, would be sufficient reward for Great Britain : "the first wish of every Englishman's heart is to see us once more fighting by their sides against France."[23] It is hardly surprising that Madison cast some doubt on the likelihood of England agreeing to these super-optimistic plans of Jefferson. Throughout September this same pattern continued. Jefferson still spoke optimistically of the prospects of a treaty of alliance with England, while Madison urged caution. Albert Gallatin, the Secretary of the Treasury, added his usual careful note, and wanted a renewal of negotiation rather than war with Spain.[24]

In the early autumn of 1805, new complications arose in Anglo-American relations when the news of the *Essex* decision reached America. Early in September Jacob Crowinshield, the prominent New England merchant and Jeffersonian, wrote to Jefferson telling him of the new British policy, and of the uneasiness of the merchants on this subject. Later in September Madison informed Monroe in London of the great alarm spread among the merchants by "this new and shameful depredation." Already Madison had started to investigate the legality of the British Rule of 1756 with a view to writing a pamphlet on the subject. Anthony Merry immediately reported the great American irritation at the *Essex* decision to Lord Mulgrave, and stated that the effect was worse because the decision was totally unexpected by the Americans.[25]

Yet in September, while the news of the seizures under the new British order slowly reached America, Jefferson still went ahead with his plans for a possible British alliance. Jefferson was always most reluctant to remove pressure from Spain and from Spanish possessions in America. The American government in the fall of 1805 did not act with the energy one would expect in reaction to the *Essex* decision. Jefferson was still dazzled by Spanish territory, and Madison was slowly gathering arguments to refute the new British pretensions while worrying about his wife's illness.[26] It took time for the full import of the new measure to be realized, and the American government only reluctantly diverted its attentions from the intricacies of the Spanish question to cope with the new problem in Anglo-American relations.

Though in time America would have had to take cognizance of the new British policy, the immediate cause of the abandonment of the idea of using English aid to obtain territory from Spain was an alteration in the European political and military situation. Early in October news arrived from Europe that Pitt had finally succeeded in drawing Austria and Russia into his third coalition, and that Napoleon was about to embark on an extensive European campaign. Madison immediately wrote to Jefferson asking him to delay his plans for a provisional arrangement with England because of the likelihood of a general extension of the war in Europe.[27] To Jefferson the news of the extension of the war came as a great relief. His fear had been that had the war in Europe come to a sudden end, the United States would have been left alone to face France and Spain. Now he was able to argue in letters to his cabinet members that the certainty of the extension of the European war gave America ample time, and placed her at her ease. While Napoleon indulged in a year of campaigning and another year of negotiations, the United States would have the opportunity to make another effort at peaceful accommodation with Spain.[28] Showing remarkable sangfroid, Jefferson added in another letter that "this new state of things is the more fortunate in proportion as it would have been disagreeable to have proposed closer connections with England at a moment when so much clamour exists against her for her new encroachments on neutral rights."[29] Nothing could show more clearly that, in spite of British action at sea between 1803 and the fall of 1805, Jefferson was quite prepared to ally with England to force concessions from Spain. This period at the close of 1805 is a striking turning point in the American attitude towards England. After this date the more restrictive policy that had been carried out by England since the renewal of the European war in 1803 forced its attention upon the American government to the exclusion of other problems.

The affair with Spain petered out inconclusively in 1806. Jefferson once again sought a peaceful conclusion, and endeavored to purchase his desires through French rather than Spanish channels. In December he sent a secret message to Congress in an attempt to obtain money for the purchase of the Floridas. Congress temporarily balked at granting this, and by the time the money was obtained and the proposition made to France in the spring of 1806, it was too late. Napoleon had decided to preserve the Spanish territory rather than use it as a source of income.[30] An important incidental result of this attempted American maneuver was that the vehement John Randolph of Roanoke broke from the administration, and later became a powerful critic of the retaliatory measures used against Great Britain. With the Spanish question fading from the public notice, there was now nothing to stop a full consideration of the new restrictive British policy as embodied in the *Essex* decision and in the numerous impressments.

The comparative moderation with which America had received the first news of the seizures under the *Essex* decision began to change to sharp protest in December, 1805. When Merry had seen Madison in the middle of October, the Secretary of State had spoken with much greater moderation than the British minister had expected on the subject of the change in the British commercial policy, but by the beginning of December this attitude was changing. Merry wrote to inform Lord Mulgrave on December 2 that the resentment at the *Essex* decision had increased considerably since his last letter, and that Madison was now treating the subject far more seriously. "We expect a boisterous session," wrote Augustus Foster, the British Secretary of Legation, "for they are angry with us about our regulations in regard to their commerce."[31]

Reflecting the increasingly bitter temper of the country, Jefferson's annual message dealt with the new infringements of neutral rights before discussing the state of affairs with Spain.

This scale of importance reversed the trend of Jefferson's private utterances to this point, and even the British minister was somewhat surprised that Jefferson gave precedence to British affairs.[32] The news from Europe could only serve to increase American despondency in December, 1805. In that month the news arrived from Europe of the British naval victory at Trafalgar on October 21. It seemed now that there was no hope of forcibly resisting England at sea. England truly ruled the waves, and in December after the battle of Austerlitz Napoleon ruled the land. With the two great European nations supreme on their own element, the war in Europe was about to enter its commercial phase of blockade and counter-blockade. The commerce of the United States was to be crushed between the two Goliaths. December also brought Stephen's *War in Disguise* to the United States. Its message of war on American commerce was well designed to cause extreme anxiety in an America already troubled by the *Essex* decision. James Monroe, minister in London, added to the general alarm. He sent Jefferson a copy of Stephen's pamphlet with the comment that it was said to have been written under government auspices. He added that if conditions were favorable, the British government was undoubtedly prepared to push measures with America to the full extent of the doctrines contained in it. "It is evident," he wrote, "that we have no sincere friends anywhere." Early in 1806 he concluded that the British government would not change its policy until America proved that she could do England so much harm that it would be an advantage to England to revert to a more lenient policy.[33]

With Congress now in session, it was only a matter of time before retaliatory action was taken against Great Britain. Petitions and memorials from all over the country, particularly from the merchants of the principal cities, urged Congress to gain redress for the many commercial injuries.[34] During the latter part of 1805 Madison had been engaged in writing a pamphlet,

which attempted to refute the theory behind the British Rule of
1756 and the interpretations put upon it in 1805. The work
attacked the Rule of 1756 as against the law of nations, and also
maintained that while Great Britain relaxed her own laws she
denied her enemies the right to do likewise. Moreover, while
England denied neutrals the right to trade with the enemy
colonies, England herself was taking part in trade with the
French.[35] Increasingly before 1812 America was to object to
England carrying on trade that she denied to neutrals. Madison
had practically finished the work by the time Stephen's *War in
Disguise* reached America in December, and in January
Madison distributed his *Examination of the British Doctrine* to
the members of Congress.[36]

Congress itself was already beginning to voice its disapproval
at British actions—both at the practice of impressment, and at
the restrictions on neutral commerce. On January 20, 1806,
Senator Wright of Maryland introduced a bill for the protection
of American seamen which would have adjudged impressment
as piracy. This bill was shelved, however, for the majority of
opinion was for a combined retaliation against both impressment and restrictions upon neutral trade. This feeling received
expression on January 29 when Andrew Gregg, a member from
Pennsylvania, moved that the House should resolve itself into
a committee of the whole to consider an act for the total prohibition of British goods, until the evils of impressment and the
violation of American commerce were corrected. Within two
weeks Joseph Nicholson of Maryland had introduced a less
sweeping resolution, which provided for the nonimportation of
only those goods that could be obtained from countries other
than England or produced at home. Though other suggestions
were made, it was the resolutions of Gregg and Nicholson that
were of primary importance. The decision was to be made between partial and complete nonimportation from England.[37]

The fact that the form of retaliation chosen against England

should have been that of economic retaliation is not surprising.
Since before the Revolution that method of resistance had been
a popular one with the Americans. At a time when England
was in complete control of the seas after Trafalgar, economic
force seemed the only possible way to challenge and change the
British policy. Jefferson himself was particularly attracted by
the idea of substituting commercial action for armed warfare.
In September, 1801, he had written to Robert Livingston, the
American minister in France, that he did not believe that war
was the most certain method of enforcing neutral rights:
"Those peaceable coercions which are in the power of every
nation, if undertaken in concert & in time of peace, are more
likely to produce the desired effect."[38] Madison too had great
faith in the possibility of coercing England through peaceful
means. In the fall of 1805 he had written to Jefferson praising
the efficacy of the embargo as a form of coercion, and arguing
that if a commercial weapon could be shaped for the executive
hand America could force all nations having colonies in the
American hemisphere to respect her rights. Even James Monroe,
far away in England, had written home to suggest the same
policy. He thought that some sort of discriminatory duty could
be levied on English manufactures—ultimately, he thought, its
effect would be beneficial to America, though its immediate
effect would depend upon the state of affairs on the Continent.
Monroe argued that the executive should be given the power
to lay embargoes or prohibit the export of American produce,
in order to hurt the British colonies.[39]

It is thus not surprising that the Congressional Resolutions of
January and February, 1806, met with the approval of the
cabinet. When John Quincy Adams dined with Madison on
February 13, he found that the Secretary of State thought that
the best means of proceeding against Great Britain was through
permanent commercial distinctions between her and other
nations—he praised a policy of discriminatory duties on articles

imported from England. This was the same policy that Monroe had suggested to Jefferson in the previous November, and was nearer in spirit to Nicholson's resolution for partial nonimportation than to Gregg's resolution for the total elimination of imports from England. Several days later, when Adams dined with the President, he found that Jefferson's preference was "manifestly for Nicholson's resolution."[40] The executive was clearly in support of any motion which attempted to force England's hand through economic pressures. This belief that peaceful coercion would, if given sufficient time, wring concession from England was of primary importance in delaying America's declaration of war upon England until 1812. The United States did not believe in this period that economic coercion would bring *immediate* concession from England. It was quite obviously a form of pressure that required time to produce any effect, and before the advocates of war in the United States could be heard, it was necessary that economic coercion should be tried and found wanting. Moreover, in this period the United States consistently tended to maintain the belief that England was almost on the point of yielding—the temptation was to give peaceful sanctions "just one more chance." Thus, in spite of disappointments, the experiments of nonimportation, embargo, nonintercourse, and Macon's Bill No. 2 followed each other in hopeful procession. The final tragedy was that when England, in the throes of an economic crisis in 1812, finally decided to yield to a major portion of the American demands, and substantially repealed her Orders in Council, America had finally lost hope and had already committed herself irrevocably to war.

On March 5, 1806, Gregg's motion for complete prohibition of imports from Great Britain was taken up by the House. Gregg in introducing his motion spoke with great moderation, and spent quite as much time attacking the practice of impressment as in attacking the new British regulations regarding American commerce.[41] He seemed confident that there would be no need to go to war against Great Britain, and that economic pressures would bring her to terms. Jacob Crowinshield, who followed Gregg in support of the measure, did however advert to the possibility of war should the peaceful pressures prove of no avail.[42] The opposition to Gregg's measure was led by John Randolph, who was now completely in opposition to the administration, and he lashed the advocates of economic coercion unmercifully. "What!" he screamed, "shall this great mammoth of the American forest leave his native element and plunge into the water in a mad contest with the shark."[43] The debate on Gregg's motion, with Randolph pitted against the supporters of the administration, continued through March 13. On this date Gregg's resolution was dropped, and Nicholson's was taken up. It had become apparent that there was more support, both in Congress and from the executive, for limited rather than complete nonimportation. On March 17 Nicholson's resolution was adopted and given over to a committee to be framed into a bill. As eventually passed by the Senate on April 15, the act prevented the importation from England of a limited list of articles.[44] By this time, however, there had been a distinct change in the political situation, and the act was not destined to come into force until the close of 1807.

The hopes of a settlement with England received a great boost in the spring of 1806 when news arrived from that country of the death of Pitt. John Breckenridge, the Attorney General from Kentucky, voiced a typical American view both of Pitt and of America's reaction to his death when he wrote, "I think it probable that our difficulties with Great Britain will be accommodated. . . . His hatred to this Country had become inveterate and his schemes to annoy and depress our commerce, systematic."[45] The good news from England was accompanied in this same month of March, 1806, by news from Europe that Napoleon had crushed the Russians at Austerlitz. Well might Jefferson write to Thomas Paine that "with England I flatter myself our difficulties will be dissipated by the disasters of her allies, the change of her ministry, and the measures which Congress are likely to adopt to furnish motives for her becoming just to us."[46] Unfortunately for America, Jefferson's hopes were to fall far short of realization.

4 *A Whig Interlude*

THE HOPES that were aroused in America by the death of Pitt in January, 1806, stemmed from the fact that it seemed likely that the King would be obliged to change the administration, and at last accept Charles James Fox. It is a strange irony that the young, rather self-consciously virtuous United States should have fastened her hopes on the prematurely old, debauched Fox. Yet the fact is that this Englishman, who had so ardently defended America's right to revolt in 1775, still embodied certain American ideals in 1806. Like America, Fox desired liberty and he desired peace. Unfortunately for America, by 1806 his first thoughts were for English liberty and for peace with France. He had only a short time to live, and his energies were so occupied with the vast problems of European affairs that America was neglected. Though Anglo-American affairs were all-important to America, in England they were of minor consideration compared to the struggle with France. In these years before 1812 the American government had great difficulty realizing this fact, and it often formulated policy as though the British government was sensitive to the least fluctuation in American affairs.

America's hopes that the King would have to accept Fox were justified. George III first tried to evade the issue by offering the premiership to the Tory Lord Hawkesbury, but when he refused the King was obliged to call on the former Pittite, Lord Grenville. Grenville, as expected, refused to form a government unless his ally Fox was included, and as a result Fox entered the administration as Foreign Secretary. Even then the alliance was not powerful enough to give the necessary voting strength to the administration. Grenville and Fox found it necessary to turn to Henry Addington, who had now become Lord Sidmouth. In return for seats in the cabinet for himself and his friend, Lord Ellenborough, Sidmouth threw the voting strength of his followers on the side of the alliance.[1] Since 1800 Sidmouth had formed his own government, allied with the Tories of Pitt, and now allied with the Whig ministry of Grenville and Fox. George Canning's comment on this new allegiance of Sidmouth was that, like the measles, everyone must have him once in their lives.[2] Owing to the diverse nature of its membership, the ministry was given the misnomer of "All the Talents."

The hopes of the Americans were given a severe blow in the very formation of the ministry. The pro-American sentiments of Fox were to be diluted by the warlike propensities of Grenville, who was devoted solely to the task of defeating Napoleon, and by the plodding caution of Sidmouth. Henry Adams in his harsh judgments on the Whig party and his indictment of its betrayal of America at this time gave too little attention to these divergences within the ministry itself.[3] Fox and his friends had to cope not only with the Pittite opposition, but also with many of those on whom they depended for their voting strength. At the time of Grenville's union with Fox in opposition to Pitt in the spring of 1804, it had been commented that the Grenville group were "uniting themselves with people to whose political opinions their own are decidedly opposite in almost all important particulars."[4] This was hardly the basis for a stable government, particularly in view of the fact that Sidmouth also had to be depended upon for support. The Whig government was in fact a motley assortment of different groups. It contained practically everyone except the Pittites, and conservatives and radicals were loosely united under the same banner.

Moreover, Fox himself, who was taking office at the end of a very full life and after a long twenty-two years of opposition, was no longer the Fox of the Revolution who with boundless energy had thundered out his friendship for America. Now a tired man, it was difficult for him to leave the peaceful pleasures of St. Anne's Hill to take on himself the rigors of office. His friends were not keen for him to serve with the conservative Grenville, but he knew it was his last chance, and when his nephew, the third Lord Holland, chided him for taking office, Fox wrote, rather poignantly, "don't think me selfish, young one; the slave trade and peace are two such glorious things, I can't give them up even to you. If I can manage *them*—I will then retire."[5] In truth, Fox was a dying man, though he refused to admit it. His end was hastened by the work he thrust upon himself as Foreign Secretary. Fox's secretary at the Foreign Office in the early months of the administration found his work there "very laborious," for "whilst light remained Fox never seemed tired."[6] Appearances were deceptive. On April 2 Fox was taken ill at the House, and he rapidly declined. On the eighteenth he was advised to give up all work, and the advice was repeated throughout April and May, but he still insisted on fulfilling his duties. In June he paid his last visit to the House, and on the twenty-ninth was declared incurable.[7] When his old friend Lady Bessborough visited him on that day she found "his face and hands are dreadfully drawn and emaciated, his complexion sallow beyond measure, his bosom sunk—and then, all at once, a body and legs so enormous that it looks like the things with which they dress up Falstaff."[8] He was suffering from the dropsy and his death was very near. From July he could not continue his work as Foreign Secretary, and the First Under-Secretary in the Foreign Department, Sir Francis Vincent, sent any instructions that were needed to America. By September 13 the "incomparable Charley" was dead, and Grenville in complete control.[9]

Hopes in the United States for a complete change of policy in England after the death of Pitt thus ignored both Fox's political and physical difficulties, as well as the fact that there was a strong Tory opposition backed by considerable influential opinion within the country bent on tightening, not relaxing, the restrictions on America. Yet the United States could hope for more from the Talents than from any other British ministry between 1803 and 1812. There was certainly influential opinion within the government in favor of a policy of friendship towards the United States. The President of the Board of Trade, the first Lord Auckland, wrote on April 7, 1806, that the American question was the most important of the moment, and he had long thought that "the prejudices or habitual opinions of some of the leading civilians at the Cockpit [Court of Appeals] tend to inflame that discussion more than in political wisdom is desirable."[10] The Lord Chancellor, Lord Erskine, whose son was to serve as British Minister in America from 1806 to 1809, went even further. He argued, in the words of the Speaker of the House, Charles Abbot, that "the judgements at the Cockpit upon neutral ships had been very mischievous; that America must be made our friend; that Mr. Fox was determined it should be so; that Lord Selkirk was a proper person to be sent there; that the Senate in America have thrown out the non-importation agreement; that they are our best commercial friends, as we export so largely to them, and their wants of us are growing, and their ties of blood, and language, and manners naturally attach them to us; that with their close alliance we shall overshadow France, &c."[11] There was friendliness towards America and a desire to avoid controversy among at least some Englishmen of influence.

The first positive step towards improving American relations was made by the appointment of a new British representative in

the United States. Fox's opinion of the present incumbent, the
tedious Merry, was not good. When the Duchess of Devonshire
mentioned to him that the youthful Augustus Foster had been
sent to the United States as Secretary of Legation to be trained
under Merry, Fox's comment was "Merry, Augustus was more
fit to train *him*."[12] On March 7, 1806, Fox wrote to Merry
that in consequence of his long continued state of ill-health, the
King was granting him permission to return to England, and
that the Earl of Selkirk was to be his successor. In a private letter
accompanying the official communication, Fox assured Merry
that his health was the reason for his recall.[13] Merry, however,
knew little of his own incapacitating illness. On June 1 he replied to Fox that he had not solicited a recall, and that his health
had not interfered with his work.[14] It is apparent that the state
of Anglo-American relations, not the state of Merry's health,
was uppermost in Fox's mind. Lord Selkirk, however, was unable to accept the appointment, and finally David M. Erskine,
the son of the pro-American Lord Chancellor, was decided upon
as the successor to Merry. His father had requested the post
for him from Fox.[15] It was a happy choice. Erskine, married
to the daughter of General John Cadwalader of Philadelphia,
was enthusiastic in his friendship for the United States. After
the fall of the Talents in March, 1807, when Madison expected
that Erskine might be recalled, he wrote that "it would be difficult to find a successor who would give or feel more pleasure
in the Station than the present incumbent."[16] Unfortunately,
Erskine's friendship for America led to divergences between him
and the home government after the Tories returned to power
in 1807, and this divergence culminated in the tragedy of the
disavowal of the Erskine agreement in 1809. Yet the appointment of Erskine was a mark of friendliness on the part of the
British government towards America, and from the time of his
arrival in Washington in November, 1806,[17] the new British
minister worked for friendship between the two countries.

In the years since 1803, the main commercial problems that had been agitated in England concerning the United States were those of the American trade between the enemy colonies and Europe, and of the American trade with the British islands in the West Indies. In regard to the second of these the controversy raged fiercely after the fall of Pitt's government. The shipping interest and the supporters of the Navigation System urged that the temporary acts which had permitted the Americans to engage in this trade since 1793 should be brought to an end, while the West India interest urged that the trade should be put on a permanent footing. Already when in opposition some of the Talents had expressed opinions favorable to the regularization of this commerce, and in language which left no doubt of their sentiments in regard to America. Lord Holland, Fox's nephew, had argued earnestly on this topic in July, 1805. "With respect to the question," he said, "though as affecting the interests of the islands of great importance, it was still of greater, as it might affect the commercial intercourse between this country and the U.S.A." The comment in Hansard on his address was that "through the whole of his speech, more especially towards the conclusion, the noble lord expiated upon the great national importance, either in a political or commercial view, of maintaining an amicable intercourse and a close connection with America."[18] The chances of the Whigs achieving legislation on this matter was much improved by the fact that Lord Grenville was in accord with the Foxites on this occasion. "My own impressions," he wrote on March 4, "have always been favourable to all questions of extended intercourse between the West Indian Islands and the United States."[19]

The President of the Board of Trade, Lord Auckland, lost no time when the Whigs came into office in sending a letter to the colonial governors directing them to continue the established intercourse with the United States, and assuring them that the usual act of indemnity would be passed in their favor.[20] With the signs so favorable, the West India interest maintained their pressure on government, and Lord Auckland at the Board of Trade was visited by the agents of various West Indian islands, who urged a more extended intercourse with the United States. In the middle of March Auckland discovered that by an oversight the usual act of indemnity, which excused the West India governors for breaches of the Navigation Acts regarding importations in neutral vessels, had not been passed since June, 1800.[21] To remedy this breach of law he prepared a bill which was read for the first time in the House of Lords on March 31, 1806. After some discussion in Parliament and among the Whig ministers, it was also decided to introduce an American Intercourse Bill to regularize the intercourse between the United States and the British West Indies.[22]

On April 22, the day that the West India Indemnity Bill was read for the third time and passed, the Intercourse Bill had its first reading. It was not an extreme bill. As finally passed by the House of Commons on July 21, 1806, it permitted for the duration of the war and for six months after the peace the import and export of certain commodities in the British West Indies in neutral ships. There were various restrictions contained in the act. Imports had to be the produce of the country to which the vessel belonged, and salted meats could not be imported at all. In addition sugar, cotton, indigo, wool, coffee, and cocoa could not be exported in foreign vessels.[23] In essence, this bill did little more than put on a more legal and regular basis a trade between the United States and the British colonies which had been carried on extensively since 1793. The whole interest of the American Intercourse Bill lies not in its provisions, but in the bitter conflict of opinion which it aroused both in the country and in Parliament. The *Annual Register* for 1806 commented with surprise that this type of measure should have aroused such violent opposition in the legislature and among the shipowners of the kingdom.[24] This is of interest because it was this

same Tory opposition that regained power from the Whigs in
1807, and formulated policy towards the United States in the
vital period from 1807 to 1812. The writings and speeches of the
opposition at the time of the American Intercourse Act give us
an excellent summary of the motives behind this policy—the
policy that finally forced America into war in 1812.

As might be expected, it was the shipping interest that made
the really co-ordinated attack on the American Intercourse Act
from outside Parliament, for it had sufficient organization to
exert sustained pressure. Quickly its pamphleteers produced
works to convince opinion, particularly parliamentary opinion,
that the proposed bill would be fatal to British interests.[25] It
was reasoned that the Whig government was attempting to
establish *"a system of suspension"* of the Navigation Laws.[26]
Lord Sheffield, in an enlarged 1806 edition of a pamphlet he
first published in 1804, put forward elaborate arguments to
prove that Britain was suffering commercially to the advantage of
the United States. He maintained that the traditional British
navigation and colonial policy was "founded in undeniable
right, policy, and wisdom," and "that it is to this policy, principally, that Great Britain is indebted for her commercial prosperity, naval predominance, and, perhaps, political existence."[27]

Another pamphleteer of this group defended Sheffield's conclusions and reiterated many of his arguments. The United
States, who was so dexterously educing advantage from the em-
barrassments of other countries, he argued, and who was entering into successful competition with Great Britain, should not
expect that England would sacrifice her laws to encourage
America's growth. "America," he concluded, "though no object
of political jealousy to England, assumes an attitude, and enjoys
a situation, which renders her, in a commercial estimate, an
object of caution."[28]

The whole group tried to prove that the proposed bill was
completely unnecessary from every point of view. It was argued

that the West Indies could be supplied from Great Britain and the British North American colonies, and that even if these supplies should prove insufficient, though in fact it was never conceded that this would be the case, *British* ships could carry the necessary supplies from the United States. If the Navigation Laws were strictly enforced, it was maintained, the British shipowners would have every inducement to enter the trade to the islands.[29]

The proposition that the American trade with the British West Indies was completely unnecessary was linked with the second proposition that it would prove fatal to British interests. Naturally, it was maintained that the shipping industry would suffer tremendously from American encroachment, but in addition an attempt was made to prove that other British interests would also feel the effects. It was argued that the United States would obviously not keep within her legal limits as designated by this bill, and that East India goods, German, and other foreign manufactured articles would be smuggled into the British West Indies. In this way, not only the shippers and the British North American colonies would suffer from American competition, but also the East India Company and British manufacturing interests. Yet the strongest weapon of the shipowners and their supporters was the argument that not only British special interests but also Britain herself was in danger. Naval power and seamen were all-important to British prosperity and to her safety in the struggle against Napoleon. The relaxation of the Navigation System was seen as a mistake from which would result a great weakening of the British economy and power—the British carrying trade would suffer a drastic reduction, and a principal source of British seamen would be lost. Lord Sheffield even went so far as to say that if the United States was allowed to supply the British West Indies, these colonies would in time become dependent on that country and would be lost to Great Britain.[30]

Of possible American retaliation for their exclusion from the

British West Indies, and of the possibility of arousing the active hostility of the United States, these writers were scornful. It was maintained that the United States was no object of jealousy except in the commercial sense, "for, whatever may be her tone, she has not yet acquired a stature gigantic enough to excite the apprehension of England."[31] Lord Sheffield supported this point of view, and argued that "if any war would be injurious to America, a war with England would be peculiarly disastrous."[32] The possibility of economic retaliation was looked upon with equal scorn. It was asserted that American retaliation in the form of discriminatory duties, embargoes, or nonimportation measures would recoil upon American trade and revenue, and that the American people would not submit to the termination of their external trade.[33] In short, "it will be better to leave America to complain of British vigilance and firmness, in maintaining British laws, than that the whole empire should be authorized to complain of the yielding weakness of a British legislature."[34]

The action of the shipping interest on the American Intercourse Bill was not confined to written pressure. A determined effort was made to exert direct pressure on Parliament through the old supporters of Pitt, who were now in opposition. On April 15, seven days before the first reading of the American Intercourse Bill, the Society of Shipowners held a meeting to take into consideration measures to prevent future suspensions of the Navigation Laws, and to combat the proposed bill. Various resolutions were passed deprecating the proposed act as injurious to the maritime interests of the country, and it was agreed that a petition should be presented to Parliament asking for a strict enforcement of the Navigation Laws, and an enquiry into the state of British shipping. These resolutions were to be submitted to the shipowners at other ports of the kingdom.[35]

This meeting inaugurated a spate of petitions to Parliament on behalf of the shipping interest and against the proposed bill.

Between May 16 and June 17 petitions were presented from Scarborough, London, Bridlington, North and South Shields, Glasgow, Greenock, and from the merchants engaged in the trade to the North American Colonies. These petitions were all along the same lines—in fact many of them were identically worded. They asked that this bill should not be passed into law, and that in future the Navigation Laws should be strictly enforced. It was stressed that the suspensions of the Navigation Laws were extremely injurious to British shipping and to the general welfare of the country. The view was clearly expounded that the Americans, if given the chance, would encroach upon British commercial supremacy. Many of these petitions also expressed the desire that the shipping interest should be heard by counsel or agents before Parliament.[36]

The hopes of the shipowners that they would be able to obtain support in Parliament were not vain ones. A hard core of Pittite Tories, who had gone into opposition on the formation of the Ministry of the Talents, were enthusiastic defenders of the British Navigation System, and the Pitt government had been moving steadily toward a stricter commercial policy in regard to America throughout 1805. Not only had they interdicted the American carrying trade from the enemy colonies to Europe in the *Essex* decision, they had also striven to tighten the regulations in regard to the American trade to the British West Indies, though pressure from the planters had prevented them from forbidding the trade.[37] George Rose, who had been Vice-President of the Board of Trade under Pitt and regained the office in 1807, wrote in June, 1806, that the bill now being discussed in the House of Commons will "do away in effect all that I was labouring to accomplish during the whole time I was Vice-President of the Committee for Trade, with Mr. Pitt's entire approbation, and for the success of which he was more than usually solicitous."[38]

On May 22, the day on which the House resolved itself into

a committee of the whole to discuss the American Intercourse Bill, the opposition made a determined effort to secure an enquiry. These efforts were continued until the second reading on June 17.[39] The Whigs, however, were particularly anxious in their somewhat precarious political position not to risk the complications of a full-scale investigation of the problem, and as a result the shipping interest was not heard before the bar of the House.[40] Yet the shipowners well realized the valuable work that was being done for them in Parliament by members of the opposition. Votes of thanks were registered at meetings of the Society of Shipowners on June 19 and on July 31 to the members of Parliament who had supported their cause, and had attempted to uphold Britain's Navigation System.[41] Among those singled out for special mention were Spencer Perceval, Viscount Castlereagh, George Canning, and George Rose. These were respectively the Chancellor of the Exchequer, the Secretary for War and the Colonies, the Foreign Secretary, and the Vice-President of the Board of Trade in the Tory government that ruled England from 1807 to 1809, and put into effect the Orders in Council policy against the United States. Moreover, Spencer Perceval was Prime Minister from 1809 to 1812. It is not without significance that the Society of Shipowners, which had as one of its avowed objects the maintenance of British maritime supremacy against American competition, should have looked upon these men who were to lead England from 1807 to 1812 as excellent exponents of its commercial point of view.

The debates on the American Intercourse Bill were characterized by their length and fervor. The Tory opposition, in its determined resistance to this comparatively insignificant bill, clearly expounded arguments that were to form the basis of policy in the years between 1807 and 1812. The whole of the fervent attack on this measure was based on twin points; that the Whigs were sacrificing the all-important Navigation System, and that they were surrendering it in favor of England's chief commercial rival, the United States. The main burden of the opposition was carried in the Lords by Sheffield and Hawkesbury, and in the Commons by Rose and Castlereagh. Sheffield had so long stressed American competition that he was well fitted for the task. Lord Hawkesbury, who was to become the second Earl of Liverpool on the death of his father in December, 1808, was an ardent mercantilist. His views were to be of importance in the years from 1807 to 1812, for at that time he first served as Home Secretary, and after 1809 as Secretary for War and the Colonies before becoming Prime Minister in June, 1812, on the eve of war. He was a somber individual. It was said of him that he always looked "as if he had been on the rack three times and saw the wheel preparing for a fourth."[42] George Rose was a lesser figure, but his work at the Board of Trade under Pitt, and again after 1807, gave his opinions weight in commercial matters. His son was to undertake an unsuccessful special mission to the United States in 1808. The austere Castlereagh, who was to become one of England's greatest foreign secretaries, was on the threshold of his career. As Secretary for War and the Colonies from 1807 to 1809, he exerted great influence on Spencer Perceval, the instigator of the Orders in Council policy. All in all, they were well placed to influence British policy in the years before the War of 1812.

The arguments of these members of the opposition in Parliament were almost identical to those used by the pamphleteers of the shipping interest. The crux of their resistance to the bill was that the Navigation Laws were essential to the greatness of England, and this was backed by the oft-repeated assertion that there was no necessity for neutral ships to be allowed into the British West Indies, as Britain and her other colonies could furnish the necessary supplies and British ships could carry them. Furthermore, the Tory speakers prophesied extensive smuggling, with losses to British manufacturers, the East India Company, the Irish provision trade, and the British North American colonies. This, in its turn, would result in an inevitable decline of the British carrying trade, and an extensive loss of British seamen to the United States.[43]

Of greater interest is the manner in which these opposition speakers paid such close attention to the commercial danger from the United States. The government was particularly attacked for relaxing the Navigation Laws in favor of the country which stood to gain most by the concessions. Spencer Perceval, the future Chancellor of the Exchequer and Prime Minister, argued on June 17 that this was the worst possible time to show weakness in regard to America, as there were so many points affecting British belligerent rights depending between the two countries. He added that England should not demonstrate to the United States that the British colonies could not exist without her—England's policy towards the United States should above all be strict.[44] This was the striking policy statement of the man who was to lead England from 1809 to 1812. His allies in the opposition agreed with him. Castlereagh on May 22 "thought it very bad policy in us to do anything, at present, that might look like concession, as the Americans might think the government was of a conceding disposition, and might presume on that temper."[45]

George Canning, who was to become somewhat notorious in Anglo-American affairs as Foreign Secretary from 1807 to 1809, added his voice to that of Perceval and Castlereagh. The young Canning, an enthusiastic Pittite, had already made himself a striking reputation with his biting, malicious wit, which he had used with devastating effect on Addington. In this debate he abandoned his witticisms to follow the opposition in warning of the great dangers of the American Intercourse Bill. Like Perceval he was afraid of the effect of the bill on the United States. He stated that Parliament should consider in regard to America how likely "considerable parties and leading individuals there,

whose sentiments towards this country are avowedly of the most
hostile nature," might consider this bill as concession on the part
of England. Canning himself had clear views. He voiced the
opinion that "a worse moment for this country to make any
concession to America could not be chosen."[46]

In the debate preceding the third reading and passing of the
bill on July 8, the opposition reiterated even more strongly its
fears regarding the United States. This is a most significant debate in revealing the views of the group that were so soon to
return to power. Sir Charles Price, who along with his London
colleague Sir William Curtis, had consistently spoken for the
shipping interest and against concession, quickly started the
opposition by stating that this was no time to discourage shipping
and navigation "and to drive still more of our sailors into the
American service."[47] Another member of the opposition continued on this theme by asserting that "the ultimate tendency of
the bill would be to place this country in a state of dependence
on the states of America." He thought America had forgotten
every feeling of amity towards England. This view seemed comparatively mild, and certainly well mannered, alongside Lord
de Blaquiere's statement that "he would ask gentlemen, and
young gentlemen in particular, if this was a time to prostrate
themselves to America, when that country had done every thing
but spit in their faces."[48] The lesser lights of the opposition having completed their sniping, some of the bigger guns were then
brought into play.

Castlereagh arose to argue that the bill assumed a far more
serious shape when considered as a manifestation of a general
relaxation of opinion on the policy of Britain's Navigation
System, and as "a disposition at the expence of that fundamental
law, unwisely, to court and conciliate the government of America
at the present moment." Castlereagh stressed the fact that the
United States was pressing her claims in opposition to "the undoubted maritime rights of this country." He acknowledged that

British prosperity was inseparably united with that of America, but it is a little difficult to imagine how he expected the ministers to conduct negotiations with the United States with friendship, as he requested, when he added that they must with "resolution and inflexible firmness" defend rights, "the maintenance of which is indispensable to our preservation as a maritime state." If the barrier which protected the British commercial marine was taken down, Castlereagh argued, "America and other countries that can build and equip cheaper than we do, will possess themselves largely of our carrying trade."[49]

The government supporters, who were in the majority, spoke far less than the opposition in this discussion of the American Intercourse Bill. Fox and his friends stressed the point that the Navigation Laws had *in fact* been suspended in the West Indies since 1793, and that this act merely established the whole position on a more regular basis. Fox stated on May 6 that the American Intercourse Bill "only transferred a discretionary power, which already existed, from one less fit to exercise that power, to one more fit."[50] This continued to be the attitude of the Whigs throughout the debates. Also, in spite of the bitter attacks of the opposition, the Whigs were not afraid to say that friendship for the United States was a factor in the opening of this intercourse. In 1805 Lord Holland had urged that this measure was of even greater importance for Anglo-American relations than for the interests of the West India colonies,[51] and the Whig President of the Board of Trade, Lord Auckland, supported this view. At the very first reading of the bill, on March 31, he argued that "the United States of America had grown with our strength, and strengthened with our strength, and had contributed much to the increase of our commerce."[52]

The American Intercourse Bill finally passed on July 8, 1806, by a vote of 85 to 30.[53] The Ministry of "All the Talents," with a majority in Parliament, was able to force the measure through in spite of the opposition of both the shipping interest and all those Englishmen, and there were many, who were convinced that England's prosperity, her greatness, and her victory over Napoleon depended upon the maintenance of England's Navigation Laws. Commercial cupidity and ardent patriotism mingled in this resistance to any infringement of the Navigation System, which had apparently given England her position of greatness. The Americans never gave the Whigs their due for this American Intercourse Bill, forced through in spite of intense opposition within England. The controversy that centered around this measure was a clear indication of the fact that any hope that the Americans might have for a more conciliatory policy from England was dependent on the maintenance of power by the Talents. The core of the Tory party had stated in no uncertain terms its belief in a firm, unyielding policy toward the United States, and once that group had returned to office there seemed little doubt that it would do all in its power to restrict American commercial activity.

On the question of extending the intercourse between the United States and the British West Indies, success had been possible because both the Fox and the Grenville wings of the Whig party had agreed on the expediency of the move. In the matter of the American trade between the enemy colonies and Europe, the Talents were presented with a far more difficult problem. In the first place, they had been presented with a *fait accompli* by their predecessors in the form of the *Essex* decision. Moreover, this trade presented the problem that by it the Americans were undoubtedly aiding Britain's enemy, and the defeat of France always had to be placed first by any British ministry. At a time when England's Continental allies had been defeated, and Britain depended upon maritime warfare in her struggle with France, it seemed paradoxical to allow American ships to replace French in Napoleon's colonial trade. This latter consideration was of basic importance to Grenville, whose dominating interest was the defeat of France. Writing to Lord Auckland in February of 1806, he attacked as a sophism Jefferson's argument that it was unreasonable for Britain to exclude America from the carrying trade at a time when Britain herself traded in colonial produce with Europe. "We have a right," Grenville asserted, "to prevent that which is injurious to us."[54] Naturally, at a time when England was engaged in a life-or-death struggle, this view had much to be said for it. England's primary concern in the years before the War of 1812 was to defeat France and the Napoleonic dictatorship. To accomplish this end many Englishmen were prepared to disregard the opinions of neutrals. To have been well regarded by the United States would have served very little purpose if Napoleon had ruled at the Court of St. James.

Fox's difficulty was thus a great one. England could afford to conciliate the United States only in so far as it did not hinder her own efforts to defeat Napoleon. To have rescinded the *Essex* decision would have seemed an action of direct aid to the enemy, and Fox would have had to face the opposition not only of the Tories and the Grenville wing of his own party, but also of all Englishmen who desired the defeat of Napoleon. Fox was obliged to compromise, and he faced the old difficulty that in compromising he was liable to please no one. At best, all he could claim was a modification of the rigor of the *Essex* decision. His Order in Council of May 16, 1806, later given the name of "Fox's blockade," proclaimed a blockade from the Elbe to Brest, but was to be strictly enforced only in the area from Ostend to the Seine. Outside this area neutrals could trade, provided that they did not carry contraband of war, and provided that they had not been laden at nor were destined to an enemy port. This meant that the trade between the enemy colonies and Europe, by way of American ports, once again became fully possible.[55] Unfortunately, America did not accept this as a concession but rather as a fresh imposition. It was looked upon as an illegal paper blockade, and attacked as much as the *Essex* decision itself.[56] The United States would perhaps have done better on this occasion to have sacrificed the principle and kept the substance, for when the Tory government regained power it was to get neither.

Later in May, 1806, the arrival of the news of the American Non-Importation Act showed once again the difficulty that any English government faced in trying to follow a policy of moderation toward America. The immediate reaction of the upholders of the Navigation System was one of intense anger. James Stephen, the author of the influential *War in Disguise,* wrote an introduction to the American John Randolph's attack on the measure, and published it as a pamphlet. He was incensed at America's attempt to force England into concessions :

> What ! is a rod to be put into the hands of a foreign minister, to whip us into submission; and are we broadly and coarsely to sell our maritime rights, for the sake of passing off a little haberdashery along with them ! ! !
>
> Are we to make a lumping pennyworth to the buyers of our leather wares, or felt and tin wares, and the other commodities enumerated in this insolent bill, by tossing our honour, our justice, and our courage also in the parcel ! ! ! I would not consent to disparage even the quality of our manufactures, much less of our public morals, by so shameful a bargain.[57]

It hardly needs to be pointed out that Stephen was interested in the preservation of the shipping interest, and of the British Navigation Laws, not in the welfare of England's fast growing industrial concerns. In Manchester, where the huge cotton industry depended for a large part of its sales on the American market, the hard-headed Lancashire manufacturers were not apt to speak so disparagingly of "a little haberdashery." Yet these aggressive sentences from James Stephen, the good friend of Spencer Perceval, boded ill for the success of American economic coercion when the Tories should return to power. They underlined the fact that there was considerable influential opinion in England that was willing to sacrifice the English manufacturers rather than make concessions to the United States.

Fox's hopes of achieving any compromise grew less and less as the news of the American reaction to the acts of his predecessors reached England. The prematurely old and dying Fox, epitome of all that was best and worst in late eighteenth-century England, indeed faced an impossible task in 1806. A warlike Napoleon, a powerful opposition, a lack of unity among the Talents, and his own health ruined his hopes. He would have liked peace with France and friendship with America, but could obtain neither. He might well have thought that the fates that had kept him from office for so long were still against him in the last year of his life. His death was a severe blow to the American cause in England.

5 *The Monroe-Pinkney Treaty*

IN AMERICA hopes were high in the spring of 1806. At the beginning of May, Jefferson looked upon the future of Anglo-American relations with a marked optimism. "The late changes in the ministry," he wrote to Monroe, "I consider as ensuring us a just settlement of our differences, and we ask no more. In Mr. Fox personally I have more confidence than in any man in England. . . . While he shall be in the administration, my reliance on that government will be solid." Jefferson went on to say that America had committed herself to a policy adopted to meet Pitt's hostility before his death, and self-respect did not permit her to abandon it afterwards. The members of the British government should not view American measures as directed against them at all, but rather against their predecessors. "No two countries on earth have so many points of common interest and friendship," this farseeing President asserted, "and their rulers must be great bunglers indeed if with such dispositions, they break them assunder." At the end of his letter he stated his creed : "We ask for peace and justice from all nations, and will remain uprightly neutral in fact, tho' leaning in belief to the opinion that an English ascendency on the ocean is safer for us than that of France."[1]

This letter of Jefferson is made even more striking by the fact that he was writing these words of friendship only a few weeks after yet another incident had occurred outside New York to inflame American passions. On April 25 the British ship *Leander*, in attempting to stop the American sloop *Delaware*, fired a shot which killed the American helmsman. Here was an act to stir national sentiment. The inhabitants of New York, enraged by this British action, stopped a boat that the purser of the *Leander* had laden with provisions, placed the supplies in carts, and paraded around the town with the British colors placed on a pole under the American flag. After giving the supplies to the Alms House, they burned the British colors.[2] Such incidents as this were inevitable at a time when the British sea captains, confident after their successes over the French, were empowered by the Admiralty to search American ships directly off the American coast. They were a constant source of iritation to the Americans.

In spite of this incident, plans for a settlement with England went ahead in the spring of 1806. On March 11, while the debates on the Non-Importation Act were still proceeding, Madison had informed Monroe that the merchants were enthusiastically advocating sending an extraordinary commission to England to negotiate difficulties. The President, Madison said, had not yet decided whether to send a mission, but it was agreed that if this step was taken Monroe would be included if he were still in England.[3] Jefferson reached a definite conclusion with rapidity, for on March 16 he informed Monroe that he intended to nominate William Pinkney of Maryland to act as Monroe's associate in settling difficulties with England. Pinkney was also to become minister to England when Monroe decided to return to America.[4] The object of the mission was to attempt to solve in one treaty the main problems of impressment and neutral rights, and to replace the commercial sections of Jay's Treaty that were to expire in 1807. On May 17 Madison sent the instructions to Monroe and Pinkney. Three essential conditions were laid down for the signing of the treaty; Great Britain would have to re-

pudiate impressment, restore the American trade with the
enemy colonies to the position before the *Essex* decision, and
give indemnity for captures made under that decision. There
was also to be discussion and bargaining concerning contraband,
blockade, East and West Indian trade, and various other less
important matters. In a private letter accompanying the official
instructions, Madison indicated that he was not quite as confident as Jefferson that England would come to an agreement,
and also indicated that he knew something of the political difficulties facing the Whigs. He said that the language of Fox held
out very favorable prospects, but that he was afraid that other
members of the cabinet might not concur in those liberal
sentiments.[5]

In London James Monroe had approached Fox after the
change of administration to investigate the possibilities of negotiation, but owing to the insistent pressure of European affairs,
and the need for careful management of the American problem,
the British government delayed coming to a decision in the
spring of 1806. Early in April Fox wrote to Merry in Washington, explained the delay, and asked him to assure the American
government of Britain's wish for friendship.[6] Throughout April
Monroe continued to press Fox to take action, though by this
time affairs were complicated by Fox's serious illness from
which he was never to recover. At the end of the month, Monroe
received preliminary news of the appointment of Pinkney to join
him in a special mission to meet with the British government,
and after this Monroe took very little action while awaiting the
arrival of his fellow commissioner.[7] Pinkney finally arrived at
Liverpool from the United States on June 19, and immediately
proceeded to London. Prompt action proved impossible, however, for a note from Fox's Under-Secretary, Sir Francis Vincent,
informed the two American commissioners that Fox was too ill
to see them. This was no diplomatic excuse. It was at this time
that Fox's doctors pronounced him incurable. Throughout July

the delay continued. Finally, at the beginning of August, Fox, who was quite unable to take part in negotiations himself, entrusted them to the care of Lords Holland and Auckland.[8]

This was probably as good a choice as could have been made for the negotiations. Lord Holland, Fox's nephew, had long been quite open in his affection for the United States, and continued his friendship even after the eventual failure of the Monroe-Pinkney negotiations. In October, 1807, after the bitterness between the two countries had considerably increased, Holland wrote to Monroe that "every day convinces me more and more that the prosperity and happiness of our two countries are inseparably united and that for their security as well as for the general interest of liberty in which all Mankind are concurred it is essential that they should not help to ruin one another."[9] Auckland too had expressed sentiments very favorable to the United States during the debate on the American Intercourse Bill, and was generally a man with a considerable sympathy for that country. He was, however, far more under the influence of Grenville than was Holland, and was apt to be somewhat more practical and hard-headed than his fellow negotiator. These two British negotiators were reasonable men, but the problems that faced them were almost insurmountable, both in regard to the complexity of the problem involved, and because of the internal opposition to an agreement in England. Even England's representatives in America had written to advise the British government against conceding anything in this negotiation with the United States. Merry wrote to Fox on May 4, and said that should the government decide that the pretensions advanced by the Americans were unjust, and be therefore disposed to resist them, "such a Resistance will only be attended with the Salutary Effect of commanding from this Government that Respect which they have nearly lost towards Great Britain." Augustus Foster, Secretary of Legation, gave as his opinion in writing home that "a mere face of anger is all we need shew to these Democrats, for a long time to come."[10]

Moreover, in England herself determined opposition had to be overcome. In writing of these events later, Lord Holland stated that during the whole negotiation for the Monroe-Pinkney Treaty "the atmosphere of the Admiralty made those who breathed it shudder at anything like concessions to the Americans."[11] At the time the much older Lord Auckland was far more aware of the practical difficulties involved than was Lord Holland. The shrewd Auckland wrote to Grenville on August 21, 1806, that Holland seemed to think the accomplishment of a treaty far easier than Auckland himself expected. He thought that his fellow commissioner was not "sufficiently aware of the expediency of carrying with us, as far as may be practicable, the concurrence and good opinion of the mercantile and shipping interests, the manufacturers, the North American Committee, the East India Company, the West India people, and others interested. A few collateral attentions very much break the attacks which will be made in Parliament with great vehemence, whatever may be the contents or merits of any treaty that can be formed."[12] In addition, the negotiation had to face the great handicap of the death of Fox on September 13, 1806. The Americans at the time may have been disappointed at the paucity of the efforts that Fox was able to make for better Anglo-American relations, but they should have made the most of them, for never again before the War of 1812 was there to be a man in high office in England so sympathetic to their cause. Lord Grenville, now undisputed leader of the Talents, was reported in December, 1806, to have called the American government "a *Mob Government* and one too weak to carry its own measures into effect."[13] A natural eighteenth-century aristocrat, immersed in the war in Europe, Grenville was growing more and more cynical in his attitude toward America. In truth, there were enough bitter events in Europe to concern him and the rest of England, and to make negotiations with America seem of comparatively minor importance.

The year 1806 had been most dismal. Since those first weeks when Nelson had been drawn through the silent streets to his last resting place in St. Paul's, and the death of Pitt had numbed the country, England's position had become increasingly precarious. Fox had desired peace with France, but in the end even he had to acknowledge that Napoleon wanted too much, and the war continued. In September Fox joined Pitt in death, and Lady Bessborough wondered: "Where, where will England ever repair such losses as Pitt and him? Two such minds, I suppose, scarcely ever enlighten'd any Country together before, and both to fail at once is dreadful, and at what a time too."[14] The situation was to become even worse, for on October 14 Napoleon continued his year of triumph by routing the Prussians at Jena.

Even the Americans thought England was finished by the second half of 1806. In December John Randolph prophesied another Austerlitz, and said that if that happened England either would become "an appendage to the continent" or would dwindle into insignificance. "Should she escape being reduced to the form of a province," he wrote, "she will go off in a political atrophy."[15] Six months before this another correspondent of Monroe, William Wirt, had decided that England was "not long for this world," and had concluded that "Mr. Pitt has made a lucky escape, if there is no hereafter."[16]

Not for the last time in British history the prophets of gloom turned out to be wrong, but the second half of 1806 was hardly a propitious time for the United States to negotiate a treaty of which the *sine qua non* was the British relinquishment of the practice of impressment. How could any government, however favorably inclined toward America, have given up the right at such a time? On the Continent Napoleon was engaged in proving that he was apparently invincible on land. The sole hope of

England waging warfare against the man who had promised to destroy her was through her navy. If she gave up impressment, it seemed likely that she would be unable to man her ships. The Admiralty had reported at the beginning of 1806 that "the demands for men have been beyond all imagination, and the want of them hampers every operation considerably."[17] No threat of economic retaliation, nor even of war itself, could make England give up the right at such a time.

Early in the Monroe-Pinkney negotiations, with the negotiators eager to compromise, it did seem that an agreement would be reached on impressment, by England giving up the right and America promising to give up deserters. The Admiralty, constantly hostile to America and also realizing that it was extremely unlikely that America could fulfill the proposed agreement, would not agree to it. This was enough to doom the proposal.[18] The dilemma of those friendly to America was clearly expressed in a statement by Holland and Auckland in October, 1806. It deserves quotation at length :

> It must be confessed that this is a question of equal difficulty and importance. If it were admitted that our Sea Faring people might transfer themselves with impunity to the American Service, our homeward bound fleets would return home manned by foreigners at the commencement of every War, and our Navy might be confined to Port for want of hands. On the other hand it is the evident Duty of the United States to protect their lawful Trade from interruption and outrage, and their citizens from being compelled to fight the battles of a foreign power.[19]

This attitude did not change in the months before the War of 1812. Only one month before America declared war, the pro-Whig and pro-American *Monthly Review* said that "our right to impress our seamen from on board the merchantmen of America, or of any country, admits of no question : but the difficulty is to exercise that right without infraction on the liberty of American citizens."[20]

The negotiations for the Monroe-Pinkney Treaty, which had finally begun on August 27, soon made it apparent that a treaty in the form desired by Jefferson was impossible. Influenced by this realization, and desirous of reaching at least some accommodation, the American negotiators decided to abandon Jefferson's *sine qua non* of the relinquishment of impressment, and informed Madison of this fact on November 11. Instead, the American negotiators accepted a British note stating that great care would be taken not to impress American citizens, and that redress would be given for injuries inflicted upon Americans while impressing British seamen.[21]

With the death of Fox in September, it seemed that both sides became doubtful of a satisfactory agreement, though in truth it seemed impossible that Fox himself could have negotiated a treaty satisfying the main American demand. On hearing of Fox's death, Jefferson wrote from America that he no longer expected an "early or just result."[22] From Jefferson's point of view, his fears were justified. Although a treaty was finally signed on December 31, 1806, it was of a type that was bound to be rejected by the President, if he maintained his insistence on the impressment clause. Even in England there was a realization that the main points had not been solved. The day after the treaty was signed, Auckland wrote that in the troubled state of the world the signing of the treaty was of great importance to England, "more especially as we have not admitted any article that is open to material attack. (Private.—In truth we have postponed the principal difficulties to quieter times.)"[23] Lord Holland's wife wrote in her journal that the treaty was signed and must be sent to America for ratification: "the only point gained is the settling the ill-humour, and fixing the continuous voyage; the seamen question is still unsettled."[24]

The obvious disastrous weakness in the treaty was the American failure to achieve a British abandonment of the practice of impressment. This was the key to its failure, though also missing was a satisfaction of the American demand for seizures made under the *Essex* decision. In regard to the trade with the enemy colonies, Britain made a substantial concession. The Americans were permitted to bring the produce of the enemy West India colonies to the unblockaded ports of France and Spain, and to return the goods of these countries to the colonies, provided that in the former case a 2 per cent, and in the latter a 1 per cent, duty was paid in the United States. These stipulations were reasonable enough to make the trade profitable to the United States, and the Americans never attained such a concession from a Tory ministry in subsequent years.[25]

Yet this was not all, for to add to the complications of the omission of impressment, Britain learned shortly before the signing of the treaty that Napoleon had issued the Berlin Decree on November 21, 1806. After defeating the Prussians at Jena, Napoleon now tried to injure England where it would do her most harm. From Berlin he issued the decree placing England in a state of blockade, and prohibiting all trade in British goods. Napoleon did not have the navy to enforce this decree, but he hoped to enforce it by control of the European ports. All trade in British goods was prohibited, and ships coming directly from British ports were to be refused access to the Continent. Napoleon was going to attempt to defeat England by control of her trade.[26] Britain's reaction to this measure demonstrates how the pressure of affairs in Europe was gradually forcing England and America into open hostility. Holland and Auckland immediately submitted a note to the American commissioners, stating that Britain expected the United States to resist the measure, or Britain would not pledge herself to uphold the terms of the treaty. Auckland so little understood the situation that he expected the note to be well received by the Americans.[27] He thought, as did the vast majority of Englishmen of this period, that if the Americans cherished liberty it would be in their interest to resist this latest act of Napoleon. In 1806 as in 1940 England found it difficult to understand why all the Americans could not immediately distinguish between good and evil, between the cause of liberty and the cause of tyranny. Unfortunately, the British note of December, 1806, given with such confidence by the negotiators, was ranked by the Americans as equally infamous to the omission of impressment in the treaty, and looked upon as another example of the British attempt to dictate to the United States.

Monroe and Pinkney transmitted the treaty to the United States on January 3, 1807, accompanied by a twenty-seven-page explanatory letter.[28] Their explanations were of little use, for the treaty was doomed before it ever crossed the Atlantic. Already on February 3, 1807, before Jefferson had received the treaty, Madison had written to the American commissioners to tell them that the President thought that "if no satisfactory and formal stipulation on the subject of impressment be attainable, the negotiation should be made to terminate without any formal compact whatever"—rather there should be just a friendly, informal understanding.[29] Jefferson, anxious for peace, realized that it was better for no treaty to be signed rather than one be signed and repudiated.

The treaty finally reached Washington early in March, 1807. David M. Erskine, the British minister, received this first copy of the treaty and immediately hurried with it to Madison. Erskine hoped that he might persuade Jefferson to detain the Senate, which was about to adjourn for the summer, to consider the treaty. Yet, in transmitting this news to Lord Howick, Fox's successor as Foreign Secretary, Erskine made it plain that Madison was dissatisfied with the treaty. Madison was "very astonished and disappointed" that there was nothing about impressment in it, and said he did not think that it would be possible to ratify it without an article on that subject. Moreover,

Madison added that the note concerning the Berlin Decree, which had been delivered to Monroe and Pinkney just before the signing, would have been enough to prevent the ratification of the treaty, even if all the other terms had been satisfactory. On the same day that Jefferson received the treaty a group of senators called on him. They were told that the treaty was exceedingly disappointing, and that the President had decided not to present it to the Senate. Erskine saw Jefferson on the following day, and the President explained that the absence of any article on impressment, and the note on the Berlin Decree delivered by Holland and Auckland, had prevented him from offering it to the Senate for ratification. Erskine, however, thought that the treaty would have been favorably received had there been a clause in it regarding impressment. A few days later Erskine was able to report to the British government that the President was determined to send the treaty back to England without ratification. He also expressed the view that American public opinion would support the President.[30]

Madison broke the news to Monroe on March 20 that, for the reasons given to Erskine, the President thought that it would be necessary to renew negotiation. He added that on the question of impressment "the public mind has reached a crisis of sensibility," and that this subject had essentially contributed both to the mission to England, and to the passing of the Non-Importation Act in April, 1806.[31] Jefferson added his explanation to Monroe in a letter he wrote the next day: "the British Commissers appear to have screwed every article as far as it would bear, and yielded nothing." He thought that if the treaty could not be put into an acceptable form, it would be better to withdraw as gracefully as possible from the negotiations while still preserving a "friendly understanding."[32] One of Jefferson's most prominent supporters in the House, Joseph H. Nicholson of Maryland, summed up the situation in a letter to Monroe in April. He said that the difficulties regarding a treaty with England were probably insurmountable, as Jefferson would not accept the treaty without an impressment clause, and Great Britain would never yield on the issue. As for American public sentiment, he thought that "the President's Popularity is unbounded, and his will is that of the nation. . . . Any Treaty therefore which he sanctions will be approved by a very large Proportion of our People."[33]

The Monroe-Pinkney Treaty foundered above all on this rock of impressment—a system, in the words of Madison, "so anomalous in principle, so grievous in practice, and so abominable in abuse." Madison used these words in a letter to his friend George Joy in May, 1807. He also stated that it was impossible to conclude a treaty with England which was silent on the subject of impressment. Though negotiations with England had been renewed, he thought any cordiality resulting from them would be of short duration unless words were transformed into deeds by "a suspension of the outrages which the naval commanders of G.B. are so much in the habit of practising on our shores, and even within our harbors."[34]

By the spring of 1807 the foundations had been laid for open Anglo-American hostility, and undoubtedly the most influential factor in the worsening of relations between the two countries in the years from 1803 to 1807 had been the question of impressment. Had there been no impressment problem, it seems likely that it would have been possible to work out some agreement between America and England in this period. The other most aggravating factor in Anglo-American relations—the American trade between the enemy colonies and Europe—had been partially solved by Fox's blockade of May, 1806, and the appropriate section in the Monroe-Pinkney Treaty. America would undoubtedly have been far more willing to accept this British compromise on neutral trade had she not already been incensed by the steady increase of impressment, and by Britain's refusal to yield any of her rights in this matter. Yet such a settle-

ment achieved in these years would not have been a permanent
one, for the war in Europe was rapidly assuming its commercial
phase, and the question of American commerce was soon to
equal in importance that of impressment. In addition, bad as it
had been, 1806 had been a year of reprieve for the Americans,
because the Whigs, impotent as they were to achieve a fundamental improvement in Anglo-American relations, were at least
making every effort to avoid increasing American irritation.
The Tories were to be far less careful when they returned to
power in 1807.

In the meantime, however, the faltering ministry of the
Talents had the problem of coping with Napoleon's new policy
as expressed in the Berlin Decree. If only for the sake of national
prestige, Napoleon's measure called for retaliation in kind. At
the close of 1806 pressure was exerted on the government for
decisive action to combat the new French decree.[35] It was quite
obvious that Napoleon's new measure could not be allowed to
pass unnoticed, but how to do this without completely alienating America was to prove an impossible problem. On January 7,
1807, the Whig government issued an Order in Council which
prohibited neutrals from trading *between* ports in the hands of
the enemy. This measure was undoubtedly harmful to neutrals,
though in comparison to later British commercial action it was
a mild form of retaliation. It bore most heavily on neutrals in
that it prevented vessels from going from port to port in the
hands of the enemy seeking the best market. It also prevented a
vessel selling a cargo in one port, and then proceeding to another
to buy a return cargo. Henry Adams took the opportunity presented by this Order to lambast the Whigs for their restriction
of American commerce, and for passing this measure while
attacking similar Tory measures at a later date.[36] He was somewhat unjust in his criticism, for, in view of the extent of Napoleon's Berlin Decree, England would have been justified in taking
far more vigorous action in retaliation to the French. The Tory

government had no hesitation in doing this later in the same year. The Whigs could not ignore Napoleon's decree, though any commercial retaliation they might make was bound to produce American opposition. The Whigs were not only criticized by the Americans for the harshness of their Order in Council, they also had to undergo attack from the Tory opposition for its weakness.

The debate on the new Order opened in Parliament on February 4, 1807, and the Tory attack on this occasion was based essentially on the grounds that the Whigs had acted with far too little vigor in retaliation to the French decree. The Tories contended that the Whigs had adopted a weak form of retaliation out of fear of offending the United States. Perceval, the future Chancellor of the Exchequer and Prime Minister, asserted in the opening debate that "we ought to have retaliated not on neutrals, but on the enemy, however hard that retaliation might prove upon neutrals."[37] This fine distinction was hardly likely to be of great significance to the Americans. Castlereagh, as in the debate on the American Intercourse Act, followed the leadership of Perceval. He stated that Britain should not be dissuaded from strict retaliation against France by any consideration of forbearance in regard to the United States. Once again in this debate he spoke of the great importance of maritime rights to England. He pointed out that in spite of the vast superiority of the British navy, France had "a surprising facility of importing the produce of her own and the Spanish Colonies, to as great an extent as during peace." America was re-exporting this colonial produce to the great advantage of France.[38]

The Tory rank and file gave full support to their leaders: "the real cause of the pusillanimous forbearance," it was asserted, "was the fear of offending America, the dread of breaking off the treaty lately pending between this country and the American Government."[39] Once again the Tory opposition was plainly demonstrating its desire to curb American commerce.

The only difference was that in the earlier debates its main arguments had been concerned with the dangers of American competition, and that now the main stress was laid on the necessity of retaliation against France regardless of its effect on America.

On their part, the Tories had no doubt as to what policy should have been adopted in retaliation to the French decree. They had no hesitation in maintaining that the best method of answering the French action would be by a total prohibition of the neutral carrying trade between the enemy West Indies and Europe. Perceval was particularly enthusiastic in supporting this plan. He made the whole matter strikingly simple. By forbidding neutrals to carry enemy colonial produce to Europe, he argued, "we should enhance the price of these articles, and enable our own commodities to meet them with advantage. We should improve the market, therefore, for our own merchants and manufacturers, and promote the sale of their goods. We should then have that trade which could be most easily interrupted, and which our enemy could not extricate from our grasp, and he would literally be made to feel the evil effects of his own injustice." Furthermore, he maintained that an effective retaliation against Napoleon's decree would be for Britain to state that no goods could be carried to France unless they first came to a British port for the imposition of a duty. This would contribute towards raising the price, and thus give a better sale in foreign markets to British commodities.[40] Perceval was advocating not only that retaliation should be made against France, but also that this retaliation should be used to give protection to British interests suffering from American competition. He was throwing his full weight on the side of those who since the beginning of the century had been protesting that America was taking advantage of the war to compete for England's commercial supremacy. In addition, he was clearly outlining the policy of the British Orders in Council of November, 1807.

4

The speeches of the Whigs on this occasion add to this impression that the January, 1807, Order was, in comparison to Tory aims, a mild method of retaliation. Moreover, these speeches are interesting in that they demonstrate the increasing link between the Whigs and the British manufacturing interests in this period. The Whig Advocate General, Sir John Nicholl, first stated in replying to the opposition that the prohibition of all commerce in the produce of the enemy would occasion tremendous distress to the neutrals. Jealousy of America, he thought, was at the bottom of the complaints regarding the weakness of Whig retaliation. He continued by arguing that Britain as well as America would suffer from a total interdiction of neutral commerce in French produce. Nicholls pointed out that though America exported to the Continent, her imports were mainly from England : "If neutrals are deprived of the continental market for their colonial produce, they will not have the means of purchasing from us."[41]

Earl Temple, the nephew of Lord Grenville and one of the paymasters general, summarized the Whig dilemma when he said that "it was agreed on all hands that this country possessed the right of retaliating; but the question was whether it would be politic in us to exercise that right to its full extent." His conclusion was that it would be impolitic to injure so valuable a friend as the United States. Temple stressed the importance of the United States to England, and the consequences that would befall British commerce and manufactures if the neutral colonial trade were eliminated. Exports from Great Britain to the United States had been worth 11 million pounds in the previous year, but only a small proportion, Temple asserted, was for American consumption. The rest was disposed of in payment for colonial produce, which was afterward brought to Europe. He argued that as the produce of the French colonies in one year was not worth more than 4 or 5 million pounds, the whole of the remainder must have been the produce of the British colonies.

Thus the effect of the stoppage of the colonial trade to Europe would be a reduction in the amount of exports from Great Britain.[42]

Though there were no firmly established English party lines in this period, it is significant how on matters concerning America a split occurred between the Pittite Tories who were to rule England from 1807 to 1812 on one hand, and the Whig alignment of Grenvillites and old Foxites on the other. Whereas the Tories in their policy since 1804 had plainly shown their sympathy with the shipping interest and the supporters of Britain's Navigation System, the Whigs were increasingly showing their interest in Britain's manufacturers. The Industrial Revolution, which was so rapidly altering English life in the late eighteenth and early nineteenth centuries, was creating a new influential class of British manufacturers. To this group America was of great importance for the excellent market it offered. Exports of British domestic goods to the United States increased from 30.5 per cent of the whole in 1805 to 33.4 per cent of the whole in 1807.[43] Whereas the shipping interest and the defenders of Britain's Navigation System had nothing to lose, in fact much to gain, from restrictions on American commerce or even war with the United States, the vast body of British manufacturers stood to lose a third of their export trade. In the years between 1807 and 1812, this division in British opinion was to prove increasingly important in Anglo-American relations. Unfortunately for the United States, the hard core of Pitt's followers regained control in England in the spring of 1807 and kept it in the period before the War of 1812. This meant that America in her economic retaliation was to face the gravest difficulties. The main British interest that America could seriously harm by economic retaliation was that of the manufacturers, and the American government was soon to discover that the government in power in England after 1807 was more interested in the fortunes of the British maritime interests than in those of the

British manufacturers. The condition of affairs in England would have to be serious enough for the opposition to be able to *force* the government to reverse its desired policy, before economic coercion would have any effect.

The January, 1807, Order in Council was the last major act of the Talents in regard to America. In March, 1807, after holding office precariously for a year, the Whig government finally fell from power, after meeting royal opposition to its plan to remove some of the disabilities from the Roman Catholics. The disciples of Pitt, who had lost power after their leader's death in January, 1806, once again regained office. The position of Prime Minister was given to a figurehead—the elderly Duke of Portland. He remained in that office until September, 1809, and during that time he was not known to have attended a debate.[44] The composition of the cabinet, however, left little hope for the United States. At the Exchequer, and leading the Commons, was Spencer Perceval; Castlereagh was at the War Office; Canning at the Foreign Office; Earl Bathurst, who had been a personal friend of Pitt, at the Board of Trade; Lord Hawkesbury at the Home Office, and at the Admiralty was Lord Mulgrave—a "complete John Bull" who "gloried in Nelson, and seemed to have an immortal hatred of Napoleon."[45] The United States could hope for no concession now. Between March and December, 1807, relations between England and the United States were to reach a deadlock from which there was no escape but American acquiescence or war.

6 *Embargo and Orders in Council*

SUCH WERE the difficulties of communication in the early nineteenth century that in March, 1807, as England was occupied with the formation of a new government, America was just recovering from the first shock of the Monroe-Pinkney Treaty. The arrival of the news of the January Order in Council at the end of March increased this shock,[1] but throughout the spring of 1807 it was the unsatisfactory treaty with England that occupied the main attention of the American government. Jefferson and his cabinet still hoped that England would agree to emendations that would make the treaty acceptable. In this spring of 1807 Jefferson and Madison occupied many fruitless weeks in a study of the rejected treaty with England. At the end of April Jefferson could only comment that "the more it is developed the worse it appears."[2] Not until May 20 was Madison at last ready to send new instructions to Monroe and Pinkney. He did this in a fifty-page letter, but in spite of all the detailed suggestions for improvement, the inexorable fact remained that America wanted England to give up impressment and England would not do it.[3] This time spent by Madison in preparing instructions to enable the American commissioners to obtain a new and satisfactory treaty was to prove of little value. News of the accession of the Tories to power had already reached America at the end of April, and if America had rejected a treaty signed

by the Whigs, what hope was there of obtaining a more satisfactory one from the Tories? Yet Madison retained hope,
though he acknowledged at the end of May that the formation
of a new government in England had increased the danger of
war.[4]

The danger to peace was nearer than Madison realized, and
it came from a source that only serves to emphasize that between
1803 and 1807 it was impressment, more than any other factor,
that was responsible for the sharp decline in Anglo-American
relations. In the early months of 1807, a British squadron was
lying at anchor in Chesapeake Bay waiting for the appearance
of two French ships that had taken refuge in United States
waters. While there, the British obtained water and supplies
from the mainland, and this presented an opportunity for British
sailors to desert. Several took the opportunity to do so, and the
matter reached a crisis on March 7 when a boat's crew of British
seamen escaped and rowed to shore. Many of them joined
American ships, including several who enlisted on board the
American frigate *Chesapeake* and flaunted their new-found freedom in the streets of Norfolk. The British officers appealed for
them without success, and then reported their grievances to the
British commander-in-chief at Halifax, Vice-Admiral George
C. Berkeley. Berkeley, angry at this flouting of British power,
issued an order to the ships of his command that should they
meet the *Chesapeake* at sea they were to search her for deserters.[5]
On June 22, 1807, the *Chesapeake* weighed anchor and put out
to sea. When she was only eight or nine miles off shore she was
approached by the British ship *Leopard,* and a man was sent on
board to request the handing over of deserters. Commander
Barron of the *Chesapeake* refused this request, and the British
ship fired first across the bows of the American vessel and then
directly into her, killing three and wounding eighteen. The
American vessel was forced to strike her colors, and the British
searched her and took off four men.[6]

The return of the *Chesapeake* to Hampton Roads produced a sensation which almost drove America into open hostility against England. The whole country cried for war with a revolutionary fervor. Augustus Foster, the British Secretary of Legation, was in the region of New York when he heard of the incident. Judging discretion to be the better part of valor, he immediately decided to travel incognito and entrusted his curricle and horses to the separate care of his groom. This proved a sound decision, as only the presence of a somewhat timid soul counseling moderation prevented the curricle and horses from being thrown into the North River. Foster revealed more than the temper of the American populace when he commented that "the ring-leader on this occasion was, as might be expected, an Irish emigrant."[7] New York's anger was paralleled throughout the country. At Norfolk a crowd destroyed the water casks of the British squadron, and the town administration forbade communication with the British ships in the bay. Even in New England, public meetings were held to denounce this latest attack on American shipping. It seemed that the injuries inflicted on America at sea between 1803 and 1807 had reached their culmination, and would at last bring open warfare.[8]

Thomas Barclay, the British consul general in New York, wrote to George Canning on July 2 and stated that "the lower order of the Americans are much irritated and inclined for violent measures."[9] Elbridge Gerry of Massachusetts well expressed the national sentiment. "The public indignation is universally excited by the repeated destruction of our unoffending seamen," he wrote, "if redress for the present, and prevention for the future, cannot be obtained, will not a state of warfare, be preferable to such a state of national insult and degredation."[10] This feeling continued throughout July, and at the end of the month Erskine informed Canning that the public excitement had still not subsided.[11] America was ripe for war.

Jefferson's first reaction was to issue a proclamation on July 2 expelling all armed British ships from American waters.[12] Yet in this moment of great crisis, the President maintained his calm and good sense. At a time when he so easily could have had war, he kept the peace. On June 29 he wrote to the governor of Virginia, saying that the decision as to whether the outrage should be answered by war rested with Congress, and that the cabinet should do nothing to commit that body. His own sentiments were expressed quite plainly by his argument that this "will leave Congress free to decide whether war is the most efficacious mode of redress in our case, or whether, having taught so many other useful lessons to Europe, we may not add that of showing them that there are peaceable means of redressing injustice, by making it the interest of the aggressor to do what is just, and abstain from future wrong."[13] Jefferson, for all his talk of war with Spain, believed essentially in achieving his ends through peaceful means. He wrote on July 9 that "both reason & the usage of nations" required that America should give Britain time to disavow the acts of her officers, and that this would also give America time to bring home her property, vessels, and seamen—"the only means of carrying on the kind of war we should attempt."[14] If war came he wanted only limited fighting, and he leaned toward the idea that nonintercourse was preferable to war. War, if absolutely necessary, could be fought by privateers.[15]

The measures taken by Jefferson were calculated to use time to assuage the temper of the country rather than to take advantage of it to produce war. At a cabinet meeting at the beginning of July, it was decided to send the *Revenge* to England to demand satisfaction for the attack on the *Chesapeake*. It was also agreed that Congress would not be called until October. This measure obviously gave time for the ardor of opinion to cool. Jefferson argued that the three months before the convening of Congress would give time for the *Revenge* to go to England and return with the answer—"Congress would not declare war without a demand of satisfaction, nor could they lay an Embargo with so much under the grasp of our adversary."[16] Madison's instructions to Monroe asked for disavowal of the act, for reparations, and for the restoration of the four seamen. Unfortunately, he also asked that this should be accompanied by an entire abolition of impressments.[17] This was to leave the *Chesapeake* incident as a running sore for four years, as Britain quite obviously was not prepared to connect the two matters. Reparation for the attack would have been distinctly possible. England, as Canning re-emphasized in a letter to Monroe on August 3, had never claimed the right to impress from American warships, but to give up *all* impressment was impossible for any British government.[18]

In the middle of July, when the *Revenge* set sail for England, America would have followed Jefferson into war. "The public mind is settling itself every where into a determined stand at the present crisis," wrote Madison, "the Proclamation is rallied to by all parties. Reparation or war is proclaimed at every meeting, or rather by every mouth, which is not British."[19] Jacob Crowinshield, the influential New England Republican, wrote from Salem that there would be no considerable opposition to any measure of retaliation, and that the New England states would support the administration in any system calculated to give effect to its just demands for reparation.[20] Even the cautious Albert Gallatin at first wanted war, and thought that it was inevitable. In July he quickly produced a plan for financing the coming war and presented it to Jefferson. Yet writing from New York in the middle of August, he expressed the view that "the people of this city do not appear to me to be in favour of war, and they fear it so much that they have persuaded themselves that there is no danger of that event."[21] This view was substantially in agreement with that of the British consul general in New York, Thomas Barclay. He expressed the opinion that the New England states, and the great proportion of the "respectable characters" in his own state of New York, were averse to war with Great Britain. He considered, however, that as one progressed southward opinions against Great Britain became warmer until in Maryland, Virginia, and the Carolinas he thought that war would be a popular measure.[22] It would seem that though some observers were inclined to disagree with the Republican Crowinshield's view that Federalist New England would support the war, or that commercial New York would give it full support, President Jefferson would have gained considerable popular support if he had decided on war in the summer of 1807.

Vice-Admiral Berkeley, whose order had produced all this agitation, showed little repentance for his action and gave a glimpse of naval attitudes in a letter to Earl Bathurst in the middle of August. He expressed the view that it was most unlikely that hostilities could be avoided, and that England needed force to awe the Americans, if not to fight. His comment on the American scene, which was described more with venom than with accuracy, was that "the violence of the American rabble still continues, and as it accords with the views of Jefferson and his party, it is not checked by Government, but is kept up by every means in the numerous newspapers which are published."[23]

In actual fact Jefferson was doing very little to take advantage of the war feeling in the country. Throughout the summer of 1807 the American government waited patiently for the return of the *Revenge* from England. Patience had been a steady characteristic of American diplomacy in the period from the spring of 1806 to the summer of 1807. For the greater part of these months America had waited for a British answer to American proposals. The Non-Importation Act, originally passed in April, 1806, had been delayed for practically a year, to await the news of the Monroe-Pinkney Treaty. And even after the bad news of that treaty had arrived, there had been a further delay as Jefferson and Madison had tried to salvage the doomed agreement. Now the *Chesapeake* affair was absorbing American opinion, and once again America settled down to await news from England. Jefferson and Madison still hoped to avoid war, and avoid it they did.

Jefferson, like so many of the early and some more recent American statesmen, hoped that the complications of European affairs would be America's salvation. He wrote on August 21, 1807, that he had never thought that he would be under the necessity of wishing success to Bonaparte, but as the English were as tyrannical on the sea as the French were on the land, he felt obliged to say " 'down with England,' and as for what Bonaparte is then to do to us, let us trust to the chapter of accidents. I cannot, with the Anglomen, prefer a certain present evil to a future hypothetical one."[24] His argument was similar to that used by the British statesmen when they said that impressment might produce a war with America, but better that more distant and problematical evil than the certainty of defeat by Napoleon if there were no seamen to man the ships. In fact, the wonder is not that England and America went to war in 1812, but that they avoided it for so long. To Jefferson, more than to any other individual, can this avoidance of war be attributed. If he had desired war, he could have had it in 1807.

Jefferson, anxious for peace, waited apprehensively for the return of the *Revenge* in the fall of 1807. He feared that war might well come, as he thought it very unlikely that England would agree to yield any of her maritime pretensions.[25] Writing to Thomas Paine on October 9, he uttered a heart cry : "If they would but settle the question of impressment from our bottoms, I should be well contented to drop all attempts at a treaty. The other rights of neutral powers will be taken care of by Bonaparte and Alexander, and for commercial arrangements we can sufficiently provide by legislative regulations, but as the practice of impressment has taken place only against us we shall be left to settle that for ourselves. And to do this we shall never again have so favourable a conjuncture of circumstances."²⁶ The importance of impressment in bringing England and America to the brink of war in the summer of 1807 was rarely, if at all, more emphatically stated than in this letter to Paine. Gallatin, however, now reluctant to commit America to a policy for which she was ill-prepared, urged caution even to the cautious Jefferson. He thought that the message Jefferson proposed to submit to Congress was too much like a manifesto against Great Britain, and that if there was a chance of accommodation, America should not ruin it. Gallatin argued that the government would obtain general support if it went to war because England refused satisfaction in the *Chesapeake* affair, but not if it went to war because of England's refusal to make the proposed arrangement regarding impressment. In the latter case, Gallatin thought that measures short of actual hostilities might become proper, leaving to England the choice of war. He made the exceedingly relevant point that America's preparations for war were meager, and that if there was immediate war America might not even be able to protect New York.²⁷

On October 26, the day Congress assembled, Jefferson perhaps reflected his own attitude in describing the opinions of Congress. He said that the members, as far as he could judge, were extremely disposed for peace, "and as there is no doubt Great Britain will disavow the act of the Leopard, I am inclined to believe they will be more disposed to combat her practice of impressment by a non-importation law than by arms." Jefferson's sympathy for this plan of action had been well illustrated in his numerous references to the possibility of nonimportation and nonintercourse in his letters since the *Chesapeake* incident. On November 1 he added that "here we are pacifically inclined, if anything comes which will permit us to follow our inclinations." By November 30 he was asserting that an embargo was the most likely action that Congress would take, though the choice lay between "War, Embargo or Nothing." At that time news arrived from England that Canning had refused to link the *Chesapeake* affair with an agreement on impressment, but that he was about to send a special envoy to America to settle the former issue.[28]

The situation seemed desperate, and on December 14 the long postponed Non-Importation Act at last went into operation against Great Britain. Yet worse was to come, for no sooner was the Non-Importation Act in force than news arrived from Great Britain that on October 17 England had made a strong reassertion of her right of impressment. On that date a proclamation had been issued recalling all British seamen from the service of foreign nations, and ordering British officers to seize such men found serving on foreign merchant vessels. It asserted that no grant of citizenship from a foreign nation discharged British seamen from their obligation to England.[29] This was nothing novel—Britain had consistently maintained this position—but coming when it did, it showed the United States quite plainly that the Tory government, in spite of such incidents as that of the *Chesapeake,* was determined to impress from American merchant ships to the full extent of its ability.

As if this were not enough, news arrived almost simultaneously from Paris that Napoleon, now in complete command of the Continent, had started to enforce his Berlin Decree of December, 1806, against American commerce. This year of 1807 had seen Napoleon consolidate his gains of the previous year and advance to new victories. In June he had faced the Russians at Friedland and had overwhelmed them. Napoleon could now make peace on his own terms. Later in the month the French Emperor and the Russian Czar Alexander met on a raft on the Niemen, and on July 7 a formal treaty was concluded at Tilsit. Russia was to join in Napoleon's plan to exclude British trade from the Continent, and as the leading commercial neutral America could expect to suffer still more from the European belligerents. America's cup of misery was full, and indeed running over, when in the middle of December strong unofficial information arrived from England that she was going to place fresh restrictions upon American commerce.[30] Official news of Britain's new Orders in Council was not to reach America for several weeks, but the new British reassertion of her impressment policy, combined with the enforcement of the French Berlin Decree and the expectation of a stricter British policy toward neutral trade, were enough to persuade Jefferson that the time had come for the total interdiction of the American trade to the outside world.

On December 17 Jefferson met with the cabinet and suggested an embargo which would coerce the European powers by preventing American shipping from sailing for foreign ports. The cabinet gave Jefferson its support, though on the following day Gallatin expressed doubts on the wisdom of the measure and argued that it would not produce a more moderate policy from Great Britain. Yet it was decided to send a special message to Congress, and after a morning meeting of the cabinet a communication drafted by Madison reached the Senate on the afternoon of December 18. It told of the danger to American vessels, seamen, and merchandise, and asked Congress to consider the total prohibition of the departure of vessels from the ports of the United States.[31] The Senate acted with great rapidity, refering the message to a committee and passing an Embargo Bill by a vote of 22 to 6 on the same afternoon that it received the President's message. The bill, which confined American vessels to American ports and permitted foreign vessels to leave only in ballast or with cargo they already had on board, was immediately sent to the House. It there passed by a vote of 82 to 44 after two days' debate.[32] Congress had concurred in Jefferson's embargo policy with the greatest rapidity. The bill received the President's assent on December 22. Erskine sent the news to England on the next day with the comment that England's proclamation of October 17 convinced the Americans that Great Britain was determined to continue her impressment policy.[33]

The American Embargo Act of December, 1807, concluded the first and contributed to the second phase of the origins of the War of 1812. The emphasis was now to change from seamen to ships and cargoes. In the Embargo Act, the gradual worsening of Anglo-American relations from 1804 to 1807, largely as a result of impressment, reached a culmination. After the *Chesapeake* incident of June, 1807, America had placed herself in a position in which, if England refused to meet the American demands, either war or some form of commercial retaliation was inevitable. Instead of obtaining a redress of her grievances, America was presented with the double blow of the statement from Canning that the *Chesapeake* incident could not be combined with a general agreement on impressments, and England's reassertion of her right of impressment in the October proclamation. When this was combined with the news of the enforcement of the Berlin Decree, and rumors of a stricter British commercial policy, it is not surprising that the reaction should have been in the form of economic sanctions rather than open warfare. The tradition of economic coercion was an old one in American history—even in the conflict resulting in the Revolution an attempt at economic coercion had long preceded actual warfare—and Jefferson and the men around him had frequently expressed their belief in the power of economic means to bring England to reason. This was the obvious occasion to give economic coercion a trial, and America, weak and uncertain of her power to wage war against the country that had defied Napoleon, attempted to defend her rights by peaceful rather than bellicose means. The reasons for the failure of this attempt are to be found in Europe, for even before America had resorted to her coercive device of the Embargo, the European war had at last developed into a vast commercial struggle between England and France. Now impressment was to take its place as only one of many American grievances. The origins of the War of 1812 were entering their second—their commercial —phase, and to understand this it is necessary to turn again to the internal politics of England.

I

The group of Tories who took office in March of 1807 had left no doubt in their year of opposition that they intended to follow and amplify the policy of Pitt's second administration in regard to America. This new government was faced with the task of waging war against the ruler of practically the entire Continent. They could afford to appease no one, least of all a commercial United States that wished to trade throughout Europe. If American trade and American ships gave aid to Napoleon, they would have to be stopped. The determination of the new government to restrict American trade was undoubtedly strengthened by the knowledge that in carrying out a strict policy toward the United States it would be pleasing the powerful mercantile interests on which the safety of the country depended. The shipping interest had left no doubt in the years since 1801 of its attitude toward America and American commerce. Since the passing of the American Intercourse Bill in 1806, it had been joined by the West India interest, which had now broken its unnatural alliance with the friends of America. It was the West India interest, even more than the shipowners, that desired the prohibition of the American carrying trade to Europe, for with the issue of Napoleon's Berlin Decree, which prevented the importation of British produce into the Continent, it seemed that it would lose the whole European market. To the West India interest it appeared essential to stop the American trade. If neutral ships were swept from the seas, Napoleon would be obliged to open his ports to British produce. Though the desires of the

West India interest had been expressed fully in 1805 by James Stephen, it was not until after the Berlin Decree that it set on foot an extensive agitation to prevent the American trade with Europe.

During their attempt to influence parliamentary opinion in 1807, the pamphleteers of the West India interest tended to use the same arguments expounded by Stephen in his *War in Disguise.*[34] Now that the complications of the American Intercourse Act had ended for the West India interest, it was able to assert with the shipping interest that the whole British Navigation System was being sacrificed to the Americans: "these invaluable rights she has now, in the plenitude of her naval power, tamely surrendered to America, who has no means whatever of enforcing her lofty demands."[35]

The anonymous author who wrote the statement above is interesting because he also elaborated the point made by Stephen that it would be far better to wage war against the United States than to sacrifice British maritime rights. He blandly stated that the interruption of the American commerce to Europe might lead to war with the United States, but he had no hesitation in arguing that "neither considerations of right, nor of interest, will warrant America in resenting the retraction of these concessions; and that even her hostility is far less formidable than such neutrality as she at present exercises."[36] The opponents of America in England had little fear of ill effects resulting from hostility with that country. This author continued by proving, at least to his own satisfaction, that war would result in ruin for the United States—her commerce would disappear, and the country would be divided. Britain, on the other hand, was represented as able to escape unscathed from war with America. In fact, she would obtain direct benefits from such a war. It was argued that encouragement would be given to the economic growth of the British North American colonies, the British carrying trade would increase, and British seamen would return from Ameri-

can service. As might be expected, the author dismissed as un-
important the loss of the British export trade to the United States.
He maintained that some British goods would still enter America
indirectly, and in any case it was either to be the loss of all profit
from the British West Indies by their ruin, or the loss of the
export trade to the United States.[37] This supporter of the West
India interest had no difficulty in making a choice between the
two evils, but it was not one to appeal to the growing industrial
areas of England.

The West India interest made no secret of the fact that its
concern was a measure which would take immediate effect in
restoring its prosperity. In its campaign it received every help
from the shipping interest, which since 1801 had pressed for the
restriction of American commerce as essential to the well-being
of England. An anonymous pamphlet of over five hundred pages,
published on behalf of the Society of Shipowners in 1807, emphasized the fact that American encroachments over a long
period of time were sapping British commercial strength. It laid
great stress on the now familiar arguments that Britain was in
danger of losing her supreme commercial position, and through
this her supreme position as a nation.[38]

The arguments of the opponents of America did not go un-
answered in London. Macall Medford's *Oil Without Vinegar*
attacked "a combination in London, that is now labouring to
bring about a war with America."[39] He was scathing in his onslaught on the West India merchants—they are "still living like
princes, but when they come before the Parliament they have
got the whining cant of beggars."[40] Medford regretted that the
two nations were being led into war by a set of interested merchants, when they might have flourished so much by maintaining a good understanding. "If war is engaged in between the
two countries," he argued, "it never will be supposed on account
of any real disagreement, but because it was thought to be convenient for Britain to prevent America, as the only Neutral, from

enjoying the advantages that must of a necessary consequence fall to her."[41] This opinion was partially true, but it ignored both the impressment problem and England's desire to wage effective war on France.

The pro-American *Edinburgh Review* in reviewing this work in October, 1807, agreed with Medford's conclusions and argued that "both nations would suffer more from a war than from any other event which can happen to them."[42] This magazine argued in favor of friendship with America, but cast an interesting light on the general state of British opinion when it conceded that "the doctrines we have now delivered, will not, we are much afraid, be very popular at this moment among the greater part of our readers," and that "we look with regret and aversion to the probable alienation of the only independent state with which we are still in amity."[43] Even the friends of America saw that they were in the minority.

The hopes of the advocates of a strict policy toward America quite obviously received great encouragement from the return of the Tories to power in March, 1807. It meant that their efforts to influence government now had a good chance of success. For some time they had been endeavoring to obtain remedies from the government for their distressed condition. As far back as June and July, 1806, in a series of conferences with the Board of Trade, they had asked for certain changes in the duty and drawback on sugar, and the substitution of sugar for grain in the distilleries and breweries. This latter application had resulted in the appointment of a committee on the subject, which had presented its report in February, 1807, without any definite result.[44] Yet the issue of the Berlin Decree at the close of 1806, and the resulting cry in England for retaliation to that measure, made the American carrying trade to Europe the more obvious and fruitful point of attack for the West India interest. On February 27, 1807, a petition was presented to the Commons on behalf of "several Planters, Merchants, Mortgagees and others

interested in the *British West India* Colonies." This petition
stressed the importance of the West Indies to Great Britain and
summarized the causes of their distressed state : increased taxes
on sugar had reduced consumption; the produce of the captured
colonies competed with the British produce; "and as if to render
the evil irreparable, and the case desperate, the great and acknowledged superiority of the *British* Navy has not been exerted
in impeding the transit of the colonial produce of the Enemy
to its European market."[45] On March 12 this petition was referred to a select committee, which also received petitions on
March 17 and March 24 from the West India interests at Liverpool and Glasgow.[46]

The report of the committee was printed on August 8, 1807,[47]
and presents an excellent summary of the ideas and interests of
the West India group in regard to the United States, and of the
manner in which Parliament was influenced by its arguments.
The committee had interviewed important planters and merchants connected with the West Indies, and had used their evidence to form its conclusions.[48] It was asserted that there had
been a progressive deterioration in the situation of the planters
since 1799, but the report did not delve with any great insight
into the fundamental causes of this depression. The committee
argued that decrease in prices had coincided with increase in
costs, and suggested as a remedy that the duty on sugar should
be lowered, and that a bounty should be given for its export. In
addition it was suggested that an encouragement should be
given to the consumption of rum in the army and navy.[49] Yet
the importance of the report from the point of view of later
Anglo-American relations was that the committee emphasized
that the above were not the original causes of the West Indian
distress. The main evil was declared to be the unfavorable state
of the foreign market, where the British colonies had once practically held a monopoly, but where they were now forced to compete with the commerce not only of the neutral but also of the

hostile colonies. There was "one grand and primary evil, from which all the others are easily to be deduced; namely, the facility of intercourse between the hostile colonies and Europe, under the American neutral flag."[50] The report stressed the advantages enjoyed by the United States as a result of the relaxation of the Rule of 1756, and the fact that the Americans were able to export enemy produce to Europe at much less cost than the British could export the produce of their own colonies. As might be expected, it was suggested that the certain way of aiding the West India interest would be to prohibit the carrying of enemy produce to Europe in neutral ships. In this way, owing to his lack of supplies, Napoleon would be forced to open his ports to British produce. It was fully realized that this might precipitate difficulties with the United States, for consideration was given to the problem of the interruption of the flow of American supplies to the West Indies. The statement was made that the West India interest would be prepared to give up this source of supplies if American competition in the European market could be prohibited.[51] The West India interest, which from 1783 had so ardently advocated a free intercourse between the British West Indies and the United States, and had thrown itself so enthusiastically into the struggle over the American Intercourse Bill in 1806, was by 1807 ready to sacrifice its victory. All it asked in return was the prohibition of the American carrying trade to Europe.

The Tory ministers had plainly shown their sympathy with the defenders of England's Navigation System in the four years before 1807. Perceval, now Chancellor of the Exchequer, had in the debate on the Whig Order in Council of January, 1807, outlined his plans for the future, and his desire to prevent American intercourse with Europe. He had defended this proposal both on the grounds of the desirability of retaliation against Napoleon, and for the protection of British interests against American competition.[52] The pressure upon the government by the West India and shipping interests after the Tory return to power gave the ministers encouragement to carry out their own earlier plans, and complete the work started at the time of the *Essex* decision in the spring of 1805. Napoleon was attempting to exclude British goods from the Continent, and now the British government, encouraged by her maritime interests, was prepared to force Napoleon to buy British goods or none at all. At one stroke American commercial competition would be eliminated, and France would feel the full weight of British naval power.

The task of designing the new Orders in Council policy fell to Perceval, and he was well fitted for the task. As a close friend of Stephen, the author of *War in Disguise,* he did not have to look far for his inspiration. In October, 1807, Castlereagh, the Secretary of State for War and the Colonies, wrote to Perceval and stated that he believed Britain would never have peace until "we have found the means of making France feel that her new antisocial and anti-commercial system will not avail her against a power that can, for its own preservation, and consequently legitimately, counteract at sea what she lawlessly inflicts on shore." He wanted Perceval to consider whether England would have to restrain herself from action owing to the American question or whether she could go ahead with her desired policy. Castlereagh thought that public sentiment was ripe for some measure, and would support the government.[53]

Perceval had already been working on this subject during the summer recess of Parliament, and on October 12 he was able to submit a long paper for the consideration of the cabinet.[54] This paper, which stressed the right of retaliation against Napoleon, has been quoted as showing that Perceval's object was to retaliate against Napoleon while hurting neutral trade as little as possible.[55] This view would seem to be somewhat generous to Perceval. There seems little question that one of his objects was to retaliate against Napoleon, but it is also quite ob-

vious from his statements, and from those of his supporters over
the previous three years, that the restriction of American commerce as a competitor to that of Great Britain was also a
definite factor in issuing the Orders in Council. Perceval, however, realized the value of maintaining peace with America.
He suggested that it would be unwise to prevent *all* American
trade with the Continent, because in that case America
might very reasonably go to war rather than submit : "I should,
therefore, wish to leave such advantages still to neutral trade,
as to make it quite clear to be the policy of America to prefer
the neutral trade which is left to her to the total stoppage of her
trade with the enemy, and with ourselves too, which a war might
occasion." He wished to permit the neutrals to have a direct
trade with the Continent in their own products, and to import
European products to their own countries. He admitted that
this would be a slight advantage to the enemy, but thought that
it would be worth it to keep America out of the war.[56] Unlike
the more extreme opponents of America and defenders of
Britain's Navigation System, who looked quite favorably upon
the possibility of war with America, Perceval realized quite
clearly that if he could restrict American commerce according
to his desires and yet still keep her out of the war, it would be of
considerable advantage to England. Thus, he inaugurated a
policy of conceding just enough to make America prefer peace
to war. The British government wanted peace with the United
States, but it wanted peace on its own terms.

Perceval in the period immediately preceding the issue of the
Orders in Council emphasized that the measures were for retaliation against France, but this should not be allowed to obscure the fact that he had already made plain his interest in
giving protection to British interests against American competition. Perceval's connection with the shipping and West India
interests was well known. Henry Brougham, the young Whig
politician who was to achieve prominence as the opponent of

the Orders in Council, wrote in September, 1807, "I am afraid
... that the West Indian and shipping interests will have great
weight with Perceval at least, and the greater part of his colleagues."[57] Perceval's great friend Stephen was particularly influential. Writing later in life, Brougham remained convinced
of Stephen's influence. He said of Perceval: "The influence of
his friend Mr. Stephen over his mind was unbounded." In particular Brougham thought that Perceval deferred to Stephen on
all questions connected with neutral rights: "Accordingly the
measure of the Orders in Council devised by him [Stephen]
was readily adopted by the minister." Brougham went on to
speak of Perceval's "scorn of the Americans, whom he disliked
with the animosity peculiar to all the courtiers of George III."[58]
These comments by Brougham, written after Perceval was dead,
must be viewed with the reservation accorded the arguments of
a political opponent, though Brougham was no unskilled political observer. William Wilberforce, who knew both Perceval
and Stephen and was a good friend of the latter, wrote in his
diary in January, 1808, that Perceval had once again offered
Stephen a seat in Parliament. Wilberforce thought that he
should accept it: "He agrees with Perceval passim, and with
the government as to their grand scheme of policy—Order in
Council; indeed it is his measure."[59] Lord Holland too, much
later in life, called Stephen "the real instigator of those impolitic
measures."[60]

The desire of the government to give protection to British
commerce was an integral part of the general desire to retaliate
against and defeat Napoleon that produced the British Orders
in Council of November, 1807. A letter from Perceval, received
by the speaker of the House, Charles Abbot, on December 1,
1807, leaves no doubt on this point. "The short principle," Perceval stated, "is that trade in British produce and manufactures,
and trade either from a British port or with a British destination,
is to be protected as much as possible." If France would not

have British trade she should have none, and the only cheap and untaxed trade that France was to have was to be either direct from Great Britain or from her allies.[61]

The Orders in Council, as finally issued on November 11, 1807, and as defined by various supplementary Orders during the rest of the month, were exceedingly long and somewhat contradictory, though their main content can be summarized quite briefly. The essential point was that all the countries from which the British flag was excluded were to be considered as if actually blockaded, and all trade with them was prohibited. There were, however, many exceptions. Neutrals were permitted to trade directly with the enemy colonies, and to take enemy produce from them to certain "free ports" in the British colonies, whence they would be shipped to England. Also, provided neutrals called first at British ports, they could trade with enemy ports in British goods, and in some cases in foreign goods, after they had paid duty on them in England.[62]

However obscure these Orders were in detail, their intent and main effect was quite plain. America was to have no trade with Europe except through Britain. The immediate reaction of France, on December 17, was to issue the Milan Decree. Since his alliance with Russia in July, Napoleon had moved even further towards the closing of the Continent. In November his forces took Portugal, and while in his Italian territories in December he issued this Milan Decree. It stated that every neutral ship that allowed herself to be searched by the British, sailed to a British port, or paid a British duty, was considered as de-nationalized and as a lawful prize for France. Any ship sailing to or from a British port, or a port occupied by British troops, was also liable to seizure by the French.[63] The chains on America were complete. No American ship could sail to a European port under the control of Napoleon without being liable to seizure : by a British ship if she had not called at a British port, and by Napoleon's officials if she had. In Europe the commercial struggle was at its height, and it is hardly surprising that in the following years this commercial issue overshadowed the old issue of impressment in Anglo-American relations.

England had secured her desires in regard to American trade, and had yielded nothing in regard to impressment. From the point of view of the British government, her relations with America were now quite satisfactory, for America had been placed in a position where she could neither help Napoleon nor harm British commerce. For the next five years the English were to play cat and mouse with the Americans. Perceval had suggested in issuing the Orders that America had been left just enough trade to make it more worth while to her to submit to British regulations and to keep the peace rather than to go to war against England. The Tory Foreign Minister, George Canning, attempted to follow that suggestion. In the next two years the young, ambitious Canning—"all froth and smoke and noise"[64]—mocked America with his confident assertions of British right, and his attempt to convince her that she had much to lose by war. On December 1, 1807, he communicated Britain's new Orders in Council to his minister in America, David Erskine. He left no doubt of the position that Erskine should adopt: "In all your Communications you will not fail so to exhibit the State in which the Trade of America will be left after this Order, as to make it Evident, that a State of War with this Country would deprive her of very great Advantages." It would then appear that he allowed his biting sarcasm to enter his official dispatch when he stated that "of course you will be cautious not to bring this Idea forward in any manner in which it could, by possibility, be received by America, in the insulting and odious Light of a Threat."[65] The English government had placed America in a situation in which she could do no harm; the aim now was to keep her out of the war, while conceding nothing. This was to remain the British policy to the very eve of the War of 1812.

7   *The Failure of the Embargo*

T HE MIDDLE phase of the origins of the War of 1812 is undoubtedly the most sterile. The period 1804 to 1807 had
produced a British policy of increasing strictness and a steadily
growing American irritation, particularly in regard to impressment, which had culminated in the Embargo. The period 1810
to 1812 was to see the development of an American demand for
war, and a fast increasing opposition in Great Britain to the
Orders in Council policy. Yet the relations of this middle phase
from 1807 to 1810 are remarkably unproductive. Stalemate had
been reached. On the one hand, England had attained her desired objectives in regard to America, and was ready to allow the
existing situation in Anglo-American relations to exist *ad infi-
nitum,* while on the other, America was at long last giving a
complete trial to her theories of economic coercion. Of necessity
a trial of economic coercion had to be given over a period of
years, not weeks, and all America could do was wait and see if
her policy was having any effect. On one side of the Atlantic
sat the American government, anxiously waiting for the first
signs of weakness in the British economy, and on the other sat
the British government, complacently watching America ruin
her own commerce. There were, however, weaknesses on both
sides. In England, the Whig opposition was gaining increasing
support from the large and rapidly growing manufacturing in-

terest that looked with anxiety at America's policy of non-importation. In America the government faced attack from two sides. On one side was the Federalist opposition, centered in New England and tied financially and emotionally to England. The Federalists were in a similar position to the Whig manufacturing interest in England, and were exceedingly desirous of peace and friendship. On the other side was a small group that objected to the apparent sacrifice of American rights and the national honor in a policy of economic coercion, at a time when it seemed that war was the only argument to which Great Britain would listen. This last group grew increasingly powerful as more and more people became disillusioned with economic coercion as a method of defending American rights; it was eventually to produce war.

The history of the American Embargo is well known.[1] Jefferson's great plan for peaceful resistance to the European powers became an abject failure. He hoped through the Embargo to provide a method by which the European belligerents would be forced to recognize American rights, but tragically brought such distress and dissension to his own country that a declaration of war, the only real alternative to a policy of economic coercion, was made infinitely more difficult. In New England, Federalism was given a new lease of life, and the friends of Great Britain were given an opportunity to belabor the government. In the South, Jefferson's own section, the Embargo gave a blow to its agricultural prosperity from which it never fully recovered. The only positive advantage gained by the Americans was that in the Middle States, and to a lesser extent in the northeastern states, a valuable impetus was given to the growth of American manufactures. Yet any slight benefit was far overshadowed by the cost of the Embargo to America. The swift American ships now rotted in port, and the once bustling seaports cursed Jefferson and his Embargo. To enforce his measure Jefferson was obliged to sacrifice his own political principles and distract America, all to no avail. Neither France nor England would rescind their decrees in order to remove the supposed burden of the American Embargo from their shoulders. Had Jefferson's measure succeeded in wringing from England the concessions in regard to neutral trade and impressment that the President hoped, there seems no reason to suppose that America would have gone to war in 1812. This being the case, the reason for its failure assumes considerable importance. Why was it that America's policy of economic coercion failed to affect England, and obliged her, after she had recovered from the enervating effects of passive resistance, to go to war?

The tragedy of the Embargo was that though it certainly caused some consternation in England, it had little effect on those who created policy. Its main repercussions were felt by the manufacturing and financial groups concerned in the American trade, and their cause was supported in Parliament by the Whig opposition. This Whig opposition strongly opposed the issue of the Orders in Council, and clearly realized the adverse effects they would have both on Anglo-American relations and on the British manufacturers interested in the American trade. The Whigs also realized that there was political advantage to be gained by attacking the government on this controversial issue. Hearing that the Orders were about to be issued, Lord Auckland wrote to Grenville and stated that "it is evident . . . that it removes one principal motive which the Americans might have had for remaining at peace with us; and it is equally evident that it increases at the moment the difficulties and distresses of our manufacturers."[2] Grenville agreed with him in this. He considered that Britain had actually helped Napoleon by her Orders in Council, which he thought would be ruinous to British prosperity.[3]

When Parliament met at the beginning of 1808 the Whigs made every effort to take full advantage of the situation. They attempted to arouse opinion by continual attacks on the Orders in Council policy.[4] This attack, though the United States did not fully realize it, was vital to her future relations with England—for it was deciding whether America could achieve her objects by peaceful means, or whether she would eventually be forced to resort to war. The Orders in Council were first laid before the House on January 26 by Perceval,[5] and from that date until the end of the session they were the subject of vigorous debate in both the Lords and the Commons. Until March the Whigs attacked the Orders primarily on the grounds of their illegality, and because of their probable adverse effect on Anglo-American relations. On legal grounds, the Orders in Council were accused of violating both the law of the land and the law of nations. The first does not concern us here, as its arguments revolved chiefly around constitutional procedure.[6] The attack on the Orders as violating the law of nations is far more interesting, as it shows that there was a notable body of opinion in England at this period that opposed the government's policy in regard to America.

The main Whig argument in these debates was that England had no right to retaliate upon America an enemy act which was directed against England.[7] Lady Bessborough, an ardent Whig, had expressed her thoughts graphically on this point in February, 1807, when she commented : "If a man who is fighting with me sets fire to one wing of my Neighbour's house, does it give me a right to set fire to the other?"[8] The Tory view that England could wage war on France, regardless of the effect of her measures upon the United States, was never accepted by the opposition. Lord Lauderdale, who had been Lord High Keeper of the Seal of Scotland in the previous ministry, stated in the House of Lords on February 15 that the Orders "injured neutrals much more than they did the enemy; and were, in his opinion, tantamount to a declaration of war against America."[9]

The Whig press and magazines tried to popularize this argument, and attempted to impress upon the public the disastrous effects that could be expected from the Tory policy.[10] The inevitable pamphlets also appeared, in the usual early nineteenth-century form of large books. The most famous of these was undoubtedly Alexander Baring's *Inquiry into the Causes and Consequences of the Orders in Council*.[11] This was the *War in Disguise* of the American interest in Great Britain, for it provides the most complete exposition of the point of view of the pro-American party in England at this period. The House of Baring Bros. and Co., which had been founded by Alexander's father in the years before the American Revolution, was one of the great financial houses of the period. It had developed extensive connections, chiefly in the United States. In fact, after the failure of Bird, Savage, and Bird in 1803, the Barings had become the general agents of the United States government in Europe. They acted in this capacity until 1835.[12] As financial representatives of the American government in Europe, they naturally looked askance at the deterioration in Anglo-American relations after 1803. Sir Francis Baring, founder of the house, had written in 1804 that "I shudder as much at a war with Scotland or Ireland, as with America."[13] His son Alexander, married to an American, was an excellent representative of the American interest in Great Britain and well able to express its arguments. Over thirty years later, as Lord Ashburton, he met with Daniel Webster in Washington and achieved a notable settlement in Anglo-American relations.

In 1808 Jefferson's hopes rested on the shoulders of the opposition in Parliament, and in the country at large on the American interest of which the Barings were a part. The London financial houses concerned in the American trade were an important part of this pro-American group. London in this period acted as the financial center for the American trade with Europe. Though the United States imported large quantities of British manufactured goods, she did not export to Britain in sufficient quantities to pay for them. This adverse balance was met by means

of the extensive American export trade in colonial produce, particularly sugar and coffee, to Europe. Financial houses in London would accept the remittances for this produce from the
Continent, and would dispose of the money according to the
instructions of their American correspondents. In this way
British manufactured goods could be paid for by the United
States. The Barings and other London houses thus had a vital
interest in the Orders in Council which restricted American
exports to Europe.[14]

Another group that had a vital interest in British restrictions
and American retaliation was the British manufacturers. The
manufacturers of cotton in Lancashire, of woolen goods in Yorkshire, and of hardware in Birmingham and Sheffield were among
those vitally concerned in the vast American market, and as they
felt the pinch of American nonimportation, they inevitably
would bring their pressure to bear on government. The industrial areas of England, along with London financial houses, had
a vital interest in friendly Anglo-American relations. It was
these groups that provided Jefferson's only hope in his embargo
policy—these were the men with sufficient interest to strive to
ensure that the government's American policy did not result
in American commercial reprisals.

Alexander Baring's pamphlet, which came out in February,
1808, was an attempt on his part to present a comprehensive
summary of the ideas of the American interest. It was an immediate success and went through three editions by April.[15]
William Pinkney, who had become American minister in Great
Britain on the departure of Monroe in November, 1807, reported the success of the pamphlet to Madison and commented
that it was being read "with avidity."[16] By the Whigs it was
considered the last word on the subject, and Lord Grenville
gave it enthusiastic praise in the Lords.[17] The main point developed by Baring in his work was that the Orders in Council had
been directed against the United States out of a mistaken

jealousy, and that if persisted in they would be ruinous both to relations with that country and to British commerce. He regarded the Orders as "purely the result of commercial calculation."[18]

Baring argued that Napoleon's policy in Europe had inevitably brought a certain amount of distress to the West India and shipping interests. Yet these groups, instead of surmising the real cause of their distress, had ascribed it all to the intercourse of the United States with Europe. They had thus set on foot an extensive agitation to improve their position by the restriction of neutral commerce. In particular, Baring blamed the West India interest: "our present measures have originated principally, if not wholly, in the persevering representations of the West India interest."[19] In a similar manner, Baring attacked the shipping interest for their shortsightedness: "A few commonplace phrases about our *Old Navigation Laws* and our *Maritime Rights,* answer the place of argument."[20] In short, commercial interests, suffering from a variety of causes such as war, and in the case of the West Indies overproduction, had laid the whole blame upon American competition, and had by extensive agitation persuaded government to act on their behalf.

In this well-argued though rather ill-organized pamphlet Baring also gave close attention to the probable effects of the Orders. His prophesy was pessimistic: "War ... there is every reason to apprehend, must be the infallible consequence of these measures."[21] This he viewed as a disaster for England. To prove his point he went into the whole question of Anglo-American trade, and attempted to show its value. He made full use of the obvious importance of America as a source of British raw materials and as a market for British manufactured goods. Also, as a representative of a leading financial house, he naturally stressed the fact that America paid for part of her British imports by the export of colonial produce to the Continent. He concluded in regard to this whole American trade: "It is impossible to conceive, upon the whole, a commercial intercourse more interesting and important in every point of view, or less deserving of being sacrificed to any other."[22]

The publication of Baring's pamphlet came at a very opportune moment, and it was not destined to fall upon deaf ears. By February, 1808, those merchants and manufacturers throughout the country who were active in the American trade were beginning to be aroused by the Orders in Council policy, and were realizing that their prosperity was in serious danger. News of the Non-Importation and the Embargo Acts had reached England by the end of January,[23] and opponents of the British Orders in Council were able to trace a direct connection between the Orders and the issue of the Embargo by the American government. William Pinkney, the American minister in England, who was in close touch with those favoring trade and friendship with America, had been expecting action against the Orders since the previous November,[24] and it was no surprise when in the new year a movement of protest grew among the interested merchants and manufacturers. By that time Whig speeches in Parliament and Whig newspapers and magazines had warned the country of the probable ill effects of the Orders, and England knew of the American reaction.

As might be expected, the port of Liverpool, a great center of American trade, became an important area of provincial opposition to the Orders. At the end of February a meeting of the "Merchants and other inhabitants of Liverpool, interested in the trade to America" decided unanimously to present petitions to Parliament against the Orders in Council.[25] Similarly at Huddersfield, a woolen manufacturing town in the West Riding of Yorkshire, when resolutions protesting against the long war were passed, the Orders were objected to as "likely to involve us in a war with America :—a Country to which British manufactured goods have been exported, annually, to an immense Amount."[26] In London, however, the strength of the pro-government sentiment was indicated when a meeting of persons interested in the trade to the United States was held at the London Tavern under the chairmanship of Alexander Baring. In response to public advertisement a crowd estimated at from 400 to 1,000 gathered at the Tavern on March 10. So many of those in favor of the Orders in Council and opposed to America attended that the original motion to present a petition against the Orders was defeated. Despite this, the American merchants went ahead and presented their petition.[27]

By March, 1808, Parliament began to receive petitions against the Orders in Council from the American interest in different parts of the country.[28] These petitions were all of the same type. They objected to the Orders in Council as likely to injure Anglo-American relations, and they emphasized the distress that would overwhelm the petitioners if, as expected, the Orders should bring about the interruption of peace and intercourse with the United States. By using these signs of opposition within the country, the Whigs were able by March 18 to secure a hearing for the petitioners before the bar of the House.[29] The petitioners put their case in the hands of the young Whig advocate, Henry Brougham, a man who was to play a vital role in the final repeal of the Orders in 1812. He was a skillful politician who never quite won the confidence of his party. The Whig Thomas Creevey commented about him that "he always has some game or underplot out of sight—some mysterious correspondence—some extraordinary connection with persons quite opposite to himself."[30] The problem of the Orders in Council presented him with his first major political opportunity. Brougham's American sympathies were well known through his contributions to the famous Whig periodical, the *Edinburgh Review,* and he now threw himself energetically into the task of organizing the pro-American feeling.[31]

The evidence of the opposition witnesses before the House in late March of 1808 was devoted to proving the value of the

American trade connection.[32] The three main types of witnesses produced were the representatives of financial houses arranging American currency transactions between the Continent and Great Britain, merchants engaged in exporting goods to the United States, and manufacturers engaged in making goods for the American market. The witnesses from the financial houses emphasized the fact that unless the United States was able to export the produce of the enemy colonies to the Continent, she would be unable to pay for British manufactured goods.[33] The other witnesses involved were naturally concerned at American restrictions on the importation of British goods into the United States, and they considered that if the Orders in Council were removed America would repeal her acts of economic retaliation.[34]

In the last days of March the opposition in Parliament made every effort to take advantage of the evidence presented by their witnesses. The Whigs stressed the commercial disaster that could be expected as a result of the Orders in Council, and asserted that England was not only losing the trade of the only important neutral but also was driving her into the arms of France. On March 22 in the Lords Lauderdale failed in an attempt to pass a resolution condemning the Orders,[35] but Holland reintroduced the question on the 29th. This good friend of America asserted that there was no more certain method of effecting ruin and destruction than by driving the people of America into hostility with the people of Great Britain. He added that it was not only in this matter of the Orders in Council that the British government was showing disregard for the friendship of the United States : "The same feeling uniformly characterised every proceeding of the king's ministers with regard to that country."[36] Though Brougham contributed an eloquent three-hour speech in the House on April 1, it was all to no avail.[37] In the first week of April the government introduced its own commercial witnesses. Examined by James Stephen, they gave the now familiar arguments of the commercial advantages gained by England as a result of the restrictions imposed by the Orders in Council.[38]

By May the opposition was beginning to realize that they could hope for no success in their onslaught on the Orders in Council, and that the government intended to stand firm. Though the Whigs had made excellent political capital out of the situation, the time had come to withdraw. Their main concern now was that it should not seem as if they were deserting the cause of the merchants and manufacturers who were interested in the American trade. The Whigs still thought the Orders mistaken, but they were in no position to alter the attitude of the government. On May 3 Auckland wrote to Grenville that "no good is to be done by a further attendance in this session."[39] With the inability of the Whig opposition to sway the attitude of the government, and its gradual withdrawal from the struggle in the spring of 1808, Jefferson's hopes for a successful policy of economic coercion were crumbling away. The opposition that had been aroused in England by the fear of the loss of American intercourse had shown that his hopes of reversing British policy by commercial means were not entirely without foundation. Yet it also raised false hopes in America that a continuation of economic coercion might still bring success.

The failure of the Embargo to influence British policy stemmed from a variety of causes. In the first place, the opposition to the Orders within England was at this time very restricted. It was comprised almost exclusively of the Whig opposition and their various organs of publicity, and of the commercial interests who were directly and intimately connected with the American trade. There was no hope of this group obtaining sufficient support in the country until there was extreme and widespread distress. This did not exist in 1808. The main groups that were suffering, or seemed likely to suffer, were those commercial interests concerned directly in the American trade, and even these had more fear of what was likely to happen than of what was actually happening. The Tory government, backed by the powerful commercial interests that had helped to produce the Orders policy, was in a strong position. It could depend on the support of these interests, and in the voting in the House it could also depend on a large body of "independents," who were impressed by the Tory argument that the Orders were essential as an instrument of belligerency against Napoleon. The Orders policy, which had been forced through only a few months earlier, was not likely to be given up because of the opposition of the Whig minority and of the American interest in the country.

The only glimmer of a chance for the opposition came in the early months of 1808, when the American interest became vocal for the first time, and the business world in general was somewhat depressed. Yet, disastrously for Jefferson's policy, at a time when the first adverse effects might have been felt by British trade as a result of nonimportation and embargo, new opportunities for trade presented themselves in South America. Any hope that Jefferson might have had of forcing England's hand in 1808 died when in spite of British restrictions the British export trade remained as substantial as the previous year. The decline in British exports to the United States was to be taken up by the increase in exports to the rest of the American continent, particularly South America.

Ironically, it was French action in the Iberian peninsula that had ultimately resulted in new trade opportunities for Great Britain in South America, and the consequent ineffectiveness of the Embargo. The first opportunities had arisen from the events of the previous November. The French invasion of Portugal, and the flight of the Portugese royal family to Rio de Janeiro in November, 1807, had opened the Brazilian trade to British merchants at a most opportune moment. Furthermore, in the early months of 1808 French troops had occupied Spain and the Spanish royal family had been deposed. In May the people of Madrid arose in revolt, and a bloody battle ensued between the Spanish populace and the French troops. Gradually the revolt spread throughout Spain. In June Spanish delegates visited England. They received a tumultuous welcome, and by July England and Spain were preparing for formal alliance. Now Spain and her colonies were to provide most attractive opportunities for English trade.

In 1808 the real value of British exports to the United States dropped from the 1807 figure of £11,850,000 to £5,240,00, but British exports to the rest of the American continent increased from £10,440,000 to £16,590,000.[40] As the new markets opened in South America, there was a burst of speculation and optimism in British trading circles. Just at the time when America wished to prove that she was indispensable to British commerce, the new opportunities seemed to prove that British trade could easily find new channels. American difficulties were soon forgotten in the fever of excitement which gripped British traders.

In January, 1808, the *European Magazine* spoke of the depressed state of trade, and advised its readers to observe the utmost caution in trading to the Brazils. In February it stated that there had been large orders for Manchester goods of every description for the Brazil market, and it conceded that it was probable that a trade "of the utmost consequence to this country" would develop in that area. By March the magazine had been completely converted. It stated that the first convoy for the Brazils was expected to sail at the beginning of the next month, loaded with all kinds of British manufactured goods. Furthermore, it advised its readers "to ship no kind of inferior goods to *Rio de Janeiro,* as they will find that *price* is no object with the inhabitants of that rich city."[41] Though this trade was not to prove as satisfactory as expected, and though there was still distress in English manufacturing areas in the spring of 1808,

American hopes of a collapse of British commercial prosperity proved unfounded. In 1808 England first looked to the Portugese and then to the Spanish colonies for new opportunities. It appeared that American trade was not indispensable. With America torn with internal strife and commercially stagnant, England, in spite of some internal discontent, happily compensated for her American losses elsewhere on the American continent. Not until the hopes of vast new markets in South America had proved overoptimistic, and depression had followed the excessive speculation, did the opposition stand any chance of convincing the country that the Anglo-American trade should be restored in full, even if it meant concession to America. But the United States would not wait for ever, and the concessions finally came too late.

With its position so favorable, the Tory government was not shaken in its resolve to maintain the Orders in Council either by opposition within the country or by pressures exerted from America. Confident of a considerable body of support, the Tories pursued a policy of supreme indifference toward the United States. In the debates on the Orders in Council in 1808, the government emphasized both that the United States had no grounds for complaint against Great Britain because of the Orders policy, and that if she did take offense her objections were insignificant beside the all-important aims of maintaining British maritime supremacy and waging the war against France. As the Orders in Council were retaliatory measures directed against France, and as suffering caused to the United States was merely incidental, the United States should blame Napoleon and not England for her present position.[42] Moreover, the government stressed that Britain had gone out of her way to avoid offending America, and Castlereagh made the exceedingly doubtful statement that if war did come about between Britain and the United States, "it would appear that no concession or submission could have prevented it."[43] Lord Hawkesbury put the matter in a nutshell when he said that he was aware of the importance of maintaining friendship with the United States, but that "he could never think of purchasing it by the surrender of any of our rights, much less of any of our maritime rights, upon which our very existence might be said to depend."[44] It becomes apparent in these debates in the early months of 1808 that the Tories were well satisfied with the British position in regard to the United States. This fact considerably helps to clarify the protracted negotiations between England and America in the years before the War of 1812. After 1807 Great Britain had no particular desire to achieve agreement with the United States; an agreement would of necessity have meant compromise, and this was the last thing the government wanted. The object became to convince the United States that she had enough advantages left to make it worth while for her to keep the peace rather than wage war, and at the same time always to hold out the hope to the Americans that there were better things to come.

The result of all this was that the American Embargo came almost as a blessing in disguise to the Tory party—America's self-imposed isolation was completely in accord with its wishes. American commercial competition and aid to Napoleon had been removed by the American government. It is true that the agitation of the British American interest gave the Whig opposition a lever to use against the government, but for the time being at least, concern was confined to those who were directly involved in the American trade, and the government had already decided that it was better to sacrifice these interests than to allow the commerce of the United States to continue unrestricted. The news of the widespread distress and discontent in America seemed to prove to the government that their policy had been a wise one. In the spring of 1808 both Canning and Castlereagh expressed their approval of the existing state of affairs. Castlereagh stated that "I look upon the embargo as operating at present more forcibly in our favor than any measure of hostility we could call forth were war actually declared." Canning's philosophy was that "above all things I feel that *to do nothing now*, at this precise moment,—absolutely nothing, —is the wisest, safest and most manful policy."[45] William Pinkney reported in August that there was a strong feeling in England that the United States would be unable to maintain the embargo policy. He pointed out that British opinion was absorbed by the Spanish resistance to Napoleon, and with the benefits this was bestowing upon England.[46] It is not surprising that when in August, 1808, Pinkney offered to remove the Embargo if England would remove her Orders in Council, Canning declined in one of his most sarcastic notes.[47] By September, Thomas Barclay, the British consul general in New York, was expressing the opinion that the continuation of the American Embargo might benefit Great Britain, as it was enabling her to export without competition to the newly opened Spanish and Portugese colonies in the New World.[48] After a whole year of trial for Jefferson's policy of economic coercion, it was written in London in January, 1809, by a member of the Whig opposition, that "the city are stark mad, and drink a continuance of the American embargo."[49]

While Jefferson's hopes faded in England as trade recovered and the Tories held firm, the President was wearily dragging out his last year of office, anxious to be rid of the complications of American foreign affairs. And the more weary that Jefferson became, the less inclined he was for war. "My longings for retirement are so strong," he wrote in February, 1808, "that I with difficulty encounter the daily drudgeries of my duty."[50] Diplomatically, America in these early months of 1808 was concerned with the visit of the special emissary, George Henry Rose. Typical of this whole period, Rose had come to solve a problem which by the time he arrived had been overshadowed by another. He was England's special emissary to negotiate a settlement of the *Chesapeake* affair of the previous June. As the eldest son of that good Pittite George Rose, the Vice-President of the Board of Trade, he could be expected to uphold the pretensions of the British government. Though himself personable and well received in America, he was on a hopeless mission.

He had been given his instructions by Canning in October, 1807; they were anything but conciliatory. He was empowered to offer reparation for the attack on the *Chesapeake,* but only if America would first accept Britain's contention that the general problem of impressment should form no part of these discussions, and if America would first withdraw the President's proclamation of the previous July by which he had ordered British ships from American waters. In addition, if Great Britain disavowed the attack on the *Chesapeake* and offered reparation, America would have to disavow the conduct of the commander of the *Chesapeake* in encouraging deserters from the British service. If these points were not agreed to by the United States, Rose was to demand his passports and return home.[51]

Rose's mission appears even less one of conciliation when it is realized that he arrived in America shortly after the arrival of the rumors of the British Orders in Council, and after Britain had also issued her October proclamation enjoining her commanders to carry out impressment strictly. Rose arrived at Norfolk on December 26, was in Washington by January 14, and was received by the President two days later. The mission was a complete failure—negotiations between Madison and Rose rapidly reached a stalemate. The United States would not meet the conditions under which Great Britain was prepared to offer reparation. By March the mission was at an end, and on March 27 Rose sailed for England. Even in a period of abortive missions, this undertaken by Rose was singularly futile.[52] England was in no mood for real conciliation, and could afford to dictate even in the matter of offering reparation. In addition, the United States was mistaken in tying the *Chesapeake* incident to the general problem of impressment. This in itself would have made an unconditional offer of reparation from Great Britain impossible.

It was not Rose's mission, however, but the fate of the Embargo that was at this period vital to the future relations between England and America, and to the question of war. Even Jefferson at this time expressed the opinion that war was preferable to a permanent embargo,[53] though he showed no enthusiasm for the logical conclusion of his own statement. He always retained the hope that his measures would ultimately force the European belligerents to yield. His beliefs on American policy, and on the continuing importance of impressment, were expressed in a letter to Madison on September 6, 1808, when he said of the British, "if they repeal their orders we must repeal our embargo. If they make satisfaction for the Chesapeake, we must revoke our proclamation, and generalize its operation by a law. If they keep up impressments, we must adhere to non-intercourse, manufactures and a navigation act."[54] Impressment and commercial problems still maintained a wide gulf between England and the United States. Jefferson's administration, which had started so brilliantly, tottered along to its close, with Jefferson still hoping for peace, and rapidly handing over control of affairs to his successor Madison. "If we go to war now," he wrote to Monroe in January, 1809, "I fear we may renounce for ever the hope of seeing an end of our national debt."[55] His hopes for economy were still with him at the close of his administration. The same hopes were to plague his followers when they tried to prepare for war.

At the end of 1808 American spirit was at a very low ebb— commerce ruined, the country split by controversy, and Britain and France apparently impervious to American threats and retaliation. America had maintained that her Embargo had been directed impartially against both belligerents, and logically she should have declared war on both of them when the Embargo failed. With good reason, however, the United States balked at this step. The Tenth Congress, which met in November, 1808, toyed with the possibility of more positive action, but the United States was a demoralized country in the winter of 1808-09. In December, 1807, America had decided that aggressions from Europe—particularly England—required retaliatory action. Following American tradition, and making allowance for American weakness, this retaliation had been in the form of embargo rather than war. One year after the adoption of America's great experiment in economic coercion, the European powers appeared to disregard it, and its main effect had been experienced in America itself, where there was widespread controversy and distress. It is hardly to be wondered at that America was in no position to take the logical step and declare war on one or both of the belligerents.

America had been greatly weakened by the Embargo, both economically and from the point of view of morale. The United States was now more disillusioned than warlike, and the initial enthusiasm had been lost. There seems little doubt that Jefferson could have carried America into war in June, 1807, at the time of the *Chesapeake* incident—a war which would have been fought primarily over the issue of impressment, with the subsidiary factor of the British commercial policy as evidenced by the *Essex* decision. But the glittering enthusiasm of the summer of 1807 had tarnished considerably by the winter of 1808-09. Not only had it lost its original brightness through the internal controversies and petty squabbles produced by the Embargo policy, it had also deteriorated from the fact that France had become much more an object of emnity after the autumn of 1807, when America received the news of the enforcement of the Berlin Decree against American shipping. This emnity increased in February, 1808, on the arrival of definite news of Napoleon's Milan Decree of December 17, which completed his Continental System. The last straw came on April 17, 1808, when Napoleon issued his Bayonne Decree. With Gallic humor, Napoleon ordered the confiscation of all American ships in French harbors, on the grounds that as American ships were forbidden by law to leave port for Europe, all these ships that were claiming to be American were really British in disguise.[56] With Napoleon's brazen humor on one side, and Canning's biting sarcasm on the other, the young United States was indeed a lamb among the wolves in 1808.

Though America was very near to declaring war upon England in the summer and fall of 1807, the position was far more confused by the end of 1808; both on account of the increased American weakness, and the new and very severe grievances against France. As a result, though the government was forced to repeal the Embargo, there was no declaration of war. Confronted by the absurdity of a situation in which a weak and disunited America was logically moving toward a declaration of war upon the foremost land and sea powers in the world, the country finally slid into an unsatisfactory compromise. By the end of February, 1809, it was finally decided that the Embargo would have to be repealed by March 4.[57] In its place Jefferson on March 1 approved a nonintercourse law which prohibited intercourse with France and England, and opened it with the rest of the world. The act was to remain in force until the end of the next session of Congress, and was eventually superseded in May, 1810. Provision was made for the President to suspend the operation of the act in favor of any belligerent that repealed its restrictive decrees.[58]

The Embargo Act had proved a failure as a weapon of retaliation—in fact it had done America much actual harm—abroad as well as at home. Canning in England greeted the news of the repeal of the Embargo with the comment that "the Yankees have been obliged to give way", and he advocated "the same firmness" in regard to Russia.[59] The effect of the Embargo in England had been to convince the government that a policy of firmness was the correct one to pursue in regard to the United States. As one contemporary British writer put it :

> The late Jeffersonian Embargo was a Rod which produced no other sensation on the rough hide of John Bull, than the pleasurable one which arises from titilation. The poor Animal was delighted, and not suspecting that this philosophical experiment on his Hide was intended to produce pain, he regretted that weariness had ultimately compelled Mr. Jefferson to cease scratching.[60]

Yet even as the Embargo faded ingloriously from the scene, new hope came to America. At the beginning of 1809 Erskine, the British minister in Washington, produced new suggestions for an agreement that seemed heavensent to the Americans. Unfortunately, the instigation came from Canning, not heaven, and the complications arising from these negotiations were to do irreparable harm to Anglo-American relations.

8 *The Erskine Agreement*

IN DECEMBER, 1808, David Erskine, the British minister in the United States, had written to Canning telling him that there was a danger of war with the United States if the Orders in Council were not repealed, but that Gallatin had suggested the possibility that some agreement could be reached between the two countries. It was also suggested by Erskine that the change of President might have some influence upon Anglo-American relations.[1] The difficulty with Erskine as British minister in the United States was that he had been sent by Fox in 1806 but had survived the fall of the Whigs in 1807. His friendship towards the United States should have proved an advantage, but as it did not reflect the attitude of the British government in the period of Orders in Council and Embargo it was in time to do more harm than good. He raised false hopes in America regarding a British policy of which he was by no means a good interpreter.

Canning reacted to Erskine's despatches of December by sending him a new set of instructions, informing him of the conditions under which Great Britain would remove the Orders in Council. These instructions contained no change of policy on the part of Canning. The conditions contained in them ensured that if America should agree to a settlement it would be on England's terms, and would produce neither aid to Napoleon nor injury to British interests. Canning did concede in regard to the *Chesapeake* affair that a settlement would not depend, as it had at the time of Rose's mission, on a formal disavowal of Jefferson's proclamation of July, 1807. He still maintained, however, that the subject of the *Chesapeake* was to be opened "separately and distinctly," and was to include no discussion of the general principle of impressment. Furthermore, Canning added in regard to the Orders in Council that the system would unquestionably have to be maintained "unless the Object of it can otherwise be accomplished." Thus, England would remove her Orders only if America would fulfill three necessary conditions. In the first place, she would have to withdraw all interdiction of her harbors, nonintercourse, and nonimportation against England, while leaving them in force in regard to France and her dependencies. Moreover, the United States would have to renounce all trade with the enemy colonies from which she was excluded in time of peace—that is, acknowledge the Rule of 1756—and finally allow the British to enforce American nonintercourse by giving them the power to capture American ships attempting to trade with France and her allies.[2] By no stretch of the imagination can this be called a serious attempt at compromise on the part of the British Foreign Secretary. He was trying, as he stated in his instructions, to secure the objects of the Orders even if the actual measures were repealed by an agreement with the United States. England was already well satisfied with her position in regard to the United States, and the only advantage to be gained by an agreement was the elimination of the risk of war and the acquisition of the support of even the British manufacturers. Canning by his instructions to Erskine hoped to attain these objects, while keeping the substance of the Orders in Council policy.

Erskine, though given permission by Canning to show these instructions to the American government, realized that he could expect no agreement based on a literal interpretation of his orders from England. Instead, he tried to work out a reasonable agreement with the Americans, while maintaining the spirit of the Foreign Secretary's instructions. This proved impossible. In his negotiations with the Secretary of State, Robert Smith, in April, 1809, Erskine was willing to accept alternative suggestions from the American, and did not insist on the letter of Canning's proposals. Regarding Canning's first point, that America should withdraw all restrictive legislation from Great Britain and leave it in regard to France, Erskine accepted the American contention that this was provided for by the provisions of the Non-Intercourse Act, by which the President was empowered to renew relations with one belligerent on the repeal of her restrictions, while leaving them in effect in regard to the other. In the matter of the American recognition of the Rule of 1756, Erskine accepted Smith's contention once again; Smith argued that the Non-Intercourse Act, which forbade intercourse with France and her dependencies, made any official recognition of the principle unnecessary. Also, details could be worked out in a future commercial treaty. On the last point, that America should allow England to enforce American regulations, Erskine again compromised by accepting the argument that Americans could not expect support from their own government while breaking American law, therefore there was no need to issue a degrading proclamation stating that Britain was to enforce American regulations.[3] Erskine, though obtaining unofficially much of what Canning had requested, was unable to extract specific promises from America on these points. If Canning had been vitally interested in obtaining a compromise settlement with America, he might have accepted the Erskine agreement. But Canning was not aiming at friendship with America at all costs. He wanted peace with her, but he wanted a peace which would satisfy all British desires in regard to the United States, both from the commercial and the strategic point of view. Moreover, between the time when he sent the instructions and the time he received the agreement, he had been informed of the repeal of the Embargo, and the subsitution not of war but of nonintercourse. It appeared that his policy of firmness towards America had proved an unqualified success. Considering the government's whole attitude towards America from March, 1807, and that of the Pitt administration from May, 1804, to January, 1806, there is no reason to be surprised by Canning's subsequent shelving of the Erskine agreement.

The notes exchanged between Robert Smith and Erskine on April 18 and 19, 1809, provided for the withdrawal of the British Orders in Council of January and November, 1807, in regard to the United States, and for the issue of a Presidential proclamation renewing intercourse with Great Britain. The date set for the renewal of open intercourse between England and the United States was June 10.[4] In the spring of 1809 the United States, economic coercion apparently having proved a failure, was looking for every hopeful sign from England. Jefferson, who left office in March, immediately wrote to the new President, Madison, expressing the hope that peace could be preserved. He offered the opinion that no government could be as embarrassing in war as the American, and peace was so important that, in the existing state of European affairs, America should not estimate her point of honor by the ordinary scale.[5]

The American government was quick to find reasons why Great Britain should have suddenly changed her policy. It was considered both that economic coercion had proved a success, and that, combined with British military reverses in Spain, had produced a policy of conciliation. Certainly in regard to economic coercion good news acted as a balm to the Americans, and for a time gave them a completely false estimate of its value as a policy. In regard to Spain, England as well as America viewed the events as a disaster. In January, 1809, Sir John Moore's army had withdrawn from Corunna, leaving its dead commander behind them. Once again British military operations on the Continent had failed. To America it seemed that England was at last weakening.

In April a newly confident Madison wrote to tell Jefferson that England had lost confidence in respect to America, and that this effect had been produced by British disasters in Spain, and by a great dread of the continuation of the Embargo.[6] Similarly, the Attorney General, Caesar A. Rodney, expressed the view at this time that had the Embargo been persisted in it would have proved successful; as it was, its effects and the British defeats in Spain would probably render England more rational.[7] The latter reason appealed to Jefferson, and he was of the opinion that if England was changing her policy it was only because of the reverses in Spain.[8]

With the accomplishment of the Erskine agreement, American joy and confidence knew no bounds. It seemed at last that America's self-denial had produced results, and England had been forced to yield. By the last week in April Madison was confident that the British cabinet had changed its policy towards the United States because of a conviction that an adjustment with America had become essential. A week later he was even more optimistic. He thought the new tone being used by Great Britain—which was in fact the tone of Erskine, not of England—made it likely that a definite agreement might be achieved. He concluded that even "the case of impressments, hitherto the greatest obstacle, seems to admit most easily of adjustment on grounds mutually advantageous."[9] There is more than a touch of pathos in the manner in which the American government so eagerly envisioned the solution of all its difficulties in the aftermath of the Erskine agreement.

The months after the Erskine agreement were indeed happy ones for America. All danger of war seemed to have passed, and ships sailed in large numbers for British ports. At the end of May Paul Hamilton, the Secretary of the Navy, wrote to Captain David Porter at New Orleans, and expressed his concern at expenditures for defense. Times have changed, thought Hamilton, and "there no longer exists a probability of war."[10] Factional differences were temporarily forgotten, and even the Federalists praised Madison. "Madison has acquired immortal honor, with his enemies," wrote Federalist Robert Troup, "for the promptitude and frankness with which he has met the overtures of the British Government: and the Jeffersonian demagogues begin to be apprehensive that the principles and measures of his administration will be too much after the school of Washington for the interests of their party."[11] For three months America lived in a fool's paradise, though an inkling of the truth came through in two.

In April, 1809, England introduced the first major changes in her system of Orders in Council. It has been maintained, and was even maintained at the time, that this Order was a substantial concession on the part of Great Britain toward America.[12] In fact, the events leading up to the Order show that, though in effect it was of some advantage to the United States, it was caused primarily by changes in the European situation. The plan for the new Order was formulated by Bathurst at the Board of Trade, and he submitted to his colleagues a private memorandum containing the reasons that led him to desire the change. The bulk of his argument was concerned with European affairs. In his reasons for revision, Bathurst frankly admitted that one of the great objects of the Orders in Council had been the encouragement of the export of British colonial produce. The main reason given for the change in the type of blockade was that the countries of Spain, Portugal, and Turkey were now in amity with the British, and they were soon to be joined by Austria. The fact that these countries had become allies meant that their trade had no longer to come through England, but could be exported directly from their own to enemy ports. The whole European situation had thus undergone a considerable relaxation. Bathurst's answer to this was to propose a stricter blockade over a more limited area. It was England's position in Europe that was of primary importance to the British government. In regard to America, England's established policy had apparently proved successful. In March news had been received that the United States was to abandon her Embargo, and Canning viewed this as a complete victory for the British policy of firmness.[13]

The new Order in Council issued on April 26, 1809, declared a strict blockade from the Ems in the north down to Pesaro and Orbitello in Italy. Ports outside this area were opened to neutral commerce, with one significant exception. American commerce was excluded from all intercourse with the French colonies. In commenting on Bathurst's original proposal, Spencer Perceval had expressed the view that America might well view her exclusion from the French West Indies as yet another imposition on her commerce. He need not have been so guarded in his conclusion. America would obviously resent the attempt to exclude her completely from the carrying trade to the Continent in French colonial produce.[14]

Canning gave a simple and significant explanation of this Order in a letter of July, 1809. He stated that the Americans had objected to the provision in the November, 1807, Orders in Council that granted them the possibility of trading to Europe by paying a duty in England. This cause of complaint he now stated was completely removed, for by the Order of April 26, 1809, all trade with France, Holland, and the ports of Italy included in Napoleon's Kingdom of Italy was now completely prohibited. America could now have no complaint regarding the payment of a transit duty in England before trading to French possessions as this option had been removed. In this matter of trading with French-controlled Europe the difficulties had certainly been removed—so had the trade. In this letter Canning also commented on the fact that in the matter of American trade with the French colonies the total prohibition had made it more restrictive than the November, 1807, Orders in Council.[15] Yet Canning realized that the opening of certain areas in Europe to neutral shipping might be thought a concession to America by certain British interests, and he was anxious to avoid this false impression. He stated to Bathurst at the end of April: "Anything is desireable that takes off the appearance of concession—which this is *not*—but which, till explained, it may be thought to be."[16]

Canning was correct in thinking that at first sight anything that produced a change in the Orders in Council would be looked upon as concession to America. There was little doubt that the American commercial position had been improved by the new Order in Council—in fact, given the status of American commerce after 1807, any change in the European situation was likely to be an improvement. Yet the fact remained that the new Order did not stem from a basic change of attitude toward America on the part of the British government but from European considerations. That this was not immediately apparent became obvious from the reception accorded the new measure. The American interest in Britain, and even Pinkney himself, who wrote to Madison that "it is universally viewed as a concession to America,"[17] regarded the new Order as a definite sign of a British intention to conciliate the United States, and received it joyfully. Sir Francis Baring wrote to Rufus King and told him: "The orders in Council are no more ... the sting is drawn."[18]

Yet though the British government naturally tried to convince the Americans that because of the new Order all American complaints should end,[19] it soon became obvious that there had been no basic change in policy towards the United States. It was in fact the news of this new Order in Council which brought the first doubts into American minds of the value of the Erskine agreement as a panacea. Madison wrote to Jefferson that "the crooked proceeding seems to be operating as a check to the extravagance of credit given to G.B. for her late arrangement with us; and so far may be salutary."[20] Jefferson, now in a pleasant retirement, was even more shocked than Madison : "I am at a loss," wrote Jefferson, "from which we have most to fear, the folly or the faithlessness of the Cannings and the Castlereaghs of the British ministry." He realized that this inconsistency boded ill for Anglo-American relations : "I fear a return of our difficulties, and it will be with increased force if they do recur."[21] Jefferson was looking into the future with more perspicacity than Madison, who thought that in spite of the seeming inconsistency, Britain would fulfill the stipulations of her minister.[22]

The hopes and fears were to continue for another month. The Erskine agreement had come as a miracle to rescue the United States from her despair at the failure of the Embargo. She could not bring herself to believe that it had been nothing but a mirage, and that all the problems of the first months of 1809 were still very much in existence. On July 21 the dreaded blow fell. News arrived that Canning had repudiated the Erskine agreement, and Erskine's rickety façade of Anglo-American friendship collapsed.[23] Canning's letters to Erskine of May 22 and 23 removed any doubt that might have remained that the April Order in Council was intended as a concession to American demands. He plainly pointed out the deviations Erskine had made from his instructions, and told him that England could not withdraw the Orders without an explicit declaration by America of the three British conditions stated in Canning's instructions to Erskine of January, 1809. In these instructions Canning had stated that the system of the Orders in Council would definitely have to be retained unless its object could be otherwise accomplished. This could be done only if America removed all restrictions regarding English commerce while leaving them in effect in regard to France, acknowledged that she could not carry on a wartime trade with the enemy colonies that was closed in time of peace, and allowed British ships to seize American vessels that traded with ports forbidden to them by American regulations.[24] It seems quite evident that England inaugurated no basic change of policy in regard to the United States in 1809—Canning's original instructions to Erskine in January had contained no real concession to the American point of view. All he did was give America a chance to yield graciously instead of ungraciously to British regulations. From the British point of view, American acquiescence would have been ideal. It would have meant that America would have still obeyed all British regulations, but there would have been no danger of war. Erskine made the mistake of trying to compromise, and immediately found himself disavowed by Canning. A new impetus was given to America for anger against England, and the stagnation of the period 1807 to 1809 was now slowly to disappear.

The chagrin and disappointment felt by America can well be imagined. To have an agreement snatched from her aroused all the old anger against England. Paul Hamilton, the Secretary of the Navy, was typical. "I am unable to express," he wrote, " . . . the affliction and indignation I feel at the additional insult to the amicable disposition manifested by the United States towards Great Britain." He thought, however, that "if, at last, the national energies shall be called out we shall have no cause to be fearful."[25] Canning had thrown away an excellent chance to gain the aid of America as a benevolent neutral in the struggle against Napoleon. He preferred America in a position of emnity than in a position to infringe upon Britain's maritime monopoly.

To add insult to injury, Canning on May 30 recalled Erskine and replaced him with Francis James Jackson.[26] Jackson was chiefly noted as being the British envoy sent to give the ultimatum to the Danes before the British fleet had bombarded Copenhagen in 1807. By his choice of a successor to Erskine, Canning clearly indicated that he had not departed from his view that America could best be treated by a policy of firmness. Jackson was the last man who could be expected to soothe the Americans after the tragic shock of the disavowal of the Erskine agreement. Even if he had been of a more yielding disposition, Canning's instructions would have prevented him from showing any mood of conciliation. Canning maintained that the American, not the British, government was at fault in the Erskine affair, for it had accepted an agreement from Erskine that the British government could not possibly have sanctioned. Canning was shocked that Erskine had reasoned throughout "as if His Majesty had proposed to make Sacrifices to propitiate the Government of the United States, in order to induce it to consent to the Renewal of Commercial Intercourse between the two Countries." He emphasized, as he had done in his instructions to Erskine, that Great Britain could only withdraw or even modify the Orders in Council if the United States should previously have taken it upon themselves "to execute, in substance, the objects of the Orders in Council." Jackson was not to propose any agreement to take the place of Erskine's, though he could refer home any American proposal that included the three conditions listed in Erskine's instructions.[27]

While Jackson was sailing towards America with his hopeless instructions, Madison and the rest of the country were endeavoring to recover from the shock of the British disavowal. Early in August Madison was obliged to return to Washington. He aptly commented that from the instructions to Erskine it would seem that Canning was as much determined that there should be no adjustment as Erskine was that there should be one.[28] On August 9 he issued a proclamation renewing nonintercourse against England, and immediately departed out of the heat of Washington to his Virginia plantation.[29]

On September 8, 1809, Jackson arrived in Washington, and conditions could hardly have been less favorable to a successful negotiation. The combination of Jackson's own character, Canning's instructions, and the bitterness of America was too much to overcome. Two days before Jackson's arrival, the Attorney General, Caesar A. Rodney, had expressed the opinion that the United States should not even deign to negotiate with a man of such obnoxious character.[30] In the United States Jackson followed the strict line laid down by Canning. He accused America of being at fault in the disavowal of the Erskine agreement, and assured a rapid termination of the negotiation. A brief, acrimonious correspondence was followed at the beginning of November, 1809, by the refusal of the American government to receive any further communication from the unpopular Mr. Jackson. Jackson was finally recalled by the British government in April, 1810.[31] Unfortunately, he stayed in America for almost a year subsidizing Federalist authors and interfering most undiplomatically in American internal affairs. Courted by the Federalists, he was reviled by the rest of the country. "God damn Mr. Jackson," shouted one Kentuckian, "—the President ought to . . . have him kicked from town to town until he is kicked out of the country. God damn him!"[32]

America was not alone in finding 1809 an unfortunate year —England too was meeting grave difficulties. While Erskine and Jackson confounded America, British endeavors on the Continent met disaster. Sir John Moore's death at Corunna in January had been followed in the summer by the dismal failure of the Walcheren expedition, and by the collapse of the fourth coalition. The only relief was in the action of the future Duke of Wellington in the Peninsula, and his limited success was not enough to appease the quarreling British cabinet. A quarrel between Canning and Castlereagh, which had been growing in the spring and summer of 1809, finally came to a head in the September of that year. Castlereagh discovered that Canning had been intriguing against him, resigned from the government, and challenged the Foreign Secretary to a duel in which Canning was wounded in the thigh. The crisis brought about the resignation of the old Duke of Portland, who had suffered a stroke in August, 1809. The changes brought no relief to America. Spencer Perceval, the author of the policy of the Orders in Council, became Prime Minister, and Lord Wellesley, who had made his reputation in India, became Foreign Secretary. Lord Liverpool, the new Secretary of State for War and the Colonies, was an ardent defender of England's maritime system. Hopes of incorporating the Whig opposition of Grey and Grenville into his government had to be abandoned by Perceval,[33] and America's chances of any new attitude on the part of Great Britain quickly faded. Yet the United States government, always anxious to make an attempt at conciliation, and always believing that some agreement with England might be possible, instructed William Pinkney to investigate the possibility of an accord with the new Foreign Secretary, Lord Wellesley. These negotiations were singularly futile, with both sides maintaining their traditional positions, and Pinkney quickly discovered that Wellesley was determined to be as unyielding as Canning. As a result no progress was made.[34]

The events of 1809 seemingly produced a deadlock, for the disavowal of the Erskine agreement, the failure of the Jackson mission, and the abortive negotiations in England marked a new low in the diplomatic relations of the two countries. Yet out of this degradation of 1809 was eventually to come a new, warlike America. The lethargy produced in the United States by the failure of economic coercion was slowly to be dispelled—between 1809 and 1812 America gradually plucked up courage to declare war on England. This movement in American history from 1809 to 1812, coming after several years of peaceful resistance to all insults, has at times been attributed to factors outside the main course of American maritime and economic history from 1803 to 1809. Great stress has been laid upon the importance of grievances against England that were peculiar to the western areas of the country. The classic statement of these factors was made by Julius W. Pratt in his famous work, the *Expansionists of 1812*. Professor Pratt argued that a factor of primary significance in the causes of the war was the western demand for the conquest of Canada to prevent British support of the Indians. This, he argued, was matched by a southern desire for the Floridas for agrarian, commercial, and strategic reasons.[35] These questions of British action among the Indians of the Northwest, and of the American demand for the Floridas, were of importance long before 1810—the problem is did they suddenly assume vital importance in forcing war with England between 1810 and 1812? Was there a sudden, unprecedented demand for the conquest of Canada in 1810 because difficulties with the Indians had reached a peak, and was this matched by an accentuation of the demand for the Floridas enough to drive America into war on England? Or was the demand for war, growing steadily from the close of 1809, intimately connected with the whole history of Anglo-American relations from 1803 to 1812, when maritime grievances had been of dominant interest to the Americans? To answer these problems it is necessary to leave the main thread of Anglo-American relations, and consider the developments that had taken place on the Northwest and Southwest frontiers in the years from 1803 to 1809.

9 The Problem of the West

WHILE ENGLAND and America clashed at sea, the frontier that separated the United States and Canada presented its own problems to the harassed governments of the two countries. As Napoleon's armies were marching and counter-marching across the Continent, American settlers were relentlessly advancing into the lands northwest of the Ohio. After General Anthony Wayne's victory over the Indians at Fallen Timbers in 1794 and the treaty of Greenville in the following year, American settlers poured down and across the Ohio River. By 1800 Kentucky had a population of 221,000. By 1810 Ohio contained 230,760 people, and settlers were thrusting onward into Indiana and Illinois. America was rapidly conquering the land between the Ohio and the Mississippi. The "permanent" boundaries between American and Indian that had been established at Greenville meant nothing to settlers eager for land, and Governor William Henry Harrison of Indiana was rapidly acquiring Indian lands in Indiana and Illinois. In these circumstances the Indians of the region were once again preparing to fight for their villages and hunting grounds. The rich lands of Ohio were practically gone, and a new, futile struggle was beginning along the Indiana frontier. For aid the Indians inevitably turned their eyes toward the British possessions to the north, to the British who had aided them in their last struggle against the Americans in the years before 1795.[1]

After Greenville in 1795, and the handing over of the western posts in 1796, the British, believing that there would be no future need for the assistance of the Indians, had been content to leave them to their own devices.[2] The attitude of the British Indian Department during this period of lethargy was succinctly summarized by Thomas McKee, the British Indian agent at Amherstburg, near Detroit, when he conceived that the object of the government was "to have as few Indians to come to the Post as possible in order to lessen the expenditure of Provisions."[3] This situation that prevailed on the Northwest frontier was not seriously disturbed until the outcry in America following the *Chesapeake* affair in June, 1807. The news of that incident, and of the bellicose American reaction, reached Canada in July and immediately produced a fear of invasion.[4]

The British and American attitude to this new turmoil in the Northwest has produced various problems. Important is the question of the exact nature of British policy in the years before the War of 1812. Did the British in Canada actively encourage Indian depredations on the American frontier, or did they attempt to restrain such attacks? Given the secrecy of much of the actual contact with the Indians, this problem has no easy solution. An additional difficulty, and one vital to the question of the origins of the war, is the extent to which British activity among the Indians dominated the interests of the westerners, and exerted a profound influence on the actual declaration of war in 1812. It has been maintained that an urgent demand for the invasion of Canada did not become apparent in America until 1810, and that before that time annexation of the area was looked upon as a matter for the indefinite future.[5] Yet British policy among the Indians of the Northwest from 1807 until the outbreak of war was based upon the fear of such an invasion. It was England's fear of an aggressive American reaction to her maritime policy that produced the British interest in the Indians of the Northwest in this period.

In the summer and fall of 1807, taking fright at the war fever in America, the Indian department in Canada began the task of regaining the affection of the Indians. Those who had gathered at Amherstburg in the fall for the annual distribution of supplies were warned before they left that they might be summoned in the near future, and messages were sent even to the nations west of Lake Michigan asking them to visit the post.[6]

The formulation of a general policy in the face of this threat of war was, however, the task of the newly appointed Governor-in-chief, Sir James Craig, who reached Canada in late October, 1807. The instructions he issued between December, 1807, and May, 1808, were the basis of British policy in the years before the spring of 1811. The philosophy behind his instructions was that in the event of war the Indians would not be idle, and that if England did not employ them there was not the slightest doubt that America would.[7] Craig himself had no desire to precipitate a conflict, but he had to ensure that if war came the Indians would flock to the British standard to aid in the defense of Canada. That the Americans would invade Canada in the event of war seemed inevitable to the British in that area. Craig's problem was to conciliate the Indians without sending them on premature attacks upon the American frontier, and thus increase the danger of war with the United States. His solution to the problem was, in effect, the suggestion of a dual policy— one public, one private. Moreover, he apparently thought that the Indians could be kept from actual warfare, if the agents could persuade them to join the British cause without any discussion of the possibility of war against the Americans. Thus he advised that the agents in contacting the Indians should, for as long as possible, avoid coming to any "explanation", as he termed it, though he was careful to qualify this with the significant "at least to any public explanation."[8]

Several weeks later, at the end of December, 1807, this hint that more could be said in private than in public received more definite expression. At this time Craig thought that there was every reason for the British to be successful in wooing the Indians; the long-lasting ties between them, the protection and supplies that could be given by Great Britain, and the obvious desire of the Americans to take the lands of the Indians were all conducive to this end. These facts were to be pointed out to the Indians not only in private councils—they should also be urged privately to some of their leading men. "Two or three gained over to us," wrote Craig, "will be of more avail than all that can be said in a Council."[9]

The reaction of Francis Gore, the Lieutenant Governor of Upper Canada, helps us to develop this theme somewhat further. He had little doubt as to how he should interpret Craig's instructions. At the beginning of January, 1808, he expressed agreement with Craig's plans, adding that they should take care "not to be too passive,"[10] and toward the end of the month, writing to the Deputy Superintendent of Indian Affairs, William Claus, he formulated more clearly the ideas of the Governor-in-chief. Claus was to proceed personally to Amherstburg and assemble the chiefs of the Shawnee and other nations. There across the river from Detroit, he was "to consult Privately" with them on the critical situation of affairs, and when there was a favorable opportunity he was to remind them of the "artful and clandestine manner" in which the Americans had taken their lands, and of the fact that the Americans ultimately intended to drive them from the whole country. The dominating theme of these instructions was secrecy. Claus was to contact the Shawnee chief Captain Johnny, and if he found him trustworthy was to use him to communicate confidentially with the other chiefs. He should, if possible, confide in only one interpreter. If he found it necessary to make a speech in public council, he was to limit his remarks to general comments on the wish of the Great Father to remain in friendship and harmony with the Indians.[11]

Thus by January, 1808, a dual policy had been inaugurated by which in public very little of importance would be said and the Americans conciliated, while in private the Indians were to be reminded of the sins of the American frontiersmen. Yet by the spring even this policy had been intensified, but not because of the fears of American invasion. This intensification of policy was brought about by apprehensions regarding French policy. The British conflict with the French, which had done so much to decide Anglo-American relations at sea, made its influence felt even on the distant frontiers of Upper Canada. In May, 1808, Craig became afraid of the arrival of French forces on some part or other of the American continent. He expressed the view that their first appearance was likely to be in the South— at New Orleans or in the Floridas—and that they would then use their skill to try to persuade the Indians to attack the "defenceless frontier" of Upper Canada.[12] Craig now reached the conclusion that the Indians were more important than even he had thought when he first arrived in North America, and that even greater efforts would have to be made to attach them to the British cause. In particular, he suggested that some means might be employed for opening an intercourse "with the nations situated to the Southward."[13] Gore was quick to oblige in Upper Canada, and in June he was able to reply that trusty and confidential persons would be employed to contact the Indians to the south and west.[14] The old bogy of Napoleon had combined with the fear of American invasion to produce a policy of active, secret communication with the tribes within American territory. To be sure, the British policy was to secure allies for a probable future war, not to precipitate war itself, but the methods used were hardly conducive to peace between the Americans and the Indians.

A danger in discussing Anglo-Indian relations in this period is the failure to realize that carrying on negotiations with the Indians was a vastly different proposition from conducting relations with a sovereign independent state. The dispatches between England and the Governor-in-chief, and between the Governor-in-chief and Upper Canada, cannot be treated as though they were part of a Bismarckian diplomacy. In this time before telegraph and telephone even the British minister in Washington was isolated, as was tragically shown by the Erskine affair, but the men who were responsible for carrying out British Indian policy had a far greater lack of supervision. Ultimately, British policy in the Northwest was channeled through two small outposts—Amherstburg, near Detroit, and St. Joseph's, near Michilimackinac. Amherstburg, the post near to the main American line of settlement, was by far the most important of these,[15] and it was from this spot on the Detroit River that the official British policy was disseminated to the Indians of the Northwest. It was here that the Indians came to receive supplies, meet in public council, and talk in confidence to the representatives of their Great Father. The Indian agent, who verbally communicated the policy of his government, held the key to Anglo-Indian relations. He had the privilege of putting the dispatches of his superiors into language that the Indians could understand, and in doing this he obviously had a power to influence policy far beyond his actual position in government. Working without adequate supervision, his character and prejudices could make or mar a policy as subtle as Craig's, whose instructions had given great power of discretion to the man on the spot.

At the time of the *Chesapeake* crisis Thomas McKee, son of the more famous Alexander of revolutionary days, was Superintendent of Indian Affairs at Amherstburg. But McKee was seldom sober, and once it became clear that there was need for intricate negotiations, the officials of Upper Canada began to exert pressure for his removal and for the appointment of Matthew Elliott.[16] Elliott, who as Superintendent at Amherstburg was to hold the key position in Anglo-Indian affairs in the years before 1812, deserves more attention than has hitherto been afforded him. An Irishman who had emigrated to America during the French and Indian War, Elliott had spent a lifetime among the Indians. As a trader in western Pennsylvania and Ohio in the 1760's and 1770's, and as a captain in the British Indian Department during the Revolution, he had lived and fought among the tribes of the Northwest, particularly the Shawnee. After the Revolution he had traded and acted as a British Indian agent in western Ohio. For many years married to a Shawnee woman, and speaking the language fluently, his sympathies were all with the Indians. In the years before Fallen Timbers he had been active in organizing resistance to the Americans. He had become Superintendent at Amherstburg in 1796, but had been dismissed two years later after a dispute over irregularities in the issuing of provisions. In spite of repeated petitions, and even a trip to England, Elliott had not succeeded in obtaining a reversal of this decision in the years before 1808.[17]

The crisis of 1807-08 found Elliott living in considerable splendor, with numerous slaves, on his farm at Amherstburg.[18] Elliott himself could not have relished the prospect of an American invasion. The Americans hated him. When he visited Detroit in October, 1807, in a futile attempt to recover some of his escaped slaves, who along with others from Amherstburg had been formed into a renegade company of militia by the Americans, he had to return home by a devious route to avoid being tarred and feathered. And in November reports came from American sources that if war came Canada would be invaded and Elliott, among others, would surely be put to death.[19] It is not really surprising that, even before his reappointment, he entered on voluntary service for Claus. When Claus arrived at Amherstburg in February, 1808, in accordance with Gore's orders, and found no one he could trust among the more than six hundred Indians assembled there, he naturally turned to Elliott. A messenger recommended by Elliott was sent to the

Auglaize in northwestern Ohio to ask the Shawnee chiefs and the Prophet to come to the post.[20]

The Shawnee Prophet and his brother Tecumseh were the leading spirits in the Indian resistance to the Americans in the years before 1812. Lalawethika, or Tenskwatawa, as he was also known, had assumed the role of Indian prophet at Greenville, Ohio, in 1805. There he had preached an Indian religious revival, urging the Indians to return to simpler ways and to throw off white influence. Under the leadership of the Prophet's brother, Tecumseh, the movement had become increasingly political, and in the years before the War of 1812 Tecumseh attempted to form a confederacy of Indian tribes to resist the advance of the Americans into the Northwest. From the end of 1807 the British started to show a marked interest in the activities of the Prophet and his brother Tecumseh.[21]

In response to the request of Elliott and Claus, a group of Shawnee chiefs, though not the Prophet, came into Amherstburg in March, 1808. Following Craig's instructions, Claus held a private meeting with three of them. He told them that the British were trying to preserve peace, but if these efforts failed their friend Elliott would send for them. He also told them how the Indians were being cheated out of their lands by the Americans. When Gore reported this visit to Craig, he spoke of the great attachment of the Shawnee to Elliott.[22]

The reason for the frequent occurrence of Elliott's name in these negotiations is not hard to understand. He had a connection with the Shawnee stretching back over forty years, and he naturally maintained it in spite of his dismissal in 1798. Two Shawnee chiefs—the Bonner and the Berry—had lived with Elliott at Amherstburg in the early years of the century; and Frederick Fisher, a half-breed interpreter and Elliott's underling, was established at Greenville in 1806.[23] Thus, in December, 1807, when Craig asked Gore for information about the Prophet, and suggested that he might be bought, Gore was able to reply that Elliott was personally acquainted with him.[24] Though the Prophet did not come into Amherstburg with the Shawnee chiefs in March, 1808, he did send a message of friendship through Frederick Fisher, who had been reappointed as interpreter at this time of crisis.[25]

Elliott himself, who had served voluntarily through the earlier part of 1808, finally regained his position in May. Craig, who had been under constant pressure from Upper Canada to reappoint him, finally yielded when he decided that there was a French as well as an American threat in the New World.[26] In the following month, in June, Tecumseh came into the post in place of his brother, who had been summoned again in May. Claus, who was still at Amherstburg co-operating with Elliott, had three hours of private conversation with Tecumseh and four other members of his band.[27] Craig's policy, transmitted by Gore, of innocuous speeches in public and weighty meetings with influential chiefs in private, was proceeding smoothly by the summer of 1808. As he had desired, confidential relations had been opened with the nations to the south, and efforts were still being made to contact the nations to the west. The tribes west of Lake Michigan, sent for the previous summer, had not yet arrived, so yet another messenger was sent to visit them.[28] It is not surprising that American records of this period are filled with references to the British agents working among the Indians.

These activities of 1808, which culminated in the visit of some 5,000 Indians to Amherstburg in the fall,[29] were apparently very satisfactory to Elliott. In February, 1809, he estimated that with only one regular regiment Detroit and all the country between it and the Ohio would soon be in British hands, and the Indians actively in support. Gore thought him too sanguine in his hopes of Indian assistance,[30] but Gore had no way of knowing what had been said in private between Elliott and his old friends.

Far away in London, Castlereagh, the Secretary of State for War and the Colonies, had no time to spare for the organization of an Indian policy in Upper Canada. Tecumseh or the Prophet seemed of minor importance beside Napoleon or Alexander of Russia. With the fate of Europe in the balance, the British cabinet could not occupy itself with the day by day events along the Detroit River. If possible, Castlereagh wanted Canada defended, but he certainly wanted to give no overt offense to the United States.[31] Far from the scene of affairs, he was obliged to depend upon the policy of the British officials in Canada. In April, 1809, he wrote to Craig agreeing with his principle that, in the event of war, if the British did not use the Indians the Americans would. He was ready therefore to support any temporary arrangements that Craig might make.[32] Castlereagh depended on Craig, Craig on Gore, Gore on Claus, and Claus on Elliott, and there was no written proof by which to check the final policy.

As Anglo-American relations worsened in the period after the *Chesapeake* affair, the British began active interference with the Indians in American territory, with the object of winning them over to the British cause and using them for the defense of Canada in the event of war with the United States. Yet though the British began to interest themselves in the Indians after 1807, American interest did not suddenly change from maritime events to the still rather obscure developments in the Northwest. The outlying territories of the United States—the exposed frontiers of Indiana, Michigan, and Illinois—were certainly becoming increasingly concerned, but the settled areas of the country were far more incensed at the stifling of American trade and the open infringements of American rights at sea. Even in the western states the warlike talk in 1807 and 1808 was primarily concerned with maritime matters, not with the secret British activities among the Indians.[33] At the close of 1808 resolutions entered into by the Kentucky House of Representatives regarding American policy concerned themselves exclusively with maritime matters. The resolutions approved of Jefferson's administration, praised the Embargo, and offered to give full support to the government in war, total nonintercourse, or a more rigid Embargo policy.[34]

It is quite apparent that in the years after 1803 the westerners bitterly resented England's maritime policy. Henry Clay, who was to become the leader of the young War Hawks in the Twelfth Congress, had said at the beginning of 1806, when the sole problems with England were those at sea, that he would "evince to the world that Americans appreciate their rights in such a way as will induce them, when violated, to engage in War with alacrity and effect."[35] A correspondent from Tennessee in August, 1807, when the reaction against the *Chesapeake* affair was still at its height, told Madison that the people of his area were for war primarily because of the problem of impressment.[36] The Senator from Ohio, Thomas Worthington, wrote to Jefferson in the same month, stating that in his region the general opinion was in favor of war with England.[37] War in actual fact did not come about at that time, owing to the fact that Jefferson was able to persuade the country to support his experiment of economic coercion, but there is little doubt that had Jefferson chosen to take the country into war, the West would have been enthusiastic in its support, though it would have been fought to rectify maritime not peculiarly western grievances.

Even more significant in this earlier phase of maritime difficulties with England is the attitude in regard to Canada. It has long been an argument of primary importance among those who would see an essential impetus for war coming from 1810 to 1812 because of peculiarly western grievances, that war was wanted in those years in order to conquer Canada and prevent British support of the Indians. It has been maintained that from 1803 to 1810 the annexation of Canada was thought of as a matter for the indefinite future, and that only the rise of Tecumseh and the danger from the Indians in 1810 produced an urgent demand that the British should be expelled from Canada.[38] This conclusion cannot be supported on the basis of the available evidence. The definite idea of invading Canada was present well before 1810, certainly as far back as 1807 and 1808. It was present during a period when it is conceded that the westerners had little thought of going to war to prevent British support of the Indians, and their primary desire for war was connected with maritime matters.

As soon as the first real threat of war with England arose after the *Chesapeake* affair, it became obvious that the one area where the United States might effectively harm England was in her North American colonies. At best, it was quite obvious that at sea America would have to depend on her privateers and on individual actions, and that in the event of war Canada was the one area where America might carry out offensive action against Great Britain with any reasonable chance of success. Thus in July, 1807, when General Turreau visited Jefferson in Washington, the President told him that "if the English do not give us the satisfaction we demand, we will take Canada, which wants to enter the Union."[39] The old warrior Lafayette was well able to grasp the strategy involved. He wrote to Jefferson in September, 1807, hoping that peace could still be kept, but urging that in the event of war Canada should be conquered to provide against all attacks from that quarter.[40] The opinion of the western country was clearly expressed by Arthur Campbell of Tennessee when he said that "a suspension of all intercourse and a battle fought on the Plains of Abraham will operate like the fall of Danzig and the late victory at Friedland," and that "it will be a sublime spectacle to spread liberty and civilization in that vast country, *Canada*."[41] The desire for the invasion of Canada was inevitably present when there was a prospect of war with England. It needed no sudden fear of Tecumseh to bring this about in 1810, though the desire to quench support for the Indians could certainly operate as an additional reason when the fear of the British action on the frontier became more acute.

In the fall of 1807 the Secretary of War, Henry Dearborn, secured a detailed description of Upper Canada, including particulars of military strength at the various forts.[42] Another cabinet member, the cautious Gallatin, had during the summer, in the weeks following the *Chesapeake* affair, drawn up a financial plan for the war that seemed so likely to occur. Among his plans were methods by which British possessions in the western hemisphere could be attacked. By the fall Gallatin doubted the wisdom of war, and in October he wrote to Jefferson suggesting that it would be inadvisable to commence war at that time owing to the inadequacy of preparations for that event, and that Canada might more easily be invaded and conquered in winter and early spring than in autumn.[43] Even in the South, the conquest of Canada was openly advocated as early as the summer of 1807.[44]

The British themselves had no doubt that the Americans would invade Canada in the event of war. In fact, it has already been shown that the reason for the renewed British activity among the Indians from the summer of 1807 was the wish to use the Indians for defense against American invasion in the event of war with the United States. Across the Atlantic, in England, Castlereagh was fully aware of the danger of an American invasion of Canada, and at the end of 1807 he was giving careful consideration to the number of troops that would be needed for its defense.[45]

The pressure for an invasion of Canada certainly existed in the United States by the summer of 1807, and both England and America realized that in the event of war this was one area in which the Americans might fight with a reasonable chance of success. It did not need a culmination of Indian difficulties and an all-pervading desire to eliminate British support of the Indians to produce this demand. The wish to invade Canada in the event of war had been present before America became actively concerned about this support. From at least the time of the *Chesapeake* incident in June, 1807, America thought of such an invasion as a positive method for resisting British restrictions at sea. In view of the strength of the British navy, land warfare against the British colonies was the only feasible alternative to economic coercion. Maritime events were influential on the Northwest frontier as well as in the Atlantic. When the irritation at British-Indian relations reached a peak in 1810 and 1811, this only added to the reasons and demand already existing for the invasion of Canada in the event of war. One can only conclude that though there was British intrigue among the Indians in the period from 1807 to 1810, and though there was also an American interest in the invasion of Canada, the main reasons advanced for this conquest stemmed from the desire to bring an end to British maritime infringements rather than to eliminate British support of the Indians. British action at sea was inflicting far more harm upon America than the British attempts to win the support of the Indians in the Northwest. Feeling against the British as instigators of the Indians was growing in this period, but it was growing because the British were becoming further and further enmeshed in activity among the Indians in order to meet the threat to Canada that was inherent in America's reaction to England's maritime policy. The root of the problems pushing England and America toward war was at sea, not on the Northwest frontier.

It has also been argued that the southern demand for the Floridas for "agrarian, commercial, and strategic reasons" was of considerable importance in the pressure of Americans for war against England from 1810 to 1812.[46] Of the interest of the United States in Florida during this whole period from 1803 to 1812, there is not the slightest doubt. The original instructions to the American emissaries Monroe and Livingston in 1803 had envisaged the purchase of the Floridas and the island of New Orleans from Napoleon rather than the vast province of Louisiana.[47] And when Napoleon decided to cede the whole of Louisiana instead of the Floridas, it did not take long for Livingston to "discover" that West Florida was included in the purchase. In the words of Henry Adams, he worked out a theory "that France had actually bought West Florida without knowing it, and had sold it to the United States without being paid for it."[48] Even France had not considered that Louisiana stretched eastward to the Perdido River, as can be seen from the instructions to General Victor in 1802.[49] Jefferson, however, had also conveniently reached the conclusion that West Florida formed a part of the Louisiana purchase. He eagerly seized on Livingston's theory, and tried to act on it for the remainder of his presidency, as did Madison at a later date. Already, in considering the American attitude towards England in 1804 and 1805, the efforts of Jefferson to obtain West Florida from Spain by diplomacy and threats have been briefly considered.[50] Though Jefferson failed in his objective at that time, he never gave up his aim of expansion into Spanish territory, nor indeed his dislike of Spain, while he remained President. At the time of the *Chesapeake* crisis in September, 1807, the President made the statement that "while war with England is probable everything leading to it with any other nation should be avoided, except with Spain."[51] Two weeks previously he had asserted that "I had rather have war against Spain than not, if we go to war against England. Our Southern defensive force can take the Floridas, volunteers for a Mexican army will flock to our standard."[52] Thus even in 1807, when Spain was still linked with France, Jefferson was contemplating a war of aggression against Spain *if* war should come with England.

The position in regard to Spain and England changed radically in May, 1808, when the Spanish revolt against Napoleon placed the Spaniards on the side of the English, and gave the latter an interest in the preservation of Spanish territorial integrity. Thus, in the years after 1808, the repeated American efforts to gain control of the Floridas were met by vigorous British protests. Canning in his instructions to Francis James Jackson in July, 1809, told him that there was no need to disguise Britain's deep interest in the affairs of Spain : "You will let it be understood that such are the ties by which His Majesty is bound to Spain that He could not see with Indifference any Attack upon Her Interests in America."[53]

Yet in spite of warnings from England, America went ahead with her infiltration into West Florida, and in September, 1810, a revolution, partially American inspired, delivered that area to the United States. In October Madison issued a proclamation commanding the occupation of the Floridas up to the River Perdido.[54] This action brought a reminder in December from the British chargé d'affaires in Washington, John Philip Morier, that Spain was intimately allied with England.[55] The Americans refused to be dissuaded by the British warnings, for the infiltration process was continued into East Florida in the period 1810 to 1812. In 1811 and 1812 illegal American efforts to gain control of East Florida, connived at by the American government, were only disavowed by Madison at the last moment in the spring of 1812. And even then, American troops were left in East Florida.[56]

The fact is that for the whole of this period from 1803 to 1812 there was a steady American demand for expansion into the Floridas. By the latter year this demand had to a considerable extent proved successful, and America was well on the way to appropriating the whole area. It is difficult to understand the view that the demand for Florida was of basic importance in *causing* the war against England. It is true that in 1811 and 1812 references can be found arguing that, should war with America come, America would be able to advance into Florida, the territory of England's ally Spain, but this discussion was of minor importance compared to the discussion devoted to English infringements of American neutral rights. The expansionist demand for Florida had been present in America since before the Louisiana purchase in 1803, and had not even produced a declaration of war upon the weak Spain. There is little reason to suppose that the desire for Florida suddenly became strong enough after 1810 to be of substantial importance in producing a war against England. There seems something incongruous in the concept of America declaring war on the greatest maritime power in the world, in order to seize an already partially conquered, long-coastlined territory from a weak and ineffectual country.[57] The conquest of the remainder of the Floridas did receive mention by the War Hawks in 1811 and 1812, for if there was going to be a declaration of war upon England it was essential to show the country how the war might be waged. That America should take advantage of a tremendously risky war against England to gain every possible advantage from England's weak ally is not surprising—how else could America win a recognition of her rights and wage effective war? Yet the fact remains that there were far easier ways of obtaining territory from Spain than by declaring war on England, and this had been well proven by 1812.

The most interesting fact about the westerners and southerners in the whole period from 1803 to 1812 is not that they were concerned with special aims of their own, but that they showed remarkable unity in their support of American governmental policy, and in their resentment of British actions at sea. The western area of the nation was particularly enthusiastic in its support of American rights on the ocean, and it is not surprising that this should have been so; cut off from the European influences of the seaboard, and creating a new, raw country, they were apt to feel insults from abroad with particular intensity. These westerners were the American empire builders, and empire builders have seldom been lacking in forceful nationalism. They felt a genuine anger that Americans should be compelled to serve on board British men-o'-war, and that American ships could sail only by permission of the British.

The westerners undoubtedly had a vital interest in the Indian problem, but one cannot separate them from the main course of Anglo-American history as though their sole concern was Indian attacks. When the Indian problem became acute in 1811 and 1812, it was of obvious importance to the West and to the rest of the nation, but it was only one interest and grievance in a variety of interests and grievances. In the period from 1807 to 1810, when the danger of Indian war was increasing, the westerners were mainly concerned not with the Indians but with the impotency of the government in the face of British maritime policy. They were concerned with the infringement of American rights, and particularly with the apparent failure of economic coercion. Both the South and the states of the Mississippi Valley were suffering economically from British commercial restrictions. A like interest in British maritime policy linked the West and the South far more effectively than any joint expansionist drive for Canada and the Floridas.

The question of overseas markets for American agricultural produce was of paramount importance to both the West and South. The factor that originally led historians to seek non-commercial causes for the War of 1812 was that in the vote for war in Congress, the Northeast, the foremost commercial and shipping area, was the section opposed to the conflict.[58] This, however, is not a reason for supposing that noncommercial causes were the primary cause of the war. The fact is that the shippers of New England, engaged in an extensive wartime carrying trade, were able, in spite of British restrictions, to make a considerable profit.[59] They were quite prepared to condone British practices and oppose war with that country, as long as these profits were available. When this was combined with their undoubted sympathy for England as the great opponent of Napoleon, there was ample reason for them to be bitterly opposed to a war with England. They realized that they had much to lose by war. Abstract questions of neutral rights bore little weight with the commercial New Englander waxing rich in spite of all foreign restrictions.

The case was much different in the West and South. These areas harbored the producers, not the carriers. They were not concerned with the vast profits of the carrying trade, but with the more marginal question of selling their produce. The South, it is commonly agreed, depended to a great extent on her export of tobacco and cotton. Planter prosperity depended upon the export of a considerable amount of the southern crop to European markets. When England hampered these overseas sales the South inevitably suffered. The area supported economic coercion in the hope of forcing England to change her policy, but only succeeded in increasing her own distress. Eventually the South was to prefer war to continued restrictions on her export trade.[60] In regard to the position of the West respecting the export of agricultural produce, there has been some disagreement. Writers have on occasion taken the view that as the West was in a primitive agricultural state it was not concerned with the matter of exporting its produce.[61] It is true that the West was not engaged in an extensive overseas export trade, but the fact that its overseas exports were small made it all the more important that this trade should not be interrupted. It has been shown quite conclusively that the farmer of the West needed purchasing power for his land, for manufactured articles, and for small luxuries in his home and diet.[62]

Moreover, in the years from 1808 to 1812 the Mississippi Valley was in a period of agricultural depression. Prices in the West reached a peak in 1805 which was never again attained before the War of 1812. By 1807 the average for prices was almost 7 per cent under that of 1805, and in 1808, the year of the Embargo, prices went sharply down; in four years the annual average for prices at New Orleans had fallen over 20 per cent. In 1809 there was an irregular recovery, but in 1810 the average was lower than 1807, which had been the poorest of the three pre-Embargo years. In 1811 conditions became even worse, and New Orleans prices were 10 per cent under those of 1810. The two Kentucky staples, tobacco and hemp, had varied fortunes in these prewar years. Tobacco was particularly hard hit. After the winter of 1805-06 tobacco prices fell repeatedly. This caused many to change to hemp, which in the years from 1808 to 1810 enjoyed high prices. In 1811, however, hemp also suffered a drastic decline. Cotton prices fell from 1805-06 to the outbreak of war. At a time when costs were remaining stationary or even rising, the prices which farmers could obtain for their produce were falling rapidly.[63]

As might be expected, the South and West did not remain impassive in the face of declining prosperity. They gave enthusiastic support to measures—first economic coercion and finally war—designed to force the European powers to repeal their restrictions on American commerce. Western and southern support for economic coercion stemmed both from a devotion to Jefferson, and from the vital interest of these areas in forcing Britain to remove her restrictions on American exports. When these efforts at economic coercion failed, only war remained as a solution to their problem.[64] Disillusionment at American efforts to resist British actions at sea by peaceful means was to inspire a growing desire for war in the West and South after 1809.

10 *The Turn of the Tide*

THE NEWS of Canning's disavowal of the Erskine agreement, which reached America in July, 1809, had the effect of awakening the country from the lethargy into which it had been lulled by economic coercion. Yet the difficulties that faced the Americans who might consider a war against England had grown immensely in the two years since the summer of 1807. Of basic importance was that in the summer of 1807 American relations with France had been relatively good, whereas two years later they were almost as bad as those with England. If America should decide to declare war on England, there was no logical reason why she should not also declare it on France. The core of feeling was directed against the former, and it was obviously completely impracticable to wage war against both European belligerents, but an excuse was needed to justify war on England alone. Jefferson shrewdly analyzed the position when he said in a letter to Madison in August, 1809, that "should Bonaparte have the wisdom to correct his injustice towards us, I consider war with England as inevitable."[1] It was to take Napoleon a year to take advantage of this fact, but when he did, he was to discover that even the shadow of a conciliation was enough to give America an excuse to fight England without fighting France. As it was, in the summer of 1809, America was in the impossible position of finding that her economic coercion had failed, and that the only alternative left was to fight against the two strongest powers in the world.

An additional source of weakness to the United States in the summer of 1809 was the general despondency that had settled on the nation as a result of the failure of the Embargo, and the bitter internal conflicts it had produced. The country seemed crushed by failure—the vigorous spirit that had been apparent after the *Chesapeake* affair in the summer of 1807 had evaporated in internal squabbles and petty bickerings. With the failure of the Embargo, and the disavowal of the Erskine agreement, America reached rock bottom diplomatically. From that time, unless the country was to lose all self-respect, a new spirit became essential. Passive resistance was an obvious failure, and the alternative of the vindication of American rights through force was apparently the only solution. But this was no easy task, for a new spirit had to overcome not only the negative attitude induced by the self-destructive Embargo, but also the entrenched opposition of Federalist New England to all forms of resistance to the mother country. Moreover, America was totally unprepared for war. Possessing completely inadequate military forces, and weakened economically by the Embargo, she was in no condition to wage war with one of the weaker powers of the globe, let alone two of the major ones. Thus, though American maritime grievances against England had been increasing steadily since 1804, and formed the basis of American anger, it was almost necessary to make a fresh start in 1809. It was now necessary to convince the country that war would succeed where economic coercion had failed. This attempt was the dominant theme after 1809. With the disavowal of the Erskine agreement, the feeling for retaliation against England, which had grown in America from 1804 to 1807 and had wilted from 1807 to 1809, gradually took fresh strength. It was a slow process, but this time its conclusion was not economic coercion, but war.

The American view of the "unprincipled rascality"[2] of Canning in disavowing Erskine brought a fresh surge of opposition to England in practically all parts of the country. In August and September meetings were held in various sections of the nation, including the West, to protest the disavowal, to support Madison's renewal of nonintercourse against England, and usually to offer support if the government should decide to take more extreme measures in retaliation.[3] The resolutions submitted from Washington County, Kentucky, suggested that if the hostile disposition of the belligerents continued American merchant vessels should be armed. There was even a marked feeling in various quarters that the disavowal of the Erskine agreement was likely to do good, as it was serving to put an end to some of the bitter internal squabbles, and helping to unite the nation in a defense of its rights.[4]

This new resolution received a fresh impetus from the brief and unfortunate mission of Francis James Jackson in the fall of 1809.[5] Even Madison, who was carrying on the traditions of the pacific Jefferson, voiced the opinion in January, 1810, that the belligerents themselves might decide the question of war or peace for America, by leaving her no choice "between absolute disgrace and resistance by force"—he thought American patience might be carried so far as to present this very dilemma.[6] Resolutions entered into at Philadelphia in the next month called for war as the only solution to the British actions since the 1790's. Every grievance mentioned was concerned with maritime affairs, and the resolutions drew an analogy between the situation in 1810 and that at the time of the War of Independence.[7] The opinion that a new War of Independence was necessary received increasing attention in the next two years. The General Assembly of Ohio, in February, 1810, proclaimed its readiness to support any government measures, and praised the government's attitude regarding the disavowal of the Erskine agreement.[8] This western state made no mention of the Indian problem, and expressed no expansionist desire for Canada.

On the same day that the Ohio Assembly was declaring its readiness to support government measures against England, young Henry Clay of Kentucky was making a momentous speech in Congress. In January he had been elected by the Kentucky Assembly to serve out the term of Buckner Thruston in the United States Senate. A Virginian who had moved west at the age of twenty, Clay had already served out a similar short term in the Senate early in 1807, before the *Chesapeake* affair and the Orders in Council. At that time Clay had spoken quite optimistically of the state of Anglo-American relations, thinking that Monroe and Pinkney were nearing a successful conclusion to their negotiations. That hope had proved false, and much had happened in the intervening years. American relations with England had deteriorated rapidly, and economic coercion had failed. The fiery Clay, only 32 years of age, was now ready to suggest the alternative to peaceful resistance.[9]

The time was certainly ripe for it. The Eleventh Congress, which had been elected in 1808 and had taken office in May, 1809, had displayed a lamentable lack of effectiveness in the first year of its existence. Facing the hostility of both France and England, the seeming impossibility of the task of resistance had reduced it to a pitiful impotence. It still clung desperately to the idea that the European powers could be forced to yield through economic pressures. Considerable time was spent in a discussion of the measure to be substituted for the Non-Intercourse Act, which was due to expire at the close of the second session in May, 1810, but when Clay arrived in Washington no definite action had been taken. In spite of the new spirit that was slowly seeping through the veins of the nation, this inept Eleventh Congress had nothing constructive to offer. It seemed mesmerized by the magnitude of its task.[10]

It was to this inept, dispirited body that Clay voiced the new fervor that eventually was to take America into the War of 1812. The dashing Kentuckian rose in the Senate chamber and lambasted the senators for their weak and vacillating course. Peaceful resistance had failed, and Clay declared he was for "resistance by the *sword*." Though America had just cause for war against both European belligerents, Clay argued that England had inflicted the worst indignities and injuries upon the United States. The catalogue of wrongs was too long and well known to be detailed, but Clay thought there was a remedy: "It is said, however, that no object is attainable by war with Great Britain. In its fortunes, we are to estimate not only the benefit to be derived to ourselves, but the injury to be done the enemy. The conquest of Canada is in your power." Clay went on to tell the Senate that it could then "extinguish the torch that lights up savage warfare," and "acquire the entire fur trade connected with that country." America could in this way regain the spirit of '76: "I cannot subscribe to British slavery upon the water, that we may escape French subjugation on land."[11]

Clay certainly mentioned British activities among the Indians in this speech, but it had not suddenly become the basic grievance. Clay was quite clear in expressing his belief that as America's efforts at peaceful resistance had failed, the time had come for resistance by war. To injure England he called for the invasion of Canada, and he mentioned the additional advantages that would accrue to America from this action. The point was that Clay was trying to show this ineffective Eleventh Congress that it was possible for the United States to wage war upon England, that there was an alternative to the indignities of peaceful resistance, and that this alternative was the American invasion of Canada. As was so often the case in the next two years, the advocates of war first considered in their speeches the reasons why war was necessary, and dwelt on maritime grievances, and then, when turning to the methods of waging war, discussed the question of invading Canada. It is true that the war party saw in the conquest of Canada an opportunity to prevent further Indian depredations, and even to gain such positive advantages as complete control of the fur trade, but there seems no reason to believe that this was in itself a sufficient reason for the war party to win enough support to bring war against England in 1812. The grievances against Britain for her support of the Indians certainly made the conquest of Canada even more desirable, but the argument that Canada was vulnerable to American invasion had been present since the beginning of Anglo-American difficulties.[12] It had been urged in sections of the country not directly concerned with the Indian menace, and indeed the West, with its meager voting resources in Congress, needed extensive support from other areas of the country. Out of 142 members of the House of Representatives, Kentucky, Ohio, and Tennessee had a total of only 10. Even including the western parts of the older states, the more recently settled areas could not muster the voting strength of the Atlantic seaboard.[13] It was a voting impossibility for the West to take America into war for grievances peculiarly its own. Clay had sounded the clarion call on behalf of the West, but for voting strength he was to depend on the intimate alliance and joint leadership of the South. And the South as well as the West had a clear realization of the strategy involved in the invasion of Canada.

It was a Southerner who made the clearest contemporary statement of the reasons for the conquest of Canada. In January, 1813, when the war was already under way, and there was little compulsion to hide motives, Matthew Clay, a veteran representative from Virginia, stated in Congress:

We have the Canadas as much under our command as she [Great Britain] has the ocean; and the way to conquer her on the ocean is to drive her from the land. I am not for stopping at Quebec or anywhere else; but I would take the whole continent from them, and ask them no favors. Her fleets cannot then rendezvous at Halifax as now, and having no place of resort in the North, cannot infest our coast as they have lately done. It is as easy to conquer them on land, as their whole Navy could conquer ours on the ocean. As to coping with them at sea, we cannot do it. We can annoy them, but not meet them on the open sea. I would meet them and hurt them, however, where we can. We must take the continent from them. I wish never to see a peace till we do. God has given us the power and the means; we are to blame if we do not use them. If we get the continent, she must allow us the freedom of the sea.[14]

Matthew Clay was rather sanguine in his estimate of American power, but it would have been difficult for him to have put his objectives and motives any more plainly. Henry Clay, in the same debate in January, 1813, exhorted the Americans to "strike wherever we can reach the enemy, at sea or on land, and negotiate the terms of a peace at Quebec or Halifax."[15] The significance of Henry Clay's earlier speech of February, 1810, was that in fiery language he had pointed out that America could injure England in war, and thus gain the recognition of her rights. Only in Canada was England vulnerable, and it was there that Clay wished America to strike. At last someone with the force and personality to inspire disciples had called for a revival of the "spirit of '76," and for war rather than submission; this cry was to become increasingly frequent during the next two years. Clay provided the leadership that had been so badly needed by the few voices crying in the wilderness, who in the years of ignominy had called for resistance by force.[16]

For the present, however, his task presented overwhelming difficulties. The defeatist Eleventh Congress, though it would have to face re-election in the summer of 1810, would not be superseded until the fall of 1811. Moreover, there was still the problem that France as yet had offered no excuse for America to declare war on England alone. Napoleon was as unyielding as

England, and offered ample opportunity for the Federalists to point out that in calling for war on England, her opponents were playing into the hands of the main threat to the liberty of the world. America was enervated by the seeming hopelessness of her position, and by her repeated failure to coerce the European belligerents. Clay reflected and directed the new spirit that was making itself felt in the country, but it was inevitably a long process to persuade a majority of the country, and even more important, a majority of the legislators, that war was the only solution of America's difficulties, and that war would succeed where economic coercion had failed. The seed was there, but it needed careful nurturing.

In spite of the efforts of Clay, the Eleventh Congress in a last despairing effort to coerce the belligerents, after a whole session of futile discussion, enacted the weakest of all the measures of economic coercion. Strangely enough, it was to prove the most significant. Macon's Bill No. 2, which was passed on May 1, 1810, decreed that all restrictions upon American commerce with Europe were repealed, but that if one of the belligerents should revoke her edicts against American commerce, the United States would, within three months, revive nonintercourse against the other, if she failed to follow suit.[17] It was, in reality, a surrender, and it could only serve to increase the feeling in America that war was to be the only escape from this humiliating position. Even Madison realized the futility of the bill. He told Jefferson on May 7 that England now had every motive for continuing her restrictions against America—"she has our trade, and our aquiescence in cutting it off from the rest of the world."[18] With France also, the last indignity was reached in the spring of 1810 when Napoleon issued his Rambouillet Decree. This act of March 23, first published in May, declared that all American vessels that had entered any port in France or controlled by France since May 20, 1809, were to be seized and the property confiscated. Thus at one blow

Napoleon seized property to the amount of some 10 million dollars.[19]

America's position was so hopeless in regard to the European belligerents that it seemed that no war could make it any worse. "In this state of things where are we to look but to ourselves," wrote Secretary of the Navy Paul Hamilton, "Is it not time for us to rouse the energies of the Nation?"[20] Hamilton's growing antagonism to England and his desire for positive action became very apparent after June, 1810, when the British ship *Moselle* attacked the American vessel *Vixen* off the American coast. The fact that the commander of the American vessel had failed to return the fire of the British ship infuriated Hamilton: "as God is my judge, if I could select one of our Commanders in whom I could safely confide, I would have this and the Chesapeake business both balanced very shortly." He issued general orders that in future not even a "menace or threat" should be submitted to from a foreign vessel.[21] Henry Clay was of a like mind with Hamilton. He also expressed disgust at the subservience of the *Vixen*: "A man receives a fillip in the nose, and instead of instantly avenging the insult, inquires of the person giving it what he means!"[22] Indeed a new spirit was making itself felt in America.

The elections of 1810 for the Twelfth Congress, which was to take office in the fall of 1811, were the clearest sign of the new trend. Many of the Eleventh Congress found that they had vacillated in the legislature for the last time, as a wave of feeling against these impotent legislators swept them out of office. Practically half of the retiring members were defeated as the country searched for new blood to inject into an anemic Congress.[23] The movement was essentially a reaction to the events of the previous six years, and particularly to the futility of the period from 1807 to 1810. The original cry had been for war or economic coercion. Economic coercion had received a long trial, and had failed. All the protests, speeches, acts, negotiations, and hopes of the previous years had come to nought. England was following basically the same policy in regard to America in 1810 as she had established in 1807. All that was left for America was war or submission. Yet war presented far more difficulties than it had in 1807, for all the dissension and internal turmoil had left America physically and morally weak. Also, feeling that was directed solely against England in the summer of 1807 had now to be shared between England and France. This latter problem was, however, to be of short duration, for Napoleon provided the solution. The opportunity offered by Macon's Bill No. 2 was too great for such an opportunist to miss.

On August 5, 1810, the Duc de Cadore, the French Foreign Minister, informed the American minister in France, John Armstrong, that the Berlin and Milan Decrees could be considered as revoked after November 1, 1810, and that England presumably would remove her Orders, or America would revive nonintercourse against her.[24] The letter was purposely made obscure, but it said enough to solve an American dilemma. It is quite apparent that throughout this period before 1810, with the exception of a Federalist minority, there was far more bitterness against British than against French actions. It is not surprising that this should have been so. Only a quarter of a century before, America had obtained her independence from England with the major aid of France. Apart from a brief period of uneasy agreement between the Treaty of Greenville in 1795 and the renewal of war in 1803, a constant series of incidents and diplomatic wrangles had marred Anglo-American relations. America naturally looked to France rather than to England, though Napoleon had done as much as any man could do to destroy that friendship. Even more important was the fact that England, with her command of the seas and her possessions in North America, had infinitely more chance of alienating American opinion. It was English not French ships that lay off the American coast to impress and search, and it was Canada not New France that bordered the United States. It was quite to be expected that if Napoleon would give the United States even the shadow of a chance, she would escape from this impossible position of facing hostilities with the major land and the major sea power simultaneously, and would turn against her traditional enemy. It was not coincidence that sprinkled references to the "spirit of '76" and the "spirit of our fathers" among the war speeches of the period from 1810 to 1812.

For three years America had faced Hobson's Choice. It is hardly surprising that Madison leaped eagerly at Napoleon's offer of a way out of the impasse. Napoleon was not to honor his promise—he rarely did—but America was given an excuse to fight England alone. In the words of Madison : "It promises us, at least, an extrication from the dilemma of a mortifying peace, or war with both the great belligerents." He wondered what England would do, but thought that whatever her immediate course "it is probable that we shall ultimately be at issue with her on her fictitious blockades."[25] On November 2, in spite of the lack of any proof that France had in fact withdrawn her decrees, Madison issued a proclamation stating that nonintercourse against England would be revived in three months unless England repealed her Orders.[26] America had baited her line to lure either France or England, and had hooked that huge shark Napoleon. Hooking was one thing, landing another. Little James Madison was now to be towed, not unwillingly, in the direction of war with England. The movement could be stopped only by British concession, and in fact the chances for this were better at the close of 1810 than ever before, though the British government was not prepared to admit it. In the period between the summer of 1810 and that of 1812, as America inched her way into war, England, beset with internal problems, was slowly forced into a repeal of the Orders in Council in an effort to restore trade with the United States.

11 *The Growth of Opposition*

I N JUNE, 1810, the news that Macon's Bill No. 2 had been passed was greeted in England by the Tory newspaper the *Courier*, with the comment that it was "a high compliment to the wisdom with which His Majesty's Ministers adopted and persevered in the system of policy towards the United States."[1] The *Sun*, another Tory newspaper, commented on June 9, 1810, that the opening of intercourse had proved that the ministers had pursued the correct policy, and had ensured that it would be a long time before the United States would try any other measure of retaliation. Indeed, it appeared that the British policy of firmness had at last triumphed, and that the United States had acknowledged the ineffectiveness of its measures by agreeing to trade on British terms. There now seemed little need for Great Britain to change a policy which had produced such favorable results.

Perhaps the most striking fact about British policy in this whole period from 1807 to 1812 was its consistency and its unyielding nature. When Augustus J. Foster, the last British minister in the United States before the war, received his instructions in April, 1811, they contained a reiteration of all the main arguments that had been used to justify the Orders since their issue in November, 1807. Wellesley, the British Foreign Secretary, concluded his instructions with words that might well have been used by Canning in 1807. He asserted that England was anxious to avoid a direct rupture with the United States, but "no Extremity can induce His Royal Highness to relinquish the ancient and established Rules of Maritime War, the maintenance of which is indispensable, not only to the Commercial Interests, but to the Naval Strength, and to the National Honor of Great Britain, as well as to the rights of all Maritime States, and to the general prosperity of Navigation and Commerce throughout the Civilised World."[2] The crux of the matter remained the same—the government wanted peace with the United States, but it had to be on British terms, for war was better than concession.

If anything, the British government had become even more scornful towards the United States in the years from 1807 to 1811. As time progressed, the government became increasingly confident that the United States had neither the power to injure nor wage war against Great Britain. The reports of the distress and disorder that flooded into England from America in this period served to convince the government that the United States was not a country to be reckoned with. The view of American conditions that prevailed in England led, in the main, to a scornful opinion of American power, and a false picture of American policy and internal conditions. Certainly by the Tories it tended to be assumed that the American government was a narrow, democratic faction ruling over a country weak and disunited by internal strife, and that this government was in addition remarkably pro-French.

Obviously a partial explanation of these views was to be found in the actual disunity present in America at that time, and in the natural irritation felt by the British against their former colonists, yet it is also clear that the American Federalist minority must share a great deal of the responsibility for giving British opinion a false idea of the state of affairs on the other side of the Atlantic. British affinity in this period was naturally with the pro-British

Federalists, and as a result considerable weight was given to their opinions of American life and policy. The English newspapers that supported the government regularly printed large extracts from the American newspapers, but the vast majority were from Federalist journals. Thus in June, 1810, the *Courier* printed an extract from the letter of a New York mercantile house, obviously the work of a virulent Federalist, as showing "the present state of the public mind in that country." The writer spoke of the United States as being swallowed up by "democracy, or jacobinism."[3] The *Leicester Journal*, a typical Tory country newspaper, stated in the same year, after receiving a packet of Federalist newspapers, that "we are happy to find that notwithstanding the proceedings of Congress, the great majority of the people of America are anxious for an amicable adjustment of the differences with this country."[4]

Americans in England commented on this influence of the Federalists. Samuel Morse, more famous for his code and for his paintings than for his political comments, said in England after the declaration of war in 1812 that the Federalists were a disgrace to their country, for their actions and words were published extensively in England: "this war will reëstablish that character for honor and spirit which our country has lost through the proceedings of *Federalists*."[5]

William Pinkney, the American minister in England, was well aware of the dangers of the popularity of the ideas of the Federalists in Great Britain, and on several occasions mentioned this problem in his letters to America. He realized that England was becoming convinced that she had nothing to fear from America and need make no concessions, and that the Federalists were helping to produce this opinion. In October, 1807, Pinkney urged Madison to send newspapers and pamphlets more regularly to England. He wrote that "a pamphlet, favorable to British pretensions, and decrying our own, is no sooner published in America than it finds its way across the Atlantic, gets

into general circulation here, and is quoted, praised, and some-
times republished; whereas those of an opposite description
either do not arrive at all, or come too late." He added in another
letter to Madison in January, 1808, that "there is an opinion
here that we are likely to become a divided people, when a rupture with Great Britain is in question," and that this opinion
was founded upon American publications. He re-endorsed this
view at the end of 1809, when he commented that "the British
government has acted for some time upon an opinion, that its
partisans in America were too numerous and strong to admit of
our persevering in any system of repulsion to British injustice."[6]

Another Federalist opinion that was of importance in England at this period, and which greatly helped to produce a hatred
of America, was the idea that the American government was
completely under French influence. Thomas Jefferson was a
favorite target for such attacks, and the Federalists undoubtedly
helped to spread the picture of a pro-French President, hated
by the majority of the American people. To Englishmen, Jefferson was "the Frenchified President,"[7] and there was hardly a
reference to him in the Tory journals that was not coupled with
the accusation that he was hand in hand with Napoleon. As
might be expected this did not add to his popularity in Great
Britain. When Sir Francis Baring gave the toast of "The President of the United States of America" at a banquet at the City
of London Tavern in August, 1808, he was greeted with a "loud
and continued hiss" from every part of the rooms. It took a
"Glee from the band of Vocal Performers" to restore the company to good humor. The banquet was attended by "the heads
of all the great companies of the first mercantile and banking
houses, together with several Ministers of the Country, Statesmen out of place, Foreign Ministers, and other illustrious
characters."[8]

The Tory *Leicester Journal* excelled itself on the subject of
Jefferson: "King Thomas I ... part fool and part knave—he

is different from Bony and from Alexander—he is neither a silly dupe, nor a determined hero; but he is a walking reasoning Philosophic *Marplot*."⁹ Occasionally it even waxed into a somewhat less than eloquent verse in an effort to do justice to its feelings for the American President:

> NAPOLEON's example to copy he strives,
> And NAPOLEON, it seems, at his project connives;
> He would quarrel with Britain, I'm sure if he durst,
> For the Corsican's friend is this—THOMAS THE FIRST.¹⁰

The influential government organ, the *Quarterly Review,* considered that the whole tenor of Jefferson's administration had excited suspicions of a secret understanding between him and France.¹¹ There was also an opinion prevalent in England that Jefferson was immensely unpopular in America. News of his decision not to stand for re-election was greeted with the comment that he "perhaps only anticipated the decision of the people, and resigned to avoid the disgrace of being dismissed."¹² William Cobbett in July, 1808, prophesied that the President would be sent from office with "an universal hiss," because "the people know, that the embargo arose out of the president's hatred of England."¹³ Madison, a less striking figure, received less personal attention from the British press. The general Tory view was that he was somewhat incompetent, pro-French, and anti-British. "His talents," it was concluded, "appear to be of a very ordinary kind indeed, and when we see him in the situation to which Washington gave such dignity and lustre, we are irresistibly tempted to, 'Wonder how the devil he came there'."¹⁴

British opinion did not confine itself to dislike of Jefferson and Madison—the Americans as a whole were disliked in England quite as much as the English were disliked in America. It was natural that this should be so. Their position as recent rebels ensured this, even without more compelling factors, and the fact that America was not opposing Napoleon at a time when Eng-

7

land was fighting for her life was enough to turn most Englishmen against that country. Though, as has been indicated, there was a minority feeling of genuine friendship in both countries, it had a most difficult task in swaying opinion. Even the friends of America in England recognized the strength of anti-American feeling.

Alexander Baring, a great friend of America, had no illusions on the state of British opinion. He argued that the achievement of American independence had left the British with a feeling of resentment, which had only increased as the United States prospered in their independent state. This sentiment had been fostered rather than checked by the government, and Baring considered that as a result the British looked upon the Americans with feelings of marked hostility.[15] A correspondent of the radical *Leicester Chronicle* endorsed Baring's opinions four years later in 1812, when he spoke of the Americans whom "in our hearts, we have never forgiven, for wresting from us their emancipation."[16] An earlier correspondent of the liberal *Examiner* had stated on August 12, 1810, that "I decidedly think the opinion very generally entertained in Great Britain of the Government and People of the United States much too unfavourable." Attacks on all aspects of American life, character, and policy abounded in the British journals of this period. Leigh Hunt, the editor of the normally reasonable and intelligent *Examiner,* showed how even the moderates found it difficult to praise the United States. After first agreeing with Jefferson's partiality for agriculture over commerce, though not with his partiality for France, Hunt stated in November, 1808 : "I would rather live in China, where the best ambition of the human intellect is respected than among the noisy and vulgar money-changers of America, whose God is a very Dagon, an image with a head of block and bowels of halfpence." In short, the United States was "the Grub-street of the world."[17] If this was the opinion of Leigh Hunt, what could be expected of the Tory squires in the House? In Liverpool on July 4, 1809, when the American ships in the harbor flew their colors, there was a near riot. British sailors and carpenters "either pulled down or compelled to be pulled down the Colours of every American Ship in the Port and in many cases they were torn or destroyed." It took two hours and the intervention of the Mayor to restore the peace.[18]

Between 1807 and 1812 the friends of America in England were swamped by an anti-American feeling, which was based on the patriotic fervor of the war against France, a commercial jealousy of the United States, and a hearty dislike of the former colonists. It was not only dislike, it was also scorn; a scorn based on the ineptness of the American defense of her own rights, and on a confidence born of resisting the all-powerful Napoleon. Why should England fear threats from the puny United States when she stood alone against Napoleon? The result was that American efforts of resistance were scoffed at, and a confidence was produced in England that helped to bring about a policy of no concession. The only people concerned about American economic coercion were the British manufacturers and exporters concerned in the American trade. Thus the biting and erratically brilliant Canning was able to reply to the proposal that Britain should withdraw her Orders in return for America removing her Embargo that it could not be done, but he would "glady have facilitated its removal, as a measure of inconvenient restriction upon the American people."[19] The *Courier* likened the United States to the man who cut off his nose to be avenged upon his face.[20]

Yet this whole confidence in regard to the United States depended upon a continuance of British commercial prosperity. Once there was a depression, for whatever reason, the Whigs could claim that all their prophesies had come true, and would be able to muster the manufacturers of the country in opposition to the government's American policy. Seemingly, Tory policy reached the height of its success in the summer of 1810, when with Macon's Bill No. 2 America acquiesced in the conditions placed by England on Anglo-American trade. Yet by the fall, the position had undergone a radical change. On November 2, following Napoleon's brilliant coup of Cadore's letter, Madison warned England that nonintercourse would be renewed within three months, unless England removed her Orders in Council.[21] Unfortunately for England, this coincided with the beginning of a commercial depression. The month of July, 1810, had seen the start of a sharp decline in British commercial prosperity, for in that month the failure of several important financial houses quickly led to a general financial crisis. The immediate cause seems to have been connected with overspeculation in the South American market. Exporters were unable to obtain payment for the large quantity of goods sent to that area in 1808 and 1809, and they in their turn were unable to satisfy the claims of the British manufacturers. The fundamental cause of the depression lay much deeper, and stemmed from many factors connected with the Industrial Revolution and with the war against France. A variety of factors had served either to bring about or heighten the distress, which was now to continue until the close of 1812 : the closing of the Continental markets, which had resulted in an excessive accumulation of colonial produce and other goods in Britain; the scarcity of specie caused by the drain of gold to pay for grain from France after the bad harvests of 1808 and 1809, and to maintain British forces abroad; the general changes associated with the Industrial Revolution; and, of course, the vast speculation in South America.[22]

The eventual renewal of nonintercourse by Congress in March, 1811, was a significant event for England.[23] For the first time since the start of American economic coercion, it was to coincide with a depression in Great Britain. This produced an immediate reaction among British manufacturers. Stocks which had been increasing since the shipment to the United States in July and August, 1810, had now no outlet. In the previous years of American economic pressure from 1807 to 1810, manufacturers had maintained employment by working for stock, as trade in general had been relatively good. Now, with all industry depressed, and the United States becoming firmer in opposition, the trade outlook could hardly have been worse. The real value of exports of United Kingdom produce decreased from £49,980,000 in 1810 to £34,920,00 in 1811, and in particular exports to the United States decreased from £10,920,000 to £1,840,000.[24] The whole position was one of the utmost gloom for the manufacturing and for the working classes. The American consul at Liverpool, James Maury, wrote to America at the beginning of 1811 about the depressed prices, and of the "continuance of failures, which for many months, have gone on to an extent unknown." In April he spoke of the "unparalleled distress to which the Trading Interest of this Country has been subjected."[25] Bankruptcies practically doubled between 1809 and 1811.[26]

Particularly hard hit by the depression were the cotton manufacturers, for the United States provided their most important overseas market. By May, 1811, the forerunners of the multitude of petitions that were to be directed against the Orders in Council arrived in Parliament from areas devoted to the cotton industry. Petitions from Scotland sketched the extreme distress of the petitioners, and the unprecedented depression in trade, which was "chiefly owing to the exclusion of our commerce from the continent of Europe, and the stoppage of our trade with America, in consequence of the orders in council and the blockading system."[27] At the end of the same month, a petition from Manchester, the center of the cotton trade, stressed the great importance of the American market. The repeal of the Orders, it was claimed, would pave the way for a removal of American nonintercourse, and considerably relieve the distress of the area."[28] These petitions were referred to a select committee on June 5, and it presented a hasty report within eight days. It made no constructive suggestions, and no definite action was taken.[29]

Yet the feeling was growing that America would have to be conciliated, and in July a petition calling for the removal of the ministers was presented to the Prince Regent from the West Riding of Yorkshire. It stated, with typical Yorkshire bluntness, that "from the apparent insensibility of the Administration to our present danger, we fear they will plunge us into a war with the United States of America, which would gratify and strengthen our enemy more than any other step they could take, would complete the ruin of our merchants and manufacturers, and expose us to danger that cannot be described."[30] Parliament recessed in July, not to meet again until the following January. The Yorkshire petition had warned the Tory majority of the attack they could expect on their return to Westminster, and in truth they were destined to encounter a veritable army of opposition to their Orders in Council policy at their next meeting. Only a revival of trade could have prevented a growth of opposition, and conditions were to get worse, not better. One visitor from distant Upper Canada wrote from London in September, 1811 : "There are now many thousands half-starved, discharged clerks, skulking about London; in every street you see, 'A counting-house to let'." He also wrote, with excusable exaggeration, that "such a time as this was never known in England," and in November he added that "things are getting worse every day."[31] Samuel Morse endorsed this view in the same period, and expressed the opinion that the people he had talked with wanted an adjustment with United States.[32] This perhaps reflects not only that Morse found his friends among those who looked with more friendship towards America, but also that economic distress was producing an increased desire for conciliation.

The Whig opposition was presented with a magnificent opportunity by the depression that began in the summer of 1810.

They had long prophesied that the Orders in Council and the cessation of trade with the United States would bring economic distress. Soon after the petitions against the Orders in Council started to arrive in Parliament in May, 1811, Alexander Baring urged a general examination of the system of the commerce of the country, and in particular the position of Great Britain in regard to the United States.[33] The whole Whig case for the conciliation of the United States became infinitely stronger at this time of intense depression than it had been in 1808, when only the interests directly connected with the United States were suffering distress. The Whigs now stressed the evil effects of the Orders, and also argued that because of the increase in the issue of licenses for trading to the Continent the Orders in Council were no longer even an effective method of retaliation against France.[34]

The system of licenses had developed owing to the inability of either England or France to carry on without the trade of the other. From the point of view of both countries, it was essential that certain British manufactured goods find their way into the Continent—to provide Napoleon with necessary articles and England with trade—and both sides, though officially prohibiting intercourse in this period, carried on an extensive trade through special licenses granted for the import or export of goods. In the same manner, in the years of bad harvests, continental grain found its way into England. In Britain, the practice of granting licenses had grown so extensive that the number had increased from 1,600 in 1807 to 18,000 in 1811.[35] In fact, it now seemed that there was little justification for claiming that the Orders were being kept in force as a method of retaliation against France. All they seemed to be doing was providing protection for British goods in European markets, and judging from the state of trade, this protection was proving of little value.

The Whigs used the license system as yet another lever to regain open trade with the United States. Joseph Phillimore's

Reflections on the Nature and Extent of the Licence Trade,
published in 1811, stressed the abuses of the trade, and its injustice to neutral commerce. The pamphlet was written at the
direct instigation of the Whigs. A letter from Auckland to Grenville on January 31, 1811, enclosed a "Minute of Instruction
to Dr. Phillimore," which was sent to Phillimore telling him to
prepare a pamphlet on this subject.[36] In his pamphlet Phillimore
maintained that the renewal of friendship between England and
America "would more effectually promote the best, and most
valuable interests of Great Britain, than any public measure
which, under the existing circumstances of the world, could
possibly be adopted."[37] In 1811 the way was being prepared
for a tremendous struggle in Parliament on the twin topics of
the Orders in Council and the commercial policy that was to be
pursued toward America. This real struggle was to start when
Parliament convened in January, 1812.

Nothing so well testifies to the faith of the British government
in the policy that it had pursued towards America since 1807
than the manner in which this policy was maintained with unyielding firmness against the rapidly rising opposition in England in 1810 and 1811. It might be said that toward the close
of 1810 and in 1811 the British government tried to observe
more care in its relations with the United States, but the heavy
atmosphere was hardly stirred by the breath of concession. The
debacle of the mission of Francis James Jackson had left England with no representative in the United States, and amazingly
enough from the time that the United States broke off relations
with Jackson in November, 1809, until the spring of 1811,
England had no accredited minister in Washington. When
Jackson was finally recalled by his government in April, 1810,
and commended for his "Zeal, fidelity, and ability," no minister
was sent to replace him.[38] In June, 1810, John Philip Morier
was appointed Secretary of Legation, but he was given no autho-
rization to propose any agreement, even of a preliminary nature.

Any proposals presented to him were to be submitted to England.[39] With commerce restored by Macon's Bill No. 2, it seemed that neither energy nor effort was needed to maintain a satisfactory position in regard to America.

The position was radically changed, though the government at first did little to acknowledge it, by the growth of depression and the rise of internal discontent in England, and by Cadore's letter on the part of France. In the late summer and fall of 1810, William Pinkney pressed the English Foreign Secretary, Wellesley, for a repeal of the Orders in Council, on the grounds that Napoleon had withdrawn his decrees. Wellesley, on his part, maintained with accuracy that in fact Napoleon had done no such thing. The impasse continued into 1811.[40] The British government, in spite of internal opposition, still had no intention of giving up the Orders in Council policy. Pinkney by this time was completely disillusioned at his prospects in England. His period as minister from 1807 had been a remarkably sterile one. All his efforts had been met with unyielding firmness. Finally, in January, 1811, convinced that there was no chance of an agreement, he requested an audience of leave on the grounds that England had no representative in the United States. This request he reiterated in February, and England and America took another step on the road to war.[41]

For one moment at the beginning of 1811 there did seem a possibility that England might change her policy. At the close of 1810, George III finally became incurably mad upon the death of his favorite child, the Princess Amelia. American hopes were based on the fact that the Prince Regent in his younger days had been a great friend of the Whigs and of Fox. If, as hoped, he would dismiss the Tory government and bring in the Whigs, there was a distinct possibility that British policy toward the United States would change, and America would be conciliated. One Tory wrote fearfully in his diary of the possibility of "the surrender of the American question" if the Whigs came into office.[42] Jefferson and Madison, perennially hopeful, wrote in March, 1811, before they knew the actual news, of the possibility of a change in British policy now that the Prince Regent was coming into office.[43] Henry Clay wrote to Caesar A. Rodney on March 7 that it was rumored that one of the first acts of the Prince Regent on ascending the throne had been to repeal the Orders in Council.[44] The Prince Regent quickly dashed all American hopes. His allegiance to the Whigs had begun to cool as early as 1807, and by 1809 he was moving toward the Tories. For a brief time in January and early February, 1811, there was the possibility of a change in government, but on February 3 a messenger brought the Whigs the news that the government of Perceval was to stay in office. With this quirk of British politics, one of the last hopes of the avoidance of the War of 1812 vanished.[45]

Ironically, one of the first acts of the Prince Regent after his accession was to receive the last audience of William Pinkney. Pinkney's determination to leave the country at least produced some effect on the British government. After Pinkney's reiteration, on February 13, of his determination to leave, Wellesley immediately replied that the British government had decided to appoint Augustus J. Foster as Minister to the United States. He also suggested that Pinkney no longer had any reason to take his leave.[46] This move—too little and too late—was typical of the Tory government in this period. Hopefully, when the possibility of war arose, it offered the shadow but not the substance of concession. An effort was made to continue negotiation—an indefinite negotiation which yielded nothing. Pinkney, however, was adamant, and left England after an audience of leave on February 28.[47]

The appointment of Augustus J. Foster as Minister to the United States could hardly be said to favor accommodation. Though connected with the Whig interest, Foster was no friend of the United States. During his period as Secretary of Legation at Washington from 1804 to 1808, his letters had been chiefly distinguished for the utter contempt and dislike they exhibited for the Americans.[48] His comment in 1805 had been that he would not come as Minister to the United States for ten thousand pounds,[49] but in 1811 his dislike for America did not extend to refusing the position when offered. After her good friend the Prince Regent had written to inform her that he had consented to the appointment of her son to be Minister to the United States, Foster's mother, who had now become Elizabeth, Duchess of Devonshire, wrote to him, "I know how you dislike that country, but it is a wonderful opportunity for future advancement."[50] Such was the inauspicious beginning of the last desperate phase in Anglo-American relations, when negotiations would have to depend on Foster, for the United States had no minister in England.

England, in spite of the increasing hostility of America, and in spite of the opposition within England herself, persevered relentlessly with essentially the same policy she had pursued since 1807. America had shown great reluctance to go to war, and England frequently expressed the desire to prevent the outbreak of open hostilities, yet the government was prepared to make no concession to attain this desirable end. To America was left the choice of peace or war.

12 *Crisis in the Northwest*

IN CANADA, too, matters were reaching a crisis in 1810 and 1811. The manner in which the British officials in Canada, driven by fear of invasion, had in 1807 and 1808 recommended a policy of cultivating the support of the Indian tribes has already been discussed.[1] There is little doubt that this policy had proved a complete success by the fall of 1810. The British task of winning the support of the Indians was not a difficult one. The insistent pressure of the frontiersmen on to the lands of the Indians ensured that the latter would look to the British for support. They would have been foolish not to have done so, for engaged in a struggle for their homes, they were obliged to take help wherever they could find it. After 1807 the British in Canada were prepared to provide both help and encouragement. Yet between 1808 and 1810 the position changed. In 1808 the British had been afraid that they had lost their influence over the Indians, and that the Indians were not sufficiently embitterd against the Americans. By the fall of 1810 these doubts were at an end—the Indians were ready for war, and the new problem was how to keep the Indians in check until the British needed them for the defense of Canada and yet still retain their friendship. Matthew Elliott, agent at Amherstburg, had already written in October, 1810, of the danger of the Indians making war on the Americans, and of the fact that the British would be blamed. In November, when Tecumseh visited Amherstburg and made it plain in his speeches that the Indians were ripe for war, Elliott wrote again and asked for detailed and explicit instructions to regulate his future conduct.[2]

Governor-in-chief Craig was now in a most embarrassing position. If he allowed the Indian Department to follow his own earlier instructions of 1807 and 1808, he ran the risk of helping to provoke the Americans into a war that his own government did not want. The result was that, for the first time, Craig was forced to maintain a true neutrality in regard to the Indians and the Americans. Already, before receiving Elliott's request for instructions, he had written to John Philip Morier, the British chargé d'affaires in Washington, asking him to warn the Americans of their danger,[3] and now he made a direct effort to prevent the impending Indian war. In his instructions of February, 1811, he stated that the officers of the Indian Department should use every effort to dissuade the Indians from war with the United States, and should make it clear that they could expect no assistance from Great Britain.[4] This conduct was above reproach, but one cannot escape the conclusion that Craig, in the early months of 1811, was desperately striving to avoid the hostilities toward which his own policy had contributed. The tragedy of the situation was that Craig himself had no desire for war with the Americans. He believed that it was in the interest of England and the United States to maintain friendly relations.[5] Yet his earlier instructions had given too much freedom to his subordinates.

Perhaps the best proof of this is to turn once again to the visit of Tecumseh to Amherstburg in November, 1810. The first point of interest is that though Elliott wrote for full instructions immediately after Tecumseh's speech, these did not reach him until some four months later.[6] Thus Elliott, in meeting with the Indians in this annual fall visit of November, 1810, was not guided by Craig's new restrictive policy, and by the next November Tecumseh was among the southern tribes and Tippecanoe was being fought. Elliott, in writing for instructions, had stated that he realized that he could do nothing overtly, but wondered whether it would not be proper to keep up "the spirit of resistance."[7] Available evidence points to the fact that, having to make the decision, he followed his own suggestion.

Colonel Isaac Brock, military commander in Upper Canada, in February, 1811, wrote to Craig on the subject of the November council. This letter was a condemnation of Elliott. Brock regretted that the Indians had retired from the council at which they had declared their intention of going to war, with a full conviction that although they could not look for active co-operation they could rely with confidence upon receiving from the British every requisite of war. How, he asked, could a cold attempt to dissuade the Indians from war be expected to succeed, when the distribution of a liberal quantity of military stores plainly indicated a contrary sentiment? If the Indians determined to commit any acts of hostility in the spring, they would be too far away for the acts to be averted by the British. Elliott, he said, was a good man and well respected by the Indians, but having lived a good deal among them in his youth, "he has naturally imbibed their feelings and prejudices, and partaking in the wrongs they continually suffer, this sympathy made him neglect the conditions of prudence, which ought to have regulated his conduct."[8]

Brock was not the first British officer to express his distrust of Elliott, and of the Indian Department at Amherstburg. At the time of Elliott's dismissal in the late 1790's, the military commandant at the post, Hector McLean, had been particularly critical of the Department's contact with the Indians. He had stated that the whole of the Indian Department at Amherstburg was connected to the Shawnee "either by Marriage or by Concubinage," and that this was the cause of that nation being more troublesome than any other, as the agents tried to prejudice the minds of the Indians against the Americans.[9] He had also attacked the veil of secrecy in which the Department cloaked its affairs, and the fact that the interpreters were all completely under the influence of Elliott.[10]

In 1811 Brock was not alone in reviving this distrust of Elliott. In fact, his letter on this subject had been prompted by a confidential letter from Craig. Only two days after issuing definite instructions that the Indians should be restrained, Craig wrote to Brock asking him to have the military officers at the various posts, particularly Amherstburg, report confidentially on what happened at the councils between the Indian agents and the Indians.[11] Once Craig had decided on a policy of absolute restraint in regard to the Indians, he considered it necessary to spy upon Elliott, though he had given him a free hand for three years. One month later, in March, 1811, Brock communicated Craig's order to Major Taylor at Amherstburg. He repeated large sections of the Governor's letter, and took the opportunity on his own account of warning Taylor about Elliott. "I should be unwilling," Brock wrote, "to place entire dependence, in an affair of such manifest importance, upon a judgement biassed and prejudiced, as his is known to be, in every thing that regards the Indians. To act with due prudence, he participates in and feels too keenly the grievous wrongs they have suffered."[12]

It may justly be observed that dependence had been placed on Elliott in this matter for three vital years, and whereas supervision might have been useful in the spring of 1808, it was a little late in the spring of 1811. What was said in confidence between Elliott and Tecumseh in November, 1810, or earlier, will never be known. It is known, however, that it was in the following summer that Tecumseh visited the southern tribes, and on that trip he was very confident of British assistance.[13] To what extent Elliott was conversant with Tecumseh's plans, then or earlier, remains an open question.

Though from early in 1811 to the fall of the year the British were genuinely trying to prevent an Indian war, there was little they could do. The Indians were too bitter, and the Americans were too frightened. On November 7, 1811, William Henry Harrison provoked the battle of Tippecanoe which was to prove so useful to him in the Presidential campaign of 1840. Here, near the Wabash in northern Indiana, the Indian confederacy was dispersed and Indian warfare became a reality, while Tecumseh was away visiting the southern tribes. Craig, from the beginning of the year until his departure for England in June, 1811,[14] made determined efforts to prevent the Indians from waging war upon the United States, but he was able to take back neither the words nor the ammunition dispensed so liberally since 1807. In fact, the new policy of trying to maintain a perfect neutrality was only of short duration. As the year progressed the British officials became increasingly convinced that war and invasion were inevitable. From August, 1811, investigations were made of defenses and posts throughout Canada with the object of strengthening them for resistance to invasion.[15] By the fall the policy of devoting all attention to the task of restraining the Indians began to crumble, and gradually gave way to the bolder policy inaugurated in 1807 and 1808. The British again became convinced that they could not risk the alienation of the Indians. In particular, during this period at the end of 1811 and during 1812, the military, in the person of Brock, became increasingly convinced that Indian co-operation was essential in the event of war, and actively set about ensuring that it would be available. It seems possible in fact that Brock in 1812 went beyond the wishes of the new Governor-in-chief, Sir George Prevost, in this matter.

At the beginning of December, 1811, Brock wrote to Prevost that he thought that the President's message to Congress justified every precaution being taken, and submitted his views of the state of Upper Canada. He considered that Amherstburg was the most important district, and that in the event of war the

British would have to reduce Detroit and Michilimackinac to convince the Indians that the war was being waged in earnest. The military force at Amherstburg should therefore be augmented.[16] Prevost's reply of late December, 1811, is significant in showing the extent to which Prevost had returned to, and depended upon, the Indian policy adopted in a similar crisis at the end of 1807. His instructions copied, at times word for word, the instructions issued by Craig on his arrival in Canada. Prevost advised that the Indians should be attached to the British cause, but that if possible no explanation should be given. Whenever the subject of hostilities was adverted to, however, it should be intimated that as a matter of course the British would expect the aid of their brothers—"I am sensible this requires delicacy, still it should be done so as not to be misunderstood."[17] Apparently, there was no great problem in securing this aid, for at the beginning of 1812 Elliott assured Claus that the majority of Indians from the St. Croix to the Wabash were on the side of the British.[18]

Another development at this time of crisis was an attempt by the British officials to integrate the work being done by British traders west of Lake Michigan and by the British officials to the south of the Lakes. In the area west of Lake Michigan it was the fur traders rather than the British officials who maintained British influence in the years before the War of 1812. Throughout this period the British traders from Canada had extensive interests among the Indians in the whole of present-day Wisconsin, Minnesota, and eastern Iowa. In 1783 the British traders had still retained an extensive trade south of the Lakes, but gradually American pressure had caused them to retreat, and by the early years of the nineteenth century the Americans had achieved a dominance in the region. The only trade left to the British south of the Canadian boundary was that west of Lake Michigan, and there too in the years before the war the traders from Canada were suffering increasingly from American pressure. After 1803 the United States pursued a policy of steady opposition to the British traders on the Mississippi and Missouri, arguing that the provisions of Jay's Treaty, which had permitted traders to pass on either side of the boundary line, did not apply to the newly purchased Louisiana Territory.[19]

Governor James K. Wilkinson of Louisiana Territory issued a proclamation in August, 1805, forbidding the subjects of a foreign power from entering the Missouri trade, and licensed traders were not to be permitted to carry the emblems of a foreign power into the area. The proclamation was aimed at the traders from Canada, and seems to have been directly inspired by the report of the Lewis and Clark expedition.[20] This was only a beginning, for in the following years a whole series of restrictions was placed in the way of British traders—from this time on they complained bitterly of the attempt to exclude them from Louisiana, the high duties exacted on the goods they sent into the United States, and a host of other minor infractions of Jay's Treaty. These grievances were communicated through the Canadian officials to the British government, and to the British minister in Washington. After the issue of the Embargo in 1807, and the seizure of the goods intended for the southwest trade, the fur traders became incensed at their ill-treatment by the Americans.[21]

It was not only official interference that the Canadian traders had to contend with after 1803, for private American trading interests were also pushing into this area of upper Louisiana. In the spring of 1807 the first attempts were made by the St. Louis traders to carry their trade to the upper Missouri, and Manuel Lisa and the American Fur Company made attempts to infringe upon the monopoly of the British in the following years. In addition, from 1807 John Jacob Astor competed with the British in Michilimackinac.[22] These private American interests were quickly followed by the American government, which in this period was extending its trading posts into the heart of the region

—in 1808 the posts of Mackinac, of Osage on the Missouri, and Fort Madison on the upper Mississippi were organized.[23]

It is not surprising that, in these years immediately preceding the War of 1812, the Canadian fur traders of the southwest country attempted to organize a resistance to the encroachments of the Americans. It was inevitable that they should strive to retain their lucrative trade. In 1805 Robert Dickson, the foremost trader in this area, organized a combination under the name of Robert Dickson and Company, but in 1806 it was merged into the far more important Michilimackinac Company. This was formed by the Montreal merchants and modeled on the North West Company, in the hope that the success of that organization could be duplicated. It proved to be a vain hope. The company was unable to cope with the American restrictions and competition, and it fought a losing battle—unable, because of the constant difficulties with the United States, to make any profit. By 1810 it was clearly a failure, and the company was dissolved. Temporarily its place was taken by the new Montreal and Michigan Company, but finally in January, 1811, the Canadian fur interests succumbed to American competition, when an agreement was made with Astor for the formation of the South West Fur Company. Astor was given a half-share in the new arrangement, and though the personnel of the trade was still largely Canadian, the Canadian fur interests had acknowledged the loss of a major part of their profits to the Americans.[24]

The reaction of the fur traders from Canada to this constant pressure by the Americans is not difficult to imagine. Having already to all intents and purposes been driven out of the trade they had formerly enjoyed through Detroit, they were now in the process of losing their hold on upper Louisiana. It was inevitable that they should show the utmost hostility to the Americans. Dickson, who had at one time co-operated with the Americans, from 1809 became increasingly bitter and antagonistic, owing to the increased difficulties in carrying on his trade.[25] What is more, apart from the obvious economic drive, these traders frequently had a genuine sympathy for the Indians —they spent their lives among them, and frequently were married to them. Dickson himself was married to a daughter of a chief of the Yankton Sioux.[26] Interest and sympathy alike combined to make these fur traders anxious to resist the Americans. The very object of the formation of the Michilimackinac Company was to provide better organization, in the hope of retaining a virtual monopoly of the trade of upper Louisiana. There was considerable truth in the statement of an American army captain at Michilimackinac: "There is not a man in the Company, who does not feel a spirit of Opposition to the American Interest; and who would not wish to Annihilate the Arm of American power, so far as it extends over the Indian Country!"[27]

The argument that the traders were a factor for peace because of the harm done to their trade by war does not seem to be valid in this case. The Canadian fur traders were already rapidly losing their profits from the southwest trade. They had little to lose and everything to gain by encouraging resistance to the Americans. This does not necessarily mean that they advocated outright war, but it does mean that they were very willing to encourage the Indians to resist American infiltration into this area.[28] The Canadian traders were hardly likely to stand idly by, and see themselves driven from the area of upper Louisiana, as they had already been driven from the area south of the Lakes.

The fur traders themselves had full confidence in their hold over the Indians. In an account drawn up in 1809 with the object of obtaining aid from the British government, the writer stressed the important role played by the traders in placing the Indians firmly in the British camp.[29] He stated of the North West Company, which traded to the very north of American territory in upper Louisiana, that "it links to the British empire a race of men (The savage nations) whom no system of Government could preserve either subordinate or faithful." He claimed that through the fur traders the Indians were kept subordinate to the British government, "and would at their desire at any moment abandon the chase and take up the hatchet." This apologist for the Canadian fur traders emphasized how grievously the Michilimackinac trade was suffering from the Americans, but gave the assurance that "even those [Indians] who by the cession of Louissiana have been transferred to the Americans, are still faithful to their old friends the British traders, and are as much as any description of Indians under their control."[30]

Thus, at the end of 1811 and the beginning of 1812, as the Canadian officials became increasingly sure of war, they turned to the fur traders for aid in controlling the Indians in the vast area west of Lake Michigan. In January, 1812, discussions were entered into with the great fur companies, the North West and the South West, in an attempt to enlist their aid in the impending conflict. The companies were not slow in offering their support. It was reported to Prevost that they would "enter with zeal into any measure of Defence, *or even offence,* that may be proposed to them." The companies seemed particularly eager to give their aid against the Americans, and it was asserted in the report to Prevost that "by means of these Companies, we might let loose the Indians upon them through the whole Extent of their Western frontier, as they have a most commanding influence over them."[31]

The two companies in addition promised definite aid in men. The South West—or, as it was still often called, the Michilimackinac Company—stated that in the event of war it could promise the support of some one hundred English and Canadians and three hundred Indians. The North West Company replied that they could promise some two hundred and fifty engagés, and three to five hundred Indians.[32] Brock was thus able in February, 1812, to assure Colonel Baynes, the Adjutant General, that in the event of war the North West Company would not object to joining their strength in the reduction of Michilimackinac.[33]

Robert Dickson had volunteered his services in 1811 before leaving for his winter quarters west of Lake Michigan,[34] and during the winter he did all he could to counter American efforts to gain the support of the Indians. This included the distribution of a large quantity of stores to the starving Indians during the long, hard winter of 1811-12—Dickson being inspired both by humanitarian and political motives.[35] While Dickson was thus employed, Brock sent him a series of questions regarding the western Indians. The crux of the matter was that the military required a knowledge of the number of Indians that could be depended upon, and the amount of supplies they would need.[36] This letter, telling much of the primitive nature of frontier communications, did not reach Dickson until the early part of June, when he was at the Fox-Wisconsin portage returning east from his winter quarters, and Dickson replied on June 18, the day that the United States declared war on England. He said that he had some two hundred and fifty or three hundred Indians ready to march when necessary—St. Joseph's would be the general rendezvous, and all "our friends" would be there about the thirtieth of the month.[37] British policy among the western Indians, carried out by the fur traders, had ensured that at the outbreak of war support was available at the strategic positions.

The British officials themselves were in 1812 once again locked in the near impossible policy of ensuring Indian support, while at the same time keeping them from offensive operations which would anger the Americans. In the case of Prevost, the receipt of instructions from England in January, 1812, strongly urging him to avoid offending the United States, made the Governor-in-chief far more cautious than Craig had been in 1808.[38] Yet, in Upper Canada, where there was a direct fear of invasion, Brock, who had become civil as well as military commander in October, 1811, proceeded rapidly with defense plans, and became increasingly impatient at the restrictions imposed upon the Indian Department by Prevost.[39] Prevost, however, urged him to exercise forbearance as Britain did not want to commit any overt act which would give the Americans justification for war.[40]

Throughout the spring of 1812 this same pattern of affairs continued. Prevost, anxious not to provoke war, urged caution, while Brock and the members of the Indian Department tried, as secretly as possible, to prepare the Indians for war.[41] They were apparently confident of success, for in May a Canadian visitor to Francis Gore in London learned that Gore, who had served as Lieutenant Governor of Upper Canada until the autumn of 1811, had received letters from the Indian Department in that province, and the visitor came away with the impression that "the Indians are all on our side."[42] At the beginning of June news was brought down from Detroit to Fort Wayne that the Indians were crossing over to Amherstburg in large numbers.[43] Thus at the outbreak of war friendly Indians were converging on British posts both in the west at St. Joseph's and in the east at Amherstburg.

British Indian policy in the years before the War of 1812 was designed to enlist the Indians for the defense of Canada against American attack. The British officials in Canada were led to expect this attack by the extent of American anger at British maritime policy. They thus sought out the Indians and endeavored to win their allegiance for a future war. In practice, it was found most difficult to keep the Indians completely defensive. Depending on agents who were connected to the Indians both by interest and sympathy, the British officials found it impossible to maintain a complete neutrality in the inevitable United States-Indian struggle. It seems very doubtful that the traders were even as cautious in their relations with the Indians to the west of Lake Michigan as were the British officials south of the Lakes. There seems little doubt that the British in Canada made use in this period of the natural animosity felt by the Indians against the Americans who were driving them westward across the continent.

British policy, both in England and in Canada, remained inflexible in the years from 1810 to 1812. It is true that in Canada for a brief period in 1811 Craig attempted to take positive action to restrain the Indians, but this policy never attained success and could not undo what had already been done. In England, though there was considerable unrest and opposition, the government was firm in the maintenance of its maritime policy. America had tried everything but war. The time was now ripe for offensive action.

13 *The War Hawks*

THAT REMARKABLY penetrating historian Henry Adams—
still in many ways the most valuable authority on this period
—said of the Congress that met in December, 1810, that "the
American system of prolonging the existence of one Legislature
after electing another, never worked worse in practice than
when it allowed this rump Congress of 1809, the mere scourings
of the embargo, to assume the task of preparing for the war of
1812, to which it was altogether opposed and in which it could
not believe."[1] Though, in the summer of 1810, the electors had
shown their disgust at the weakness of the Eleventh Congress by
deposing practically half of its membership, the new Congress
was not to meet until the fall of 1811. As a result, yet one more
session of futility was to wend its weary way before Henry Clay
and his colleagues were to infuse Congress with the new enthusiasm that had elected them. But the Eleventh Congress was
to take America still nearer to war before its moribund body
finally expired.

Madison's proclamation of November, 1810, had established
by executive act that nonintercourse against England would be
renewed unless that country repealed her Orders in Council.
The problem still remained of whether Congress would confirm
this act, for very little proof was forthcoming that Napoleon had
actually repealed his decrees. The available evidence apparently

217

proved the contrary. Congress spent the first two months of its session in discussing the action to be taken in West Florida, and the question of the rechartering of the United States Bank, and it was not until the President's proclamation had actually come into force against England in February that Congress took up this problem. In the ensuing debates on nonintercourse, the absence in the House of an enthusiastic leader such as Clay or of any organized warlike group is particularly striking. Clay was still in the Senate serving out his partial term, and there his fiery oratory was making its effect felt throughout the country. In the debates on the annexation of West Florida, which Clay enthusiastically supported, he took the opportunity to lash out at British influence: "Is the time never to arrive when we may manage our affairs without the fear of insulting his Britannic Majesty? Is the rod of British power to be forever suspended over our heads? Does Congress put on an embargo to shelter our rightful commerce against the piratical depredations committed upon it on the ocean? We are immediately warned of the indignation of offended England. Is a law of non-intercourse proposed? The whole navy of the haughty mistress of the seas is made to thunder in our ears." He continued in a like vein— protesting at the deference that had been shown to England, and calling for a vigorous defense of American rights.[2] The words rang around the nation, and this eloquence was to fall on fruitful ground in the House of Representatives, when the Twelfth Congress met in the fall of 1811.

The rejected Eleventh Congress, constantly swept by the scathing onslaughts of John Randolph, had little that was constructive to offer in the way of a policy to be pursued towards Great Britain. The main objection that was raised to the enforcement of nonintercourse against England was that there was no proof that France had in fact repealed her decrees. In the long run, however, the hopelessness of being placed in a position of hostility to both major powers bore considerable weight, and on

February 27 complete nonintercourse was passed against Great Britain.[3] In these debates there were some signs of the vigor that would be felt when the new Congress came into power, and some of the future War Hawks made it quite clear in which direction their sympathies lay. There was even a minority move to make it obligatory upon England to give up impressment as well as her Orders in Council if America were to give up non-intercourse, but this suffered a heavy defeat—obtaining only 21 votes in support.[4] Among this small group were names that were to make their reputation in the next Congress. John Rhea, representative from Tennessee, gave his support to this motion concerning impressment, and urged the necessity of taking strong ground in regard to Great Britain, who had so unceasingly injured the United States.[5] Langdon Cheves of South Carolina, later to be an important member of the war party, said that he had only approved of Macon's Bill No. 2 for one reason : "He believed it would make the country act a part more worthy of its character; it would precipitate us on a particular enemy—and this he believed the country required. He believed a more direct and proper course should long ago have been resorted to."[6]

Once the Non-Intercourse Bill had passed the House, it quickly proceeded to the Senate, and was passed there two days later.[7] The Eleventh Congress was a futile body that had outlived its usefulness, but at least in passing the Non-Intercourse Bill, and making its repeal contingent upon a British repeal of the Orders in Council, it moved the United States firmly in the direction of war. Now the doubt as to whether to fight England or France was practically solved, though the possibility of fighting both was once again toyed with in the spring of 1812. The protagonists of war against England knew that France also was injuring American rights, but they thought that England was injuring them far more deeply. They preferred to cope with the one they considered most guilty, rather than attempt the impossible task of resisting both.

The Eleventh Congress expired immediately after the passing of the Non-Intercourse Bill, and there was now a hiatus until the meeting of the new Congress in the fall. In the months between May and November, 1811, nothing was done to ease the growing tension in Anglo-American relations. In fact a steady deterioration had set in—a deterioration toward war. Madison was no longer deluded by any false hopes. He compared the mission of Foster, the new British minister to the United States, to the abortive one carried out by George Henry Rose on the subject of the *Chesapeake* in 1807 and 1808. The British "Cabinet is inflexible," he wrote, "in its folly and depravity."[8] What small hope Foster might have had of his success in his mission was considerably diminished even before he arrived in the United States. In May, 1811, yet another of the numerous maritime incidents occurred, and once again increased the complications of Anglo-American relations. The incident stemmed, as was so often the case, from the British blockade off the American coast. On this occasion, however, reflecting the new fighting spirit that was making itself felt in the United States, the American ship was the aggressor. On May 6, 1811, Secretary of the Navy Paul Hamilton, who in the previous year had made it clear that he believed in a more active resistance to Britain on the ocean, ordered the American ship *President* to sea to protect American shipping.[9] On May 16 occurred the inevitable incident. The *President* fired a broadside into a British sloop, the *Little Belt*. To the Americans it seemed that the *Chesapeake* was avenged, though in fact the *President* had fired into a ship of far weaker firing power.[10] In England the government press raged : "The blood of our murdered countrymen must be revenged and war must ensue.—The conduct of America leaves us no alternative; ... We have behaved towards America with unexampled forbearance; but that forbearance has produced insolence, and that insolence must be punished."[11] America was at last taking the offensive.

It was at this point that the new British minister, Augustus Foster, arrived in the United States bearing only one concession, and that a belated one. He had been given permission to offer compensation for the *Chesapeake* affair.[12] This concession came far too late. It was recognized for what it was—a move designed to deflect American anger, while conceding none of the basic points at issue. Concession in the affair of the *Chesapeake* at this point could mean nothing to an America bent on either securing a repeal of the Orders in Council and an agreement on impressment, or in vindicating its rights by force of arms. The *Chesapeake* affair was finally settled on November 12, 1811,[13] but by that time the settlement meant nothing.

In July, 1811, Foster started his negotiations with Madison. Once again things settled down into their old pattern, with Monroe, who had become Secretary of State after the dismissal of Robert Smith, maintaining that England should repeal her Orders, and Foster maintaining that France had not repealed her decrees.[14] Foster argued that England could not repeal her Orders until Napoleon admitted British goods to the Continent, thus proving that he had repealed his Continental System. This placed America in the position of having to force open the Continent not only to American but also to British ships, in order to secure a repeal of the Orders.[15] England's position was strengthened by the fact that America could offer no real proof that Napoleon had repealed his commercial decrees. Impasse was once again reached, as the British government, in the face of growing internal and external opposition, still clung to the commercial policy inaugurated in 1807.

All was now ready for the meeting of Congress in November, 1811. A year had passed since its election as a reaction to the disavowal of the Erskine agreement and the final breakdown of the policy of economic coercion, but there had been no accommodation between Britain and America. It seemed that however America protested, whatever peaceful pressures she employed, the basic British policy remained unchanged. A trifling concession was offered here, another there, but nothing that brought any fundamental change in British policy. France, not America, determined the British attitude in this period—to defeat France was all-important. For America nothing remained but active resistance, and as the time neared for the meeting of the Twelfth Congress it became increasingly obvious that momentous decisions were to confront that assembly.

Matthew Lyon of Kentucky, who was very doubtful of the wisdom of war upon Great Britain, wrote to Monroe in September, 1811, of the "approaching war" and its object. "If it can have any object," he wrote, "it must be that of preventing and punishing the British in and for their encroachments on our Maritime rights, and can this object be attained by any forcible means in our power?" He went on to say that all eyes were turned towards Canada as a means to attain this end, but that he himself, though he had advocated it in 1808, now thought it a far more difficult proposition. His only suggestion was that if war came, America should take the British possessions near Detroit to prevent tampering with the Indians.[16] In this whole period from 1807 to the meeting of the Twelfth Congress, when the injuries from Britain were debated unceasingly, it is striking how little attention was paid to the British action among the Indians as a reason for waging war. Though the conquest of Canada was discussed throughout the whole period, it was discussed essentially as a means of waging war—a war which had become necessary as a means of resisting British maritime policy. The question of British incitement of the Indians was certainly to arise in the Twelfth Congress, but to assume that this suddenly became the reason for war it is necessary to ignore the pattern of American protest from 1807 to 1812, and in particular the connection between the growth of war-feeling and the disillusionment at the failure of peaceful methods of resistance.

Undoubtedly the battle of Tippecanoe, which was fought in Indiana Territory on November 7, 1811, had a profound effect on American sentiment, and helped to bring it to the pitch necessary for war, but it should be remembered that even before Tippecanoe was fought the country was becoming convinced that war would result from the meeting of the Twelfth Congress. A westerner wrote to Andrew Jackson from Tennessee on October 12 to tell him that all the members of Congress from the area had set off for Washington. "I presume," he wrote, "Mr. Madison's first bulletin will be the most important state paper since the Declaration of Independence." He went on to say that "we have no alternative between War, submission, and perpetual embargo—and as no American can or dare submit, War or Embargo is the question—I think a little blood-letting would relieve the system and therefore at present I should prefer hearing that the *Guerrier* and *President* had been alongside."[17] The desire for war here is very plain, but this westerner was apparently most concerned with maritime affairs, and surely was not suggesting "War or Embargo" as a solution for the Indian problem.

The question of American concern with the Indian problem has exerted a profound influence on historians. To some it is the key factor in the coming of the war, to others it is of practically no significance.[18] There seems little reason to doubt that the presence of hostile Indians on the frontier was of great importance to the westerners. Any careful study of the records of this period inevitably leads one to that conclusion. The debates of the Twelfth Congress and the territorial papers of Indiana, Michigan, and Louisiana-Missouri have frequent references to the Indian problem.[19] One has only to read the letters of Governor William Henry Harrison of Indiana to the War Department to realize the extent to which the thinking of certain areas of the West was dominated by this factor.[20]

Even more important from the point of view of this study is that there was no doubt in the minds of the settlers that the British were instigating the actions of the Indians. On July 31, 1811, the citizens of Vincennes, Indiana, adopted a series of resolutions to petition the President regarding the danger from the Indians. The third of these petitions stated : "That we are fully convinced that the formation of this combination headed by the Shawanese prophet, is a British scheme, and that the agents of that power are constantly exciting the Indians to hostility against the United States."[21] In August the *Kentucky Gazette* stated that "we have in our possession information which proves beyond doubt, the late disturbances in the West to be owing to the too successful intrigues of British emissaries with the Indians."[22] The encounter at Tippecanoe crystallized this western sentiment, and convinced the settlers that British intrigue among the Indians was bringing desolation to the frontier.

Yet even if one grants that the British officials in Canada were not maintaining a complete neutrality in regard to the Indians, and that the westerners were convinced that the British were actively inciting the Indians, it does not necessarily mean that this was the main reason for going to war. This view fails to take into consideration several relevant facts. In the first place, the core of feeling against the Indians was in the exposed northwest frontier—in the Indiana, Michigan, and Illinois territories, and it should be remembered that these areas did not command one Congressional vote. It is true, of course that the anger against the supposed British inciting of the Indians to war was felt deeply outside the immediately exposed area—Kentucky was much incensed at the Indian depredations and Kentuckians fought and were killed at Tippecanoe; also, Andrew Jackson wrote from Tennessee offering Harrison the use of his forces after that encounter.[23] Yet it is essential to realize that of the 79 votes for war in the House only a total of 9 votes came from the states of Kentucky, Tennessee, and Ohio, while a total of

37 came from the South Atlantic states of Maryland, Virginia, North and South Carolina, and Georgia. Pennsylvania, a state of very limited frontier area by this period, alone provided 16 votes for war.[24] In fact, the actual vote for war depended on nonfrontiersmen. The Indian menace undoubtedly influenced frontier areas, and in some exposed regions must have been the dominating factor in the minds of the inhabitants, but it seems unlikely that the large vote for war in nonfrontier regions was inspired by a desire to protect the northwest frontier from Indian depredations. The core of the support for war was to come from the West and South—the regions that had supported economic coercion because it had been in their interest to secure, if possible, freedom of the seas without war. When economic coercion failed, it was quite logical that support for war should come from the same regions.

The Congressmen that assembled at Washington early in November, 1811, were much different from those who had departed in March of the same year. The House of Representatives now became the forum for a group of young men, led by Henry Clay, who became known as the War Hawks. There had been advocates of a strong policy in Congress since 1806, and some of the same men now among the War Hawks were not new Congressmen, but never before had there been enough at one time to form a cohesive group bent on arousing the country from its lethargy. The leader of the group was thirty-four-year-old Henry Clay, who had already made a reputation as an eloquent advocate of strong measures, and he gathered a powerful group around him. From the West came Richard M. Johnson and Joseph Desha of Clay's own state, and Felix Grundy of Tennessee. From the South came John C. Calhoun, Langdon Cheves, William Lowndes, and David R. Williams of South Carolina, and George M. Troup of Georgia. And from other regions came equally able supporters—Peter B. Porter of New York, and John A. Harper of New Hampshire being two of the

8

most prominent.[25] Youth had for the first time assumed control in American politics.

These young men, who formed the core of the war party in the Twelfth Congress, supported the particular interests of their regions and demanded war to protect those interests, but they also had a genuine feeling that American national honor had suffered as a result of the events of the previous four years. The country which only a quarter of a century before had dared to fight for its independence against the might of England had made an ignominious surrender of its rights. The leaders of the War Hawks were young men who had been raised on the traditions of the War of Independence. The older generation were the "first generation revolutionaries"—men who had gambled for independence, had won, and were in their later years little inclined to risk their winnings in an uncertain war with England. Henry Clay and his young allies were the "second generation revolutionaries"—young men who were willing to take chances to defend the hard-won gains of their parents. They had grown to manhood hearing oft-repeated tales of the War of Independence, but they themselves had long been compelled to suffer without retaliation the constant infringement of American rights. Now they called for war, and in their enthusiasm they were to take many of their fathers along with them.

The spirit of the new Congress was quickly in evidence when Clay, on his first day as a representative, was elected speaker of the House on the first ballot.[26] On the following day Madison delivered his annual message. He clearly indicated the trend of American policy. After telling Congress that the British cabinet was persevering in its wrongs, he stated : "With this evidence of hostile inflexibility in trampling on rights which no independent nation can relinquish, Congress will feel the duty of putting the United States into an armor and an attitude demanded by the crisis, and corresponding with the national spirit and expectations."[27] In a private letter to John Quincy Adams less than two weeks later, he stated the problem quite plainly: "The question to be decided therefore by Congress ... simply is, whether all the trade to which the orders are and shall be applied, is to be abandoned, or the hostile operation of them, be hostilely resisted. The apparent disposition is certainly not in favor of the first alternative." Madison had no illusions regarding the reparation for the *Chesapeake* incident. He thought that though it "takes one splinter out of our wounds," it was too tardy, and too much like an anodyne to soothe Congress and the nation to have much effect.[28]

Clay left no doubt as to his reaction to the question posed by Madison in his organization of the committees of the House. He made sure that the War Hawks predominated on all those of primary importance. On the nine-man Foreign Relations Committee, five were War Hawks, including the chairman, Peter B. Porter. He was supported by John C. Calhoun, Felix Grundy, John A. Harper, and Joseph Desha. David R. Williams and Langdon Cheves of South Carolina were made chairmen of the Military Affairs and Naval Committees respectively, and Ezekiel Bacon of western Massachusetts became chairman of the Ways and Means Committee.[29] Clay had ensured that the drive for war would have enthusiastic leadership.

The first important concern of the House was to deal with the part of the President's message that was concerned with foreign relations, and this was referred to the newly appointed Foreign Relations Committee.[30] By the end of November its report was ready, and on November 29 it was presented to the House. Late the previous night, after returning home from the meeting of this committee of which he was a member, that ardent War Hawk Felix Grundy had written an account of its proceedings to Andrew Jackson. "If the opinion of that Committee is to prevail," he wrote, "I may say the Rubicon is pass^d." He told Jackson that the Committee had a full determination to report in favor of war at a given period, and that for the present it was going to recommend various additions to America's military forces. In regard to the attitude of Madison, Grundy made the significant comment that the Committee's action "meets fully the approbation of the Executive, and indeed the co-operation of that department in ulterior measures was promised before a Majority of the Committee could be brought to so mild a Course." Grundy was for war, but in his own words "still I could not think of War untill I saw something like the means provided." These War Hawks would have liked immediate war, but they could plainly see that America would have to increase its strength before war could be declared. This delay to raise forces did not mean there was any lessening of the desire for war. Grundy concluded his letter with the ominous statement: "Rely on one thing, we have War or Honorable peace before we adjourn or certain great personages have produced a state of things which will bring them down from their high places."[31]

One could not ask for a clearer exposition of the determination of the War Hawks than is to be found in Grundy's letter to Jackson, and the Foreign Relations Committee's report, which was presented on the next day by Peter B. Porter, was in the same vein. It bluntly stated that the time for submission was at an end, and recommended war preparations for the United States. The report is a particularly significant document. As the opening salvo of the war Congress, issued only three weeks after the battle of Tippecanoe, one would expect it to contain the essence of the grievances against Great Britain. It did do this, but significantly in this report which was at last taking America away from economic warfare and into open conflict, there was no mention of British incitement of the Indians. The report concerned itself exclusively with maritime matters, though this fact has received too little attention from historians. After asserting that the French decrees were at an end, the committee stated that Great Britain was still impressing American seamen, and seizing the products of American soil and labor off the American coast. The essential cause of complaint against England was summarized with the argument that the United States claimed the right to export her products without losing either ships or men. Injury had been borne, it was asserted, until forbearance had ceased to be a virtue. The report concluded by recommending six resolutions to raise military forces and prepare the country for war.[32]

The arguments of the War Hawks in the ensuing debates clearly followed the line of reasoning laid down in the report. They agreed that war was necessary against Great Britain for the defense of American maritime interest and honor. Southerners and westerners united in demanding a market for their produce and a vindication of American rights. Throughout the debates of the Twelfth Congress in 1811 and 1812 it is apparent that the westerners and southerners were convinced that the British were ruining the overseas market. Frequently, in later works stressing western expansionist urges as the basic cause for war, the words of Henry Clay and Richard M. Johnson of Kentucky, of Peter B. Porter of western New York, and of Felix Grundy of Tennessee have been quoted. These men have been taken as living proofs of the dominating urge of the West to take Canada and subdue the Indians. A careful consideration of their speeches in Congress, however, shows that though they spoke with feeling and eloquence of the atrocities of the Indians and of taking Canada, the *dominating* themes of their speeches were the questions of maritime rights, especially the right to export American produce.

On December 6, 1811, Peter B. Porter opened the debate on the report of the Foreign Relations Committee, of which he was chairman. He stated : "The committee thought that the Orders in Council, so far as they go to interrupt our direct trade, that is, the carrying of the productions of this country to a market in the ports of friendly nations, and returning with the proceeds of them—ought to be resisted by war."[33] He was not asking America to go to war to defend the New England carrying trade, nor to prevent British incitement of the Indians, but was maintaining that the United States should fight for the right to export her produce. As for the methods of waging war, Porter thought that it could be done by the action of privateers at sea, and by an attack on Canada: "By carrying on such a war as he had described, at the public expense on land, and by individual enterprise at sea, we should be able in a short time to remunerate ourselves tenfold for all the spoliations she [England] had committed on our commerce." He concluded by urging that if there were any gentlemen in the House "who were not satisfied that we ought to go to war for our maritime rights" he should not vote for these measures.[34]

Porter's brother War Hawks gave him full support. The greatest War Hawk of them all, Henry Clay, contended that "to-day we are asserting our right to the direct trade—the right to export our cotton, tobacco, and other domestic produce to market." Clay's whole argument in this speech, which he delivered on December 31, was for the necessity of war to defend American maritime rights. "What are we not to lose by peace?" he asked, "—commerce, character, a nation's best treasure, honor!"[35] Clay was echoing the sentiments of his fellow Kentuckian, Richard M. Johnson, who as far back as April 16, 1810, had argued that there was no doubt that America had just cause of hostility: "At this moment France and Great Britain have decrees in force, which regulate at their pleasure the exportation of our own produce—the produce of our own soil and labor."[36] Johnson developed his views on Britain's infringement of America's maritime rights in his speech on December 11, 1811. In this he certainly discussed Canada, but previously he had stated: "Before we relinquish the conflict, I wish to see Great Britain renounce the piratical system of paper blockade; to liberate our captured seamen on board her ships of war; re-

linquish the practice of impressment on board our merchant
vessels; to repeal her Orders in Council; and cease, in every
other respect, to violate our neutral rights; to treat us as an
independent people." He ended his speech with a fine rhetorical
flourish about the massacre on the Wabash, but before he had
reached the peroration he had outlined quite clearly the essential reasons why America would have to declare war on England.[37] Felix Grundy also spoke of the recent action on the
Wabash in his speech on December 9, but previously in his
speech he had stated that the point of contention between the
United States and Great Britain "is the right of exporting the
productions of our own soil and industry to foreign markets."[38]

Orders in Council, illegal blockades, impressment, and the
general terms of neutral rights and national honor, dominated
these arguments of the Twelfth Congress. The speech of Joseph
Desha of Kentucky on December 12 well showed a westerner's
awareness of maritime questions. He said though America had
negotiated for fifteen to twenty years, and insult had been heaped
on injury, he would not fight for the carrying trade. What he
would fight for was the direct trade—the right to export American produce.[39] On January 4, 1812, John Rhea of Tennessee
spoke solely of maritime matters. "But it is asked, will you go to
war for commerce?" argued Rhea, "It is answered, England
has been at war for commerce the greatest part of two hundred
years; and shall not the United States protect their commerce,
in which is involved the safety of their seamen and the rights of
the people?"[40]

The arguments of the westerners for the defense of American
maritime rights were repeated almost verbatim by their allies
from the south, who had the same interest in the export of
American produce. Robert Wright of Maryland bitterly
attacked British restrictions, and stated that "we are to look for
the cause of the reduction of the prices of our cotton and tobacco
in the political and commercial history of Europe."[41] Langdon

Cheves of South Carolina, speaking for the enlargement of the naval force on January 17, stated: "No proposition appears to me more true or more obvious, than that it is only by a naval force that our commerce and our neutral rights on the ocean can be protected. We are now going to war for the protection of these rights."[42] Speaking of the people of the South, John C. Calhoun asserted that "they see in the low price of the produce, the hand of foreign injustice."[43]

The commercial desire of the war party did not go unnoticed by the opposition. Historians have been fascinated by John Randolph of Virginia, who so passionately denounced the westerners for seeking a war of aggression. A favorite quotation is his famous "we have heard but one word—like the whip-poor-will, but one eternal monotonous tone—Canada! Canada! Canada!"[44] It is forgotten that in his wandering, half-demented diatribes Randolph attributed practically every reason for desiring war to the War Hawks. Other less vehement, but perhaps more sane, members of the opposition saw other motives behind the desires of the war party. On December 13, 1811, Adam Boyd of New Jersey stated bluntly: "You go to war for the right to export our surplus produce—tobacco, cotton, flour, with many other articles."[45] Daniel Sheffey of Virginia, in a long and penetrating speech on January 3, 1812, came to this conclusion: "No! the nominal repeal of the Orders in Council is not your object. It is the substantial commercial benefit which you conceive will follow that act, that forms the essence of the controversy. The unmolested commerce to France and her dependencies is the boon for which you are going to war. This is the real object, disguise it as you will."[46] Such observations of the opposition may of course have been completely unfounded, but it is at least possible to give them as much weight as has been given to the utterances of Randolph.

In the West itself there seems much evidence that the representatives in Congress were, as might be expected, reflecting the views of their constituents. Bernard Mayo in his excellent biography of the young Clay states, after an examination of Kentucky newspapers, that "unprecedented hard times" caused by Britain's illegal monopoly was the constant theme of distressed farmers in this period from 1810 to 1812.[47] On December 10, 1811, the *Reporter* of Lexington, Kentucky, stated: "It appears that our government will at last make war, to produce a market for our Tobacco, Flour, and Cotton."[48] A particularly significant series of petitions was presented to Congress from Mississippi Territory in September and November, 1811.[49] There were two petitions from the inhabitants of the Territory, and one from the Territorial legislature. All the petitions requested that the payment of installments on the petitioners' lands should be deferred until a later date, owing to a lack of specie. The petitioners stated that they were dependent upon foreign commerce for money, and that the price of cotton had been so reduced that they could not discharge the annual expenses of their families, much less pay for their lands. All three petitions attributed this to the destructive effects of foreign restrictions upon American commerce. The petition of November 11 admirably summarized the importance of foreign commercial regulations to this area of the West:

> The Severe pressure of the times arising from the unjust Edicts of Foreign Governments, and the unpresedented State of the world ... the Violation of the legitimate and well Established Rights of neutral Commerce on the high seas, to which the Belligerents of Europe have resorted Are not confin'd in their Destructive consequences to the Commercial enterprize of our Country—But their effects are seen and Felt among the humble Cultivators of the Soil—Who Depend for the reward of their laborious Occupations on an Oppertunity to convey the Surpless Products of their Industry to Those Countries in which they are consumed.[50]

In Ohio too there was the same concern with commercial matters. A resolution of the Ohio General Assembly of December 26, 1811, spoke at length of the violation of American neutral rights, and of the mission that had followed mission—all to no avail. The Assembly considered that the report of the Foreign Relations Committee, which had concerned itself exclusively with maritime matters, "breathes a spirit in unison with our own."[51] There seems ample evidence that the West and South were voicing a genuine interest in British commercial restrictions in this period. In particular, they were attributing the loss of a satisfactory export market, and the subsequent decline in prices, to British action at sea. It is not surprising that the Congressmen of 1811 and 1812 spoke vigorously of the need to defend American maritime rights—this was not simply a façade, hiding a real western desire to conquer Canada; it was a genuine feeling that if the West and South were to have a market for their produce British restrictions would have to be resisted.

One of the best summaries by a westerner of why the West wanted to fight was that given by Andrew Jackson on March 12, 1812, when, as commander of the militia for the western district of Tennessee, he issued a call for volunteers from this area. In this document, if in no other, one would expect to see reflected the ideas and aspirations of the people of the West; a commander calling for volunteers does not use unpopular arguments. Under the heading "For what are we going to fight?", Jackson wrote these words: "We are going to fight for the reestablishment of our national charector, misunderstood and vilified at home and abroad; for the protection of our maritime citizens, impressed on board British ships of war and compelled to fight the battles of our enemies against ourselves; to vindicate our right to a free trade, and open a market for the productions of our soil, now perishing on our hands because the *mistress of the ocean* has forbid us to carry them to any foreign nation; in fine, to seek some indemnity for past injuries, some security against future aggressions, by the conquest of all the British dominions upon the continent of north america."[52]

The fact that the conquest of Canada was viewed as an excellent way of retaliating against the maritime restrictions of England came out just as clearly in the debates of the Twelfth Congress as it had in the utterances of American leaders since 1807. The southerners, who themselves had no particular reason to desire the conquest of Canada, urged it as a method of retaliation against England. Calhoun clearly stated the reasons for the southern support of Canadian conquest in his speech on December 12, 1811. In answering Randolph's taunt that the Canadas bore no relation to American shipping and maritime rights he stated: "By his system, if you receive a blow on the breast, you dare not return it on the head; you are obliged to measure and return it on the precise point on which it was received. If you do not proceed with mathematical accuracy, it ceases to be just self-defence; it becomes an unprovoked attack."[53] This gives the essence of the matter. Once the War Hawks had decided they wanted war, they were obliged to face the problem of where they could injure their mighty foe. Apart from the activities of American privateers there seemed little hope of waging effective war against Great Britain on the sea. Britain's vast navy was to be matched against a handful of American frigates. The conquest of Canada was the obvious, if not the only method of injuring Britain.

Two representatives of North Carolina—Israel Pickens and William R. King—well summarized the essential reasoning behind the demand for Canada. King stated on December 13, 1811, that he was not enamored of conquest but this war had been forced upon America: "We cannot, under existing circumstances, avoid it. To wound our enemy in the most vulnerable part should only be considered."[54] Pickens less than a month later answered the opposition that, though the contemplated attack on the British Provinces was called a war of offense, "when it is considered as the only mode in our reach, for defending rights universally recognized and avowedly violated, its character is changed."[55] Even calm and honest Nathaniel Macon of North Carolina, whose opinion can surely be given as much weight as the impassioned and half-mad Randolph, contended that the war which the United States was about to enter was not a war of conquest—"Its object is to obain the privilege of carrying the produce of our lands to a market"—but he considered that no war could long continue to be merely one of defense.[56]

Yet, though the members of the Twelfth Congress were determined on positive action when they came to Washington, and though they reiterated their reasons for war on England once they had arrived, the actual realization of their hopes was not an easy task. The fundamental problem was American weakness. Until measures had been taken both to pay for the war and to provide America with the forces to fight it, even the War Hawks had to acknowledge that hostilities would have to be delayed. They meant to have war before the end of the session, but exactly when depended upon the adoption of effective measures to wage it. No nation could have been less fitted to wage war than America in 1811, and they were contemplating attacking the power that had defied Napoleon for over a decade. From November, 1811, to June, 1812, Congress ineffectually attempted to remedy this problem.

14 *America Goes to War*

THE REPORT of the Foreign Relations Committee on November 29 had recommended specific measures to prepare the country for war. The addition of 10,000 men to the regular army for a term of three years, a volunteer force of 50,000, the arming of the merchantmen, and the outfitting of ships of war not in active service were the four essential suggestions. These resolutions were adopted by the House on December 16 and 19 by large majorities.[1] To pass the bills needed to give practical reality to these resolutions was to prove a far more difficult task. Already on December 9, Senator William B. Giles of Virginia had introduced a bill calling for a regular army of 25,000 men. On December 19, after Giles had earlier attacked the executive for the weakness of its measures and claimed that at least 25,000 regulars would be needed to wage effective war, the Giles bill passed the Senate.[2] It was now sent to the House Committee on Foreign Relations, where it was quickly decided to compromise between the original recommendation and the Senate bill, and to ask for a measure calling for 15,000 regular troops. In these last days of December the Committee on Foreign Relations was busily occupied not only in discussing the army bill, but also in preparing bills calling for the formation of a volunteer corps, the arming of merchantmen, and a measure authorizing the President to call out detachments of militia. So immersed was the

Committee in its various tasks that it spent Christmas Day in drawing up these measures.[3]

Grundy in reporting the progress of these events to Andrew Jackson told him that it was hoped that by increasing the already existing regular army to its full force of 10,000, a total force of 25,000 regulars could be provided by the Committee's compromise proposal. At this time Grundy was confident of the determination of Congress. "I firmly believe," he wrote, "that G. Britain must recede or this Congress will declare war—If the latter takes place the Canadas and the Floridas will be the Theatres of our offensive operations." Later in the letter he invoked the spirit of independence: "Our fathers fought for and bequeathed liberty and Independence to *us* their children —shall they perish in our hands? No, a firm and manly effort now, will enable us to transmit to *our children* the rich inheritance unimpaired."[4] Another westerner, writing to Jackson on this same Christmas Eve, agreed with Grundy on the nearness of war. "From present appearances it is extremely difficult to perceive," wrote George Washington Campbell of Tennessee, "how war can be avoided without degrading the national character still lower than it now is—which certainly cannot be desirable—For there is no ground to expect G. Britain will abandon her system of depredation on our commerce, or the habitual violations of the personal rights of our citizens in the impressment of our seamen."[5] Campbell reflected the deep interest of the West in a change in British maritime policy.

The practical difficulties of raising military forces was making prompt action against England extremely difficult. The Senate bill for raising regular forces, which was put before the House in its amended state, brought immediate controversy as to the number of troops that should be raised. Henry Clay, however, threw his weight behind the original Giles figure of 25,000 men, and commanded enough support to bring about the adoption of his views. At the same time he offered one concession to the financial qualms of the traditionally economical Republicans. Only the officers for eight of the proposed thirteen regiments were to be appointed immediately—the others were to be commissioned only when three-quarters of the men for the original eight regiments had been recruited.[6] Even this was not enough, and when on January 6, 1812, the amended bill was passed by the House, it was stipulated that only the officers for six regiments were to be raised immediately.[7] The bill was now sent back to the Senate, but there the main amendments were immediately struck out.[8] The bill once again returned to the House for further discussion, but fortunately for the progress of the war preparations, the House decided on January 9 to accept the Senate bill without amendment, and on the eleventh it received the President's signature.[9] A total regular army of 35,000 had been provided for on paper; to raise it was to prove a more difficult matter.

The next problem was that of the militia bill, empowering the President to raise 50,000 volunteers, which had been reported on December 26.[10] The bill was taken up on January 10, and immediately was disputed. The question of whether this militia could be used outside of the country—for the invasion of Canada or Florida—absorbed the attention of Congress.[11] Clay and Langdon Cheves adopted the attitude that for the legitimate purposes of war these militia could be used on foreign soil, but other War Hawks such as Porter and even the enthusiastic Grundy retained enough of the old Republican principles to object to this unlimited view of the government's power to wage war. The only way in which agreement could be reached was by leaving the problem unresolved when the bill passed the House on January 17. After passing the Senate, the bill was approved by the President on February 6.[12] America's rusty war machine was laboriously creaking into motion. A quick declaration of war had proved impossible, and though the principle of war had been approved, there was considerable doubt as to whether the means of waging it could be found. In a letter to Jefferson on February 7 Madison waxed into sarcasm. He said of Congress that "with a view to enable the Executive to step at once into Canada they have provided after two months parlay for a regular force requiring twelve to raise it, and after three months for a volunteer force, on terms not likely to raise it at all for that object."[13] Madison was justified in his criticism of the dilatory attitude of Congress, though in truth Madison himself had neither the dynamic qualities of leadership nor the singleness of purpose required of a war leader.

Madison was not alone in his irritation at the ineffectiveness of the effort to prepare America for war. Not for the first time, nor the last, in American history, while the executive blamed the legislature, the legislature blamed the executive. Grundy wrote on February 12 that though the bill for raising 25,000 regulars had been law for six weeks, not a single officer but the commander-in-chief had been appointed. "Is there nothing rotten in Denmark?" he asked. Of the difficulties faced by even the most ardent War Hawks, Grundy gave full testimony when he admitted: "This Congress will do more *harm* or *good* than any that has preceded for some years—how things will end God only knows, for I am sure no man here can tell how this Session will end." Grundy, who was one of the fiercest supporters of war, and one of the "inner circle" with Clay, went on to tell Jackson: "Shall we have War? That is the question you want answered— *So do I*—I thought some time ago there was no doubt—But if in six weeks only one man out of 25,000 is furnished, how long will it take to furnish 25,000."[14] America, who had for so long attempted to keep the peace, was finding she had lost the ability to prepare for war. Even now, when sentiment was in favor of the conflict, the problems were proving almost insuperable. Even the most ardent advocates of war were doubtful whether it would actually be declared.

The internal difficulties that confronted the War Hawks became even more apparent in the next debates that absorbed Congress in January, 1812. After passing the militia bill, the House faced the problem of enlarging the navy. Here there were grave difficulties, for the Republican party was the traditional opponent of a large navy. Could the War Hawks forget the Republican dogma in which they had been reared long enough to vote for this measure? On January 17 Langdon Cheves introduced a bill asking for an appropriation to build twelve ships-of-the-line and twenty frigates.[15] He met immediate opposition, for the westerners feared that the bill would add to the influence of the commercial class, without providing anything like the force necessary to defeat England on the sea. Many of the War Hawks were convinced that they could force England to change her commercial policy far more simply by the invasion of Canada than by trying to defeat the all-powerful British navy. Though Grundy, Rhea, and Johnson were all opposed to the Cheves measure, Clay proved his passion for war, and his independence of opinion, by speaking ardently for the new navy. On January 22 he enthusiastically urged the necessity of defending America's maritime rights at sea. Even after America had taken Canada, he argued, the war would have to be continued on the ocean.[16] His eloquence was not enough, however, to defeat the entrenched prejudices of the Republicans against a large navy, and on January 27 the bill was defeated. Clay's force of personality had failed to carry the day—the measure was lost by the narrow margin of 62 to 59.[17] If the Republicans were determined to maintain their traditional principles in this way, they were going to face the gravest difficulties in preparing for war. This became very apparent with the introduction of a bill to finance the war, for once again it became necessary to overcome traditional Republican scruples.

On February 12 Felix Grundy had already expressed his fears of heavy taxation. Ezekiel Bacon, the chairman of the Committee on Ways and Means, had told him that he was determined to push through heavy internal tax bills. Grundy, paradoxically, preferred war before the money was raised to pay for it : "What if we get taxes, and do not go to War," he argued, "will the taxes then become permanent."[18] On February 17 his fears of heavy taxation came near to realization. Bacon introduced a series of resolutions designed to double the customs duties, lay a direct tax of 3 million dollars on the individual states, levy direct taxes on various articles, including salt, and to raise a loan of 11 million dollars.[19] After considerable discussion, Congress agreed to these resolutions on March 4.[20] It was a great success for the war party, though the condition was imposed that the taxes were only to become effective on the outbreak of war against a European nation. "You will see that Cong.ˢ or rather the H. of R.ˢ have got down the dose of taxes," wrote Madison, "It is the strongest proof that they could give that they do not mean to flinch from the contest to which the mad conduct of Great Britain drives them."[21] Paul Hamilton, the Secretary of the Navy, wrote on March 8 that it was a source of great satisfaction to him that amid all the indecision of Congress, the President was consistently promoting measures of warlike character. "I can say with confidence, that if war were determined on tomorrow, it would have his ready concurrence."[22] Madison, though never providing striking leadership, in this winter of 1811 and 1812 apparently determined to support war if Congress would provide for it.

At the beginning of March, 1812, Madison made a disclosure that was of great aid to the war party. On March 9 he laid before Congress the instructions and dispatches of John Henry, who in 1808 and 1809 had sent Sir James Craig, the Governor-in-chief of Canada, information concerning the eastern states of the United States.[23] The information contained in the letters apparently showed that Great Britain had intrigued with the leading Federalists, and Madison charged in his message to Congress that the documents showed that Britain had conspired to bring about the dismemberment of the Union.[24] Inevitably, the effect of these disclosures was to increase the anger of America against England, though it seems doubtful whether these letters, which were not even exact copies of the originals, were worth the $50,000 that Madison paid for them. Yet these Henry letters were used as one more method of driving America into war, and Madison by purchasing them and laying them before Congress had given an added incitement to war at just the right moment.

The rest of March saw the movement stumbling forward to its conclusion. On March 15 Henry Clay spoke to Secretary of State Monroe, and later in the day wrote to him suggesting that the President should recommend an embargo of thirty days, and that the termination of this embargo should be followed by a declaration of war. He also advocated the raising of 10,000 volunteers for a short period.[25] Peace-loving Jefferson on March 26 wrote to Madison that everybody in his quarter expected war as soon as the weather would permit the entrance of the militia into Canada, and that though they might desire peace they would disapprove of its continuance "under the wrongs inflicted and unredressed by England."[26] War feeling was growing so strong that the news of the French burning of American ships even brought demands for war on France as well as England, on the theory that France had made it evident that she had not repealed her decrees. Clay's reaction to this French action was recorded by Augustus Foster, the British minister, on March 25. Clay told Foster that if it is true that the French have burned the American ships, "he will be for war on France as well as England (in a softer tone)."[27] Yet it was against England that the main sentiment of this period 1811-12 had been expressed, and the impractibility of waging war against two major adversaries was to make the Americans acquiesce in all indignities from France. It was against England that the War Hawks wanted war, and whatever Napoleon did, he seemed comparatively immune from American attack so long as England's Orders in Council remained in operation.

On April 1 Madison, after prompting from the House Committee on Foreign Relations, sent a secret message to Congress recommending a sixty-day embargo.[28] On the same day Foster visited the President, and commented in his diary that Madison was "very warlike." He also commented that Senator Varnum of Massachusetts thought that English policy was actuated by jealousy of American commerce, and that he was for war with England even if it lasted twenty years.[29] Madison's message recommending an Embargo was presented in the form of a bill by Porter, chairman of the Foreign Relations Committee, on April 1. Clay and Grundy both spoke enthusiastically in favor of the measure on the grounds that it was the immediate precursor of war, and significantly the measure passed on the day it was presented by a vote of 70 to 41.[30] On the next day the measure was also passed by the Senate, but not without considerable opposition. Before it was passed by a vote of 20 to 13 the Embargo had been extended by the moderates from sixty to ninety days. The House approved this emendation, and on April 4 the President signed the Embargo measure.[31] On April 3 he had written to Jefferson telling him that he had recommended the Embargo as a step to war. As Britain apparently preferred war to a repeal of her Orders in Council, he wrote, there was nothing left but to prepare for it.[32] George Washington Campbell of Tennessee told Andrew Jackson in his letter of April 10, 1812, that preparations for war had continued to progress, and that an Embargo had been laid for ninety days. "It is considered by those who supported it as a precursor of war—There is not the slightest ground to hope that G. Britain will revoke her orders in council."[33] It is apparent from American comments in the early months of 1812 that a repeal of the British Orders in Council could still have checked the movement toward war.

The war was now very near. On April 15 the imperturbable British minister Foster was rather strangely placed at dinner between Clay and Calhoun. His comment was that "Clay was very warlike," and that Calhoun had the cool, decided tone of a man resolved. The South Carolinian observed that "the Merchants would put up with any wrong and only talk of Gain, but a Government should give Protection."[34]

From November through April Congress struggled toward war, convinced that it could hope for no change in British policy. Of a relaxation of the British policy in regard to impressment there was never any hope, but even in regard to the Orders in Council, which were encountering considerable opposition in England, the Americans despaired of a change in the British attitude. That this was the case is not surprising. Even as late as April 20, 1812, the American consul at Liverpool, James Maury, was writing to Madison that "it daily appears more and more the determination of administration to continue the orders in council."[35] In actual fact, England was in a state of considerable turmoil in these early months of 1812. Slowly the country was moving towards a repeal of the Orders in Council—unfortunately, even more slowly than America was moving towards war—but the British government still refused to admit the fact.

I

The distress in England that had caused the growth of opinion against the Orders in Council in 1811 showed no sign of relenting as the time drew close for the meeting of Parliament in January, 1812. The fears of those interested in a repeal of the Orders had been increased by the fact that relations with America had deteriorated rapidly as 1811 drew to an end. For the first time since the issue of the Orders in 1807, it seemed that the United States was likely to declare war on England. The *Times* of January 4, 1812, printed the warlike report of the Foreign Relations Committee of November, 1811, with the comment that it was more hostile toward Great Britain than any other document previously received : "It should seem,—in truth, so warm in its temperament,—to be immediately introductory to a declaration of hostilities." One day later the *Examiner* printed the same report with the comment that "a war with the Republic, it is lamentable to observe, appears every day more and more likely." The situation was arising in which war seemed likely with the one nation that the manufacturers thought could provide relief for the depressed condition of Great Britain. The increasing threat of war with the United States, when taken in combination with the depressed state of trade and the riots and disturbances in the country, convinced the manufacturers that it was necessary to repeal the Orders in Council. The Whigs were ready and anxious to organize this growing opinion, and to direct it towards securing a repeal of the despised measures.

Henry Brougham, who in 1808 had won a considerable reputation as advocate for the petitioners against the Orders, was the major link between the Whigs and the manufacturing districts, and an important instigator of the extensive number of petitions against the Orders in Council. "Throughout the early part of 1812," Brougham stated in his memoirs, "I had been in constant correspondence with leading men in the manufacturing districts, not only on the state of trade and the distresses, but on the not ill-grounded apprehensions of a war with America."[36] At a time when the manufacturing districts were earnestly seeking the best method of securing relief for their distresses, a suggestion from Brougham was likely to have striking results. The form his suggestions took is well illustrated by his letter to a leading clothier in the important woolen manufacturing center of Leeds in March, 1812. He stated that to relieve their present unexampled distress, it was necessary to make "a firm and united representation of those distresses to

Parliament." In this way, Brougham stated, a war with the United States might be avoided. He gave considerable general advice on the best procedure to influence Parliament, stressing that all violence should be avoided and that all internal political topics should be kept out of the petitions. He emphasized that quick and unanimous action from all parts of the country would prevent hostilities, and preserve good order at home.[37]

From the time when Parliament opened at the beginning of the year, the Whigs repeatedly emphasized in that body the distressed state of the country, and the fact that war with the United States was likely if England should persevere in her system of Orders in Council.[38] By the end of February the opposition considered that it was ready to try a test of strength with the government. It was confident of considerable support from the merchants in the House, and on this occasion also hoped for help from a very unexpected source. George Canning, who since his resignation in 1809 had retained his own small group of friends, had now gone completely into opposition. That this old supporter of the Orders should have become their opponent, even if for political reasons, was a great coup for the opposition.[39] On March 3 Brougham inaugurated his great effort to obtain a committee on the state of trade. He spoke at length, discussing the effect of the Orders on relations with the United States, and on the prosperity of Great Britain. Above all he advocated the conciliation of the United States. To close the debate he stated that "if any man there was desirous of preserving peace with America, he would vote for the inquiry; and every one who gave such a vote might go to his home, and lie down with the consciousness that he had done his utmost to avert the greatest evil with which the people of England could be menaced."[40]

The motion was lost by the Whigs by 72 votes, and one Tory commented: "We triumphed last night solely through the country gentlemen, who came up on purpose to vote."[41] The opposition had lost, but they had made a good showing. On the next day, in a letter to a merchant at Liverpool, Brougham was optimistic. "Our division is a good one," he stated, "and by following it up with petitions an American war may be prevented."[42] In the following months Brougham made unceasing efforts to muster this support, and his letters circulated throughout the manufacturing districts.[43] The Whig journals and pamphleteers echoed Brougham's premonitions of ruin to Great Britain if the Orders were not repealed, nor an American war avoided.[44] James Phillimore argued in a pamphlet published in February that the Orders in Council were directly responsible for the annihilation of British trade with the United States—"a trade of all others, the most advantageous to Great Britain, and the most congenial to the habits and propensities of her people."[45] The general Whig appeal did not fall upon deaf ears, for after March, 1812, as America moved nearer and nearer to war, petitions for the repeal of the Orders in Council flooded into Parliament from all areas of England.

Numerous petitions testified to the belief that the trade of the United States was vital to Great Britain, and that at all costs war between the two countries should be avoided. The movement that in 1808 had been confined to isolated centers of the American interest in Great Britain now contained all the main manufacturing areas. With trade at a standstill and distress widespread, some method of relief had become essential, and the Whigs had given extensive publicity to the fact that the obvious method of obtaining this desired relief was through the reopening of trade with the United States. In the spring of 1812 the repeal of the Orders in Council became the supreme object of the manufacturing interests of the kingdom. The manufacturers became convinced that trade with America was essential to their prosperity.

The five great centers of opposition to the Orders were the Birmingham hardware district, the Staffordshire potteries, the cutlery district of Sheffield, and the woolen and cotton centers of Yorkshire and Lancashire. In April petitions from Birmingham and nearby Walsall argued that the cessation of intercourse with the United States was the principal cause of their distress, and that a repeal of the Orders in Council would bring about a repeal of American nonintercourse.[46] The Staffordshire potteries used the same arguments—in that area even the journeymen potters added a petition to that of the manufacturers.[47] Elsewhere in the Midlands the same concern was to be found. The Leicester framework-knitters stated their distresses, and urged the repeal of the Orders in Council in regard to the United States, for they feared that war might result if this step were not taken.[48] In a similar way, the manufacturers of glass and porcelain ware at Worcester, and of woolen and linen cloth, flannels, and hose at Shrewsbury, who depended to a great extent on the trade to the United States, added their appeals to the general demand for the repeal of the Orders in Council.[49]

The North too united in opposition to the policy of the government. The cutlers of Sheffield, as closely linked to the United States as were the hardware manufacturers of Birmingham, urged "that of all foreign markets yet discovered for the sale of our manufactures the U.S.A. has been the most important."[50] The woolen manufacturers of the West Riding of Yorkshire urged the government to repeal the Orders in Council, or to take any steps which would "open and establish our commerce with the whole Continent of *America*."[51] Across the Pennines in Lancashire, the inhabitants of Blackburn, Chorley, and Chow Bent, who were concerned in the cotton industry, all attributed their distress to the cessation of commercial intercourse with the United States, and advocated a policy of conciliation.[52] The inhabitants of Blackburn clearly showed that the Tory party and its supporters in their policy of firmness towards the United States represented only one segment of

British opinion. They argued that their distress stemmed from "the impolicy which suggested, adopted, and still continues unrevoked the Orders in Council, in the absence of conciliatory measures towards the United States, and in the want of clear prompt, and satisfactory explanations in diplomatic negotiations with that country."[53]

Liverpool, as might be expected from the center of commerce with the United States, petitioned at great length. The main petition from the town on April 27 traced in detail the extreme distress of the area, and emphasized that the prosperity of Liverpool depended upon the trade with the United States.[54] Even further north, the manufacturers in Scotland used the same arguments as their English compatriots, and petitions from Glasgow, Dunfermline, and Paisley added their weight to those of the English manufacturers.[55]

The expression of such decided opinions by manufacturing centers of the country had exactly the result that the Whigs had expected. In spite of Tory opposition, the Whigs had by April 28 forced them to accept the appointment of a committee to consider the petitions against the Orders in Council.[56] From the time of Brougham's unsuccessful attempt to secure the appointment of a committee on March 3, the Whigs had maintained a steady attack on the policy of the government in both Houses of Parliament.[57] Every petition presented provided them with fresh material for argument, and the government became increasingly concerned at conditions in the country.

The spring of 1812 was a bleak one for the manufacturing districts of England. In April riots and disorders testified to the extensive unemployment and poverty of the industrial workers, and troops had to be used to keep an uncertain peace. On April 17 Thomas Ridout wrote to his father in Upper Canada and told him of conditions in England: "Nottingham, Manchester, Leeds, Birmingham and Sheffield have been scenes of the utmost confusion within these few weeks past. In consequence of the scarcity of provisions and an almost total failure in the manufactories and flatness of trade, the workmen are thrown out of employ, and fill the poor-houses."[58] Two nights later a dinner guest at the Home Secretary's found that because of the scarcity "he would give no pastry, and set the example of rice flour."[59] While the Home Secretary made his gesture the unemployed were desperate for work and for food. In their anguish they attacked the new machines that they thought had helped to produce their distress, and with the memory of the French Revolution still fresh in their minds the forces of order began to fear for their position. There was talk of the possibility of "rebellion and revolution,"[60] and even in an age when governmental reaction to popular pressures was comparatively slight, the threat of internal disorder turned the thoughts of government to remedial measures.

The general concern of increasingly influential manufacturers aided by internal unrest in the country forced the government to yield to Whig pressure for a committee of enquiry. After a debate on April 28 the government conceded that a committee should be appointed, and the Vice-President of the Board of Trade, George Rose, at least testified to the extent of opposition opinion when he stated : "With regard to the question immediately before them, there seemed to be a general delusion in the country as to the Orders in Council. 'Repeal them and all will be well : persist in them, and ruin must ensue.' That was the general language held upon the subject."[61] Indeed, this had become the case and the manufacturers saw in the repeal of the Orders in Council, and the renewal of trade with the United States, the supreme panacea.

This was well illustrated by the examination of numerous merchants before the committee on the Orders in Council, which began its sittings on May 5. While America debated war, England debated the conciliation of America. For the Whigs, the examination of the witnesses from all parts of the country was carried out by Henry Brougham and Alexander Baring, and they took full advantage of the mass of evidence. An adequate summary of the variety of information placed before Parliament at this time is difficult, in that over one hundred witnesses were examined, and the minutes of their evidence covers over seven hundred pages.[62] Over eighty of these witnesses supported the case for the repeal of the Orders in Council, and they represented practically every branch of trade with the United States. Fittingly, the Birmingham area provided most witnesses, over twenty, for even the fervent Tory George Rose at the Board of Trade had admitted in debate that : "As for the iron manufacturers in Dudley and Birmingham, he knew, that they felt the existing pressure more than any other description of persons, as their articles were limited to the American market."[63] Yet there were very few manufacturing districts unrepresented, and almost all the areas which had petitioned against the Orders in Council sent representatives to put their point of view before Parliament.

Out of all this mass of evidence two significant facts emerged; in the first place, industry was so depressed and distress so widespread that immediate remedial measures were needed, and in the second, the manufacturers considered that their distress had been produced by the Orders in Council. Time and time again it was emphasized that the Orders had produced a cessation of British trade with the United States, and that this trade was essential to British manufacturing.

There could be no doubt of the extensive distress in the country. The manufacturers stressed that since the loss of the Continental market, the American market had become increasingly important. Since February, 1811, nothing had been sent to the United States, and as a result the manufacturers had been unable to keep their workmen in full employment. In Birmingham, it was estimated that between 20,000 and 25,000 men were working half the week, and that in the nail trade only two-thirds or three-quarters of the men were employed at all. In the potteries, it was estimated that out of a normal 14,000 at work, only about 10,000 were now employed, and these were working part time. In Sheffield, the poor rates had jumped from over £11,000 in the year ending April, 1807, to over £18,000 in that ending April, 1812. It was the same all over the country; in Manchester, London, the West Riding, Leicester, and the other districts represented among the witnesses, the tale was one of reduced employment and pauperism.[64]

The remedy for all this was unanimously stated to be the renewal of commercial intercourse with the United States. Repeatedly the manufacturers stated that if the American trade was reopened, their huge stocks would be sold and industry would revive.[65] It was generally agreed that if the Orders were removed the United States would, as a matter of course, open trade with England—a direct connection was traced between the issue of the Orders in Council and the beginning of complications in trade with the United States. The intricacies of the question held no concern for these witnesses. The arguments were the simple ones used by two Birmingham manufacturers—"before these Orders in Council I had a good trade, and since then my trade is gone," and the similar: "We have not received American orders in the same way as we used to, since the Orders in Council were issued."[66] Most of the manufacturers testified that they had orders for goods from America, which could be sent when the Orders in Council were repealed.

The manufacturers' anxiety was increased by the fact that they were apprehensive of a permanent reduction in their trade to America, as the isolated United States was being compelled to manufacture for herself. From the time of the first introduction of American economic retaliation at the end of 1807, the news that America was developing her own manufactures to compensate for the lack of those from overseas had been well publicized in Great Britain,[67] and the evidence in 1812 shows that the manufacturers had taken these warnings to heart. In order to convey to Parliament the danger of this American industrial expansion, three witnesses who had recently lived in the United States were introduced to testify to the growth of American manufactures.[68]

The acute depression in England had convinced the manufacturing interests that friendship with America was essential to their prosperity, and in the spring of 1812 they desperately tried to force this view upon the government. Everything depended upon the degree of stubbornness of the Tory government. In Washington, the War Hawks were uncertain whether war could be effected by the end of the session. Any clear mark of conciliation on the part of Great Britain, such as the repeal of the Orders in Council, could still have placed a fatal block in the path of the stumbling American war machine. Yet with extensive opposition at home, and the threat of war abroad, the Tory government still clung grimly to its Orders policy. It was holding firm with the full knowledge that, though the manufacturers might be against its policy, the commercial interests which had helped to bring about the Orders in 1807 were still firm in their support.

At this time, in the spring of 1812, when petitions against the Orders were flooding into London, and the War Hawks were striving for war in Washington, the British shipping interest was making its last stand against any concession to the United States. In April and May the defenders of the Orders in Council petitioned Parliament on their behalf.[69] The arguments were old ones—they were those which had been urged since before the adoption of the Orders in Council policy. Both in their petitions, and in the evidence that was given by the shipowners and their allies the West India interest before the committee on the Orders,[70] it was argued that a continuation of the policy was essential for the war against France, and that in addition a repeal of the Orders would throw the carrying trade into the hands of the neutrals. The protection of British commerce and the war against France still provided the supporters of the Orders with the most cogent reasons for their continuance.[71]

Since the spring of 1811, when the British government had despatched Augustus J. Foster as Minister to the United States, it had done little else to avoid the war that was approaching. Foster throughout 1811 protested, with good reason, that the French decrees had not been repealed, and that Great Britain could not repeal her Orders.[72] In fact, French repeal or no French repeal, the Tory government had no desire to change its Orders policy—while the British government stood firm against extensive opposition in its own country, it could hardly be expected that it would yield to American diplomatic pressure. That its basic attitude had not changed was made quite clear early in 1812 by the issue of a pamphlet entitled *A Key to the Orders in Council*. This work was written by John Wilson Croker, Secretary to the Admiralty, at Prime Minister Perceval's request, and was printed at the expense of the Treasury.[73] It endeavored to explain the policy of the government. It was made quite plain in this work that the government had two main reasons for its refusal to repeal the Orders in Council: first, the great benefit that would accrue to France from a repeal, and second, the great benefits that would accrue to American commerce at the expense of Great Britain. In regard to France, it was stressed that all pressure would be removed from England's great enemy, that her trade would be carried on under the American flag, and that raw materials and colonial produce would be supplied to her in abundance.[74] More surprising than this is that it was argued quite openly in this government-sponsored pamphlet that if the Orders were repealed, the United States would become the carrier of the world, and the British shipping interest would be annihilated. This in its turn would mean that the exports of all British produce and manufactures would decline and in time expire, with the sole exception of exports to the United States, for American ships would take manufactures from France in exchange for produce carried to that country.[75] When that happened, it was argued, British products would not long remain supreme even in the United Kingdom itself. "Gold may be bought too dearly," this government-sponsored pamphlet argued, "and the immediate loss of all our European trade, and the eventual diminution of that which we should have with her, is rather too much to pay for a temporary accommodation with America."[76] These words sounded a death knell to hopes of peace.

Yet in spite of this Tory conviction that their policy was the correct one, the increasing distress and discontent in England was gradually forcing the government to the wall. On April 10, 1812, Castlereagh informed Foster that he should do all he could to keep the peace between England and America: "Whilst no injurious concession is made to the United States, nor any necessary exertion against the Enemy relaxed, it is not essential to the interest of Great Britain that America should be urged to an immediate decision."[77] It was the old policy of delay and interminable negotiation, but Castlereagh did concede that Britain would resort to a policy of limited strict blockades, and issue no more licenses, if the United States would reopen intercourse with Great Britain. On April 21 this was followed by the official declaration that if France should publish an official repeal of her decrees, England would withdraw her Orders in Council.[78] Inch by inch the government was yielding, but unfortunately the process of yielding in England was moving even more slowly than the process of declaring war in America.

At this point fate intervened; several months too late to be of use. On May 11 as Spencer Perceval, the British Prime Minister, entered the lobby of Parliament, he was shot by a lunatic, inspired by personal, not public, motives. Such was the temper of the country that the coach carrying this news to Leicester was cheered on its arrival.[79] At Nottingham the news was re-

ceived with "the most enthusiastic demonstrations of joy"—
"The bells were rung, bonfires were lighted up, and a tumultuous
crowd of people assembled in front of the guard room with
drums beating, flags flying. . . ."[80] When Perceval's assassin, John
Bellingham, was executed on May 18 at Newgate, he was greeted
by an immense mob which extended from Fleet Street into
Smithfield and the adjoining streets. On his appearance they
doffed their hats and uttered a great cry of "God Bless You."[81]
At a critical juncture of affairs England was left without a
prime minister, and for almost a month until the Tory Lord
Liverpool accepted the task of forming a government on June 8,
England was without effective leadership.[82] Though this crisis
occurred while the committee on the Orders was in the midst
of its work, and though all other business was suspended,
Brougham insisted on carrying on with the enquiry.[83]

With the author of the Orders dead, and the country in open
opposition, it was unlikely that the new government would dare
to continue the measures. On June 16, after weeks of evidence,
Brougham introduced his motion asking for their repeal. He described in detail the distressed state of the country, and accused
the government of a "perpetual jealousy" towards the United
States. His long and fervent speech was unnecessary, for in the
same debate on that day Castlereagh intimated that the Orders
in Council would be withdrawn.[84] The new Liverpool government had decided that it could not take office with the millstone
of the Orders in Council around its neck, and the official revocation followed on June 23.[85]

The excuse for the repeal was that France had at last produced the authentic act by which she had withdrawn her
decrees.[86] This so-called decree of St. Cloud, dated April 28,
1811, was produced by the French on May 11, 1812, apparently
in response to the British declaration on April 21 that England
would withdraw her Orders in Council if the authentic French
act of repeal was produced.[87] It was generally known to be

9

spurious, but undoubtedly provided a convenient excuse for the government to cite as a reason for the withdrawal of the Orders. William Wilberforce's description of a private meeting at Lord Castlereagh's is particularly illuminating, for Castlereagh's reply to the assertion that the French decree was spurious was: "Aye ... but one does not like to own that we are forced to give way to our manufacturers."[88] Jefferson's policy of economic coercion had won a belated and ironic success.

The repeal of the Orders brought considerable rejoicing in England, for the workmen as well as their employers had become convinced that a repeal of the Orders would bring them relief. News of the repeal was greeted with the "ringing of bells, Bonfires, Roasting Sheep, Processions, Public Meetings, Votes of Thanks—not to the Ministry, but to Mr. Brougham and his colleagues."[89] In the center of Birmingham a large crowd gathered in heavy rain and, preceded by a band, marched to the outskirts to meet the representatives who had given evidence before Parliament. They took the horses from the shafts, and drew the carriages through the crowded streets.[90] Throughout England merchants and manufacturers voted thanks to the opposition, and particularly to Henry Brougham, who was looked upon as the leader of the opposition campaign.[91] As late as August 3, 1812, *Aris' Birmingham Gazette* printed an account of a public dinner held to celebrate the repeal of the Orders in Council, at which was given the toast: "May the Revocation of the Orders in Council be the means of establishing permanent friendship between Great Britain and the United States." The toast was a bitter one, for the same paper contained news of the American declaration of war. Concession had come too late.

II

The ninety-day Embargo, which was passed by Congress at the beginning of April, was regarded in America as the immediate precursor of war. Augustus J. Foster, the British minister, stood by helpless through April and May, and watched America go to war as England prepared to make her greatest concession of the whole period. It was obvious now that war would not be long delayed—indeed in the middle of April the possibility was once again mooted that France as well as England should be included in the war measure. In private, the French minister, Sérurier, sarcastically commented that he would have to seek an interview with Foster, so that the two powers could concert measures of defense against "so alarming a power."[92]

Foster's comments at this time showed the importance of both impressment and of the Orders in Council in the minds of the American legislators. Impressment, which had been somewhat eclipsed in the years immediately preceding the war by the problems caused by the Orders in Council, still rankled deep in the hearts of the War Hawks. Foster informed Castlereagh that the Congressmen who were in favor of peace had told him that they had more trouble explaining impressment to their constituents than they did the Orders in Council.[93] Foster in these months immediately preceding the war emphasized impressment and the Orders in Council as the main American grievances, and his reports of conversations with various Congressmen showed that it was these questions that absorbed their interest. When on May 18 he asked Senator Chauncey Goodrich of Connecticut what was required of England by men of fair views, Goodrich replied "take off the orders in Council and come to some Arrangement about Impressment."[94] Had the good senator but known it, one-half of his desires was to be accomplished within a month. Foster himself seemed strangely unperturbed by the likelihood of immediate war on England. At the end of May, he was writing anxiously to his mother of his desire to see Annabella, the girl he had left behind in England, and commenting: "No Minister ever had such temptations to break up a negotiation."[95] Augustus Foster was not the man to entrust with the difficult task of maintaining peace in the crisis in the spring of 1812.

In May the American government waited for its last dispatches from Europe. The *Hornet* arrived on May 19, but it brought nothing to warrant a delay in the declaration of war—if it could have brought news of the repeal of the Orders in Council war might still have been delayed for further negotiation. As it was, the main question posed by the arrival of the *Hornet* was the old one of whether war should be declared on France as well as England, for there was no sign that France had in fact repealed her decrees.[96] The long-lasting grievances against England, and the implausibility of war against both great European belligerents, however, ensured that the transgressions of France would be ignored until a reckoning had been made with England. While in England the climax of the struggle against the Orders in Council was reached, in America came the climax of the struggle for war.

On June 1 Madison sent his war message to Congress. This document presented a very accurate summary of the grievances that had driven America to make war on England. After stating that he did not intend to discuss American grievances for the period before 1803, Madison clearly outlined the main problems that had beset Anglo-American relations in the years from 1803 to 1812. First, he stressed the grievance that had been the original cause of difficulties between the two countries in the years following 1803—impressment, which he called "this crying enormity." He then continued with the British practice connected with impressment—the hovering of British cruisers off the American coast to stop and search American ships. The next section of his message dealt with the problem of illegal blockades, and with the system of Orders in Council. Madison stressed the fact that America had tried every expedient short of war, and that England had proved inflexible in the face of all American efforts. Finally, at the end of his list of grievances, he mentioned briefly that he could not omit the recent revival of Indian warfare, which he connected with British influence. His conclusions, however, were concerned solely with maritime problems. He reiterated that impressment still continued, and that American ships, laden with American products, were still being seized: "We behold, in fine, on the side of Great Britain a state of war against the United States, and on the side of the United States a state of peace toward Great Britain." He called for Congress to consider the necessary measure.[97]

On June 3 the bill for war was reported.[98] There was little need for discussion. This war was no sudden decision, for the whole problem had been debated time and time again in the preceding years. The War Hawks had journeyed to the Twelfth Congress determined that unless there was a radical change of policy on the part of Great Britain, America would defend her rights by war. In the debates of the Twelfth Congress the War Hawks had made it quite plain why they wanted war, and the delay until June, 1812, had been occasioned not by any lack of desire, but by the fact that an attempt had to be made to supply the means for waging the war before it was actually declared. In addition, it was not a unanimous America that declared war in 1812, and this was well reflected in the vote for war. There were certainly enough votes to carry the bill in the House on June 4, only one day after it was reported, but over one-third of those who voted were opposed to war—the margin of 79 to 49 reflected the hard fight that had been needed to bring America to the point of open conflict.[99] The western states—Kentucky, Ohio, and Tennessee—that had little voting power, but considerable enthusiasm and powers of leadership, cast 9 votes in favor of war and none against it. They were aided by the 3 to 1 vote of the northern frontier state, Vermont, but the mass of the support they needed came from the southern states—Georgia, Maryland, North Carolina, South Carolina, and Virginia—which voted 37 to 11 in favor of the war, and from Pennsylvania whose delegates supported the measure by a vote of 16 to 2. Opposition was centered in the northeastern seaboard—the six seaboard states from New Jersey northward were opposed to war by a vote of 34 to 14. Yet, even if these six states had cast all these 48 votes against war, it would not have been enough to prevent it.[100]

In the Senate, action was taken with more deliberation, and it was not until June 17, one day after Castlereagh had announced that the Orders were to be withdrawn, that the bill finally passed by the narrow margin of 19 to 13.[101] The President signed it on the next day, and at long last America sought through open warfare what she had failed to achieve through peaceful resistance.

I 5 *Conclusion*

THE CONFUSION concerning the origins of the War of 1812 has stemmed primarily from the lack of attention paid to the position of England in the causes of the conflict, and from the overemphasis that has been placed on "western expansionist" factors. Historians have expended considerable effort in an attempt to differentiate between a number of possible "American" causes of the war, but have tended to ignore the fact that the basic cause of the war is to be found not in America but in Europe. When America went to war in 1812 she was reacting to certain British policies—she was not acting in a vacuum—and whether one decides that western expansionists, southern planters, American nationalists, or any other group were responsible for the war, the results are incomplete unless the situation in Europe is taken into consideration. Unless one accepts the view that the War of 1812 was a war of pure aggression on the part of America, it is essential to study the motives behind British policy in order to understand the reasons for America going to war in 1812.

It is quite evident that British policy in this period was dictated to a great extent by European, not American, considerations. Great Britain was fighting a war for her existence. To fight Napoleon she needed every resource she could muster. From her point of view, it was essential to prevent American commerce from aiding France, and it was essential to prevent the wholesale desertion of seamen to the Americans. The British government preferred to risk war with the United States than to risk defeat by Napoleon. If possible, England wished to avoid war with America, but not to the extent of allowing her to hinder the British war effort against France. Moreover, the additional factor existed that a large section of influential British opinion, both in the government and in the country, thought that America presented a threat to British maritime supremacy. It would be a mistake to consider that this feeling was restricted solely to a self-interested commercial jealousy on the part of the shipping interest and its allies, although this group was undoubtedly influential in organizing opinion. Many who had no monetary interest in British shipping believed that British wealth, and Britain's greatness as a nation, rested on maritime supremacy. At a time of all-out war with France such considerations carried great weight in Great Britain. There was undoubtedly commercial jealousy of the United States in England, a jealousy increased by America's late colonial position, but there was also the feeling that only England could resist Napoleon and his threat to freedom. To many Englishmen this last consideration justified any restriction imposed upon neutrals. British commercial policy in this period stemmed both from the need for survival in the struggle against France, and from a commercial jealousy of America.

It is only after 1803 that a steady deterioration towards war can be discerned in Anglo-American relations. Though the problems bequeathed to the two countries by the Revolution were to be an aggravating factor in relations from 1803 to 1812, there was little reason to suppose in the former year that the two countries would be at war within nine years. If England and France had maintained the peace which existed in a precarious fashion from 1801 to 1803, it seems unlikely that there would have been war between England and America in 1812. The renewal of the war in Europe in May, 1803, decided the future course of Anglo-American relations. From 1803 to 1812 England, by her maritime policy, attempted to wage effective war against Napoleon. Impressment, which was the main point of contention between England and America from 1803 to 1807, was made necessary primarily because of England's great shortage of seamen for the war against Napoleon. In a similar manner the restrictions on American commerce imposed by England's Orders in Council, which were the supreme cause of complaint between 1807 and 1812, were one part of a vast commercial struggle being waged between England and France. Some restrictions on neutral commerce were essential for England in this period. That this restriction took such an extreme form in the period after 1807 stemmed not only from the effort to defeat Napoleon, but also from the undoubted jealousy of America's commercial prosperity that existed in England. America was unfortunate in that for most of the period from 1803 to 1812 political power in England was held by a group that was pledged not only to the defeat of France, but also to a rigid maintenance of Britain's commercial supremacy. The Whig government that held office from February, 1806, to March, 1807, was more sympathetic towards American problems, but discovered that it was impossible both to please America and to wage effective war against France. It was not until the years of bitter commercial depression in England in 1811 and 1812 that the Whig opposition obtained enough support to force a change in the government's policy towards the United States. By that time it was too late. America had already decided to defend her rights by force.

The American protest at British maritime policy can be traced as a continuous process from at least 1805 to 1812, and any attempt to trace the rise of American war feeling from 1810 to 1812 without reference to the earlier developments is inevitably inadequate. Bitterness against Great Britain had become extreme by 1807, and the five-year delay in the outbreak of war is explained primarily by the determination of Jefferson and his followers to attempt peaceful means of coercion before embarking upon an extremely dangerous war. That America should have tried peaceful means of coercion is not surprising. Jefferson himself, who could muster the support of a majority of the country, believed that it could succeed. Moreover, the seeming impossibility of America waging war against the might of England made the trial a practical necessity. By its very nature, peaceful coercion had to be tried over a matter of years, not months, and its supporters could always urge its continuance on the grounds that only persistence was needed to bring success. The trial and failure of economic coercion made its alternative —war—even more difficult, for the Embargo produced both economic weakness and political dissension. Those who saw war as the only way out of the morass had to contend not only with the supporters of peaceful resistance, but also with a Federalist opposition which wanted neither war nor economic sanctions. The commercial New Englanders were tied emotionally and financially to England.

Yet the failure of economic coercion made war or absolute submission to England the only alternatives, and the latter presented more terrors to the recent colonists. The main support for war in the years from 1809 came from those areas—the West and the South—that had supported economic resistance, and that were suffering the most from British restrictions at sea. The commercial classes of America were making ample profits from the wartime carrying trade, in spite of the numerous captures by both France and England, but the producers, who looked longingly at the export market, were suffering a commercial depression in the years before 1812. British commercial decrees provided a convenient scapegoat for all the ills of American farmers and planters. Though France was also abusing American neutral rights in these years, it was against England that the chief anger was felt. The reason for this is not hard to find. It was England, not France, that controlled the seas, and it was English ships that harassed the American coast, stopping American ships and removing seamen. Moreover, independence had been won from England, with French aid, only thirty years before, and the traditions of the War of Independence had not been forgotten. There was considerable bitterness against France in the years before 1812, but it was far more practical from the American point of view to attempt to relieve the immediate and more pressing injuries from Great Britain than to attempt a totally impractical war against both European belligerents.

The bitter anger that arose in America at Indian hostilities on the Northwest frontier, and the belief that the British officials in Canada were instigating Indian attacks, undoubtedly added to the irritation at Great Britain, and helped to win popular support for the war. Yet there seems no reason to suppose that this was either the basic cause of the war, or even the factor that finally impelled America into open hostilities. Even had there been no Indian problem, it seems likely that America would have gone to war in 1812. The increasing demand for war after 1809 arose naturally out of the failure of economic coercion as a means of resisting British maritime policy. The same areas that had desired to change British policy by economic means also supported warlike means of achieving the same ends when peaceful methods failed. The idea of conquering Canada had been present since at least 1807 as a means of forcing England to change her policy at sea. The conquest of Canada was primarily a means of waging war, not a reason for starting it. America in 1812 was acting essentially in reaction to British maritime policy. This British policy, though influenced by jealousy of American commercial growth, stemmed primarily from the necessity of waging war against France. Had there been no war with France, there would have been no Orders in Council, no impressment, and, in all probability, no War of 1812.

Bibliography

There is an abundance of material relating to the origins of the War of 1812, and a comprehensive bibliography would fill a separate volume. The following bibliography is intended as a guide to the materials that have proved most useful in the preparation of this study. Though it is not exhaustive, it lists the essential materials on which the study is based.

1. SOURCES
Though there are numerous printed sources relating to this period, indispensable material is still to be found only in manuscript form.

A. *Manuscript*
   Burton Historical Collection, Detroit Public Library:
   George Ironside Papers, Box 1, 1790-1820. Ironside was storekeeper for the British Indian department at Amherstburg in the pre-1812 period. Previously he had been a trader along the Maumee.

   Clements Library, Ann Arbor, Michigan:
   United States Office for Indian Affairs. Fort Wayne Indian Agency. Letterbook, 1809-1815.

   Indiana University Library, Bloomington, Indiana:
   War of 1812 MSS. These consist of various letters for the period prior to and during the War of 1812. Some are of great interest.

   Library of Congress:
   Henry Clay Papers. Disappointing as a source for the pre-1812 period.

Joseph Desha Papers. These are also disappointing.

Augustus John Foster Papers. A valuable collection which includes Foster's "Part of a Journal in the United States of America, 1811-1812."

Andrew Jackson Papers. Some important letters from Felix Grundy are found in this collection.

Thomas Jefferson Papers. Essential both for the understanding of Jefferson and of American policy.

James Madison Papers. As necessary to an understanding of the period as the papers of Jefferson himself.

James Monroe Papers. As both Minister to Great Britain and Secretary of State in this period, Monroe's papers are of great value.

Caesar A. Rodney Papers. Includes some letters from the War Hawks.

National Archives, Washington (Department of State):

Consular Letters 2-3, Liverpool, 1801-1825.

Consular Letters 8-9, London, 1799-1825.

Dispatches from the United States Minister to Great Britain.

Instructions to Ministers.

Public Archives of Canada, Ottawa:

Canada. Miscellaneous Documents, vol. 8 (1805-1812).

Claus Papers, vols. 1-10 (1760-1816).

Dispatches to the British Minister at Washington, vols. 1 and 23. Photostats of these dispatches are in the Library of Congress.

Governor General's Papers. Series G.

Indian Affairs. RG 10, Series 1, vols. 1-4, 8-12, 486.

Military, Series C.

Public Record Office, London:

Admiralty 1/495-502. Admirals' Dispatches, 1800-1812.

Admiralty 2/932-933. Letters of the Secretary of the Admiralty to the Commander-in-chief of the North American station, 1808-1815. Transcripts in the Library of Congress.

Colonial Office. Transcripts in the Public Archives of Canada, Series Q.

Foreign Office

F.O. 5/38, 1-42, 45, 48-49, 52, 54, 56-58, 62-64, 68-70, 74-77, 83-88.

F.O.115/11, 13, 16, 18, 20, 23. Transcripts in the Library of Congress.

Wisconsin State Historical Society Library, Madison:

Draper MSS. Tecumseh Papers 1YY-13YY. This contains Draper's extensive notes and letters together with some original material.

B. *Printed*

(a) GOVERNMENT—AMERICAN

*American State Papers. Class I. Foreign Relations, v*ols. II-III, Washington, 1832-1833.

American State Papers. Class II. Indian Affairs, vol. I. Washington, 1832.

American State Papers. Class IV. Commerce and Navigation, vol. I. Washington, 1832.

Annals of the Congress of the United States, 1789-1824. 42 vols. Washington, 1834-1856.

Carter, Clarence E. (ed.), *The Territorial Papers of the United States.* Washington, 1934-

vol. VI, *The Territory of Mississippi, 1809-1817.* Washington, 1938.

vol. VIII, *The Territory of Indiana, 1810-1816.* Washington, 1939.

vol. X, *The Territory of Michigan, 1805-1820.* Washington, 1942.

vol. XIV, *The Territory of Louisiana-Missouri, 1806-1814.* Washington, 1949.

vol. XVI, *The Territory of Illinois, 1809-1814.* Washington, 1948.

Manning, William R. (ed.), *Diplomatic Correspondence of the United States: Canadian Relations, 1784-1860,* vol. I. Washington, 1940. This collection has been extremely well edited.

(b) GOVERNMENT—BRITISH AND CANADIAN

Brymner, Douglas, Arthur G. Doughty, and Gustave Lanctot (eds.), *Report on the Canadian Archives*. Ottawa, 1872- . This annual publication contains valuable calendars of material in the Canadian Archives.

Hansard, Thomas C. (ed.), *The Parliamentary Debates from the Year 1803 to the Present Time*, vols I-XXIII, 1803-1812. London, 1812.

Journals of the House of Commons

Journals of the House of Lords

Mayo, Bernard (ed.), *Instructions to the British Ministers to the United States, 1791-1812*. American Historical Association, *Annual Report, 1936*, III. Washington, 1941.

Minutes of Evidence upon Taking into Consideration several Petitions, Presented to the House of Commons, Respecting the Orders in Council. London, 1808.

Minutes of Evidence Taken before the Committee of the Whole House, to whom it was referred to consider of the several Petitions which had been Presented to the House, in this Session of Parliament, Relating to the Orders in Council. London, 1812. This bulky publication, together with the one above, were consulted in the Goldsmith Library of the University of London. They contain considerable information both on the discontent against the Orders in Council, and on the general state of commerce and industry in Great Britain.

Robinson, Christopher (ed.), *Reports of the Cases Argued and Determined in the High Court of Admiralty*. 6 vols. London, 1799-1808.

(c) PRIVATE PAPERS, MEMOIRS, ETC.—AMERICAN.

Adams, Charles F. (ed.), *The Memoirs of John Quincy Adams*. 12 vols. Philadelphia, 1874-1877.

Adams, Henry (ed.), *Documents Relating to New England Federalism, 1800-1815*. Boston, 1877.

Bassett, John Spencer (ed.), *The Correspondence of Andrew Jackson*. 7 vols. Washington, 1926-1935.

Brown, Everett S. (ed.), *William Plumer's Memorandum of Proceedings in the United States Senate, 1803-1807*. New York, 1923.

Collections of the State Historical Society of Wisconsin. 31 vols. Madison, 1854-1931. These contain a wealth of material, particularly on the fur trade.

Donnan, Elizabeth (ed.), *Papers of James A. Bayard, 1796-1815.* American Historical Association, *Annual Report, 1913,* II. Washington, 1915.

Edwards, Ninian W., *History of Illinois, 1778-1832; and Life and Times of Ninian Edwards.* Springfield, Illinois, 870. Edwards was the territorial governor of Illinois. This volume contains a selection of his correspondence.

Esarey, Logan (ed.), *Messages and Letters of William Henry Harrison.* 2 vols. Indianapolis, 1922. This is volume VII and IX of the Indiana Historical Collections.

Ford, Paul L. (ed.), *The Writings of Thomas Jefferson.* 10 vols. New York, 1892-1899.

Hamilton, Stanislaus M. (ed.), *The Writings of James Monroe.* 7 vols. New York, 1898-1903.

Harden, Edward J., *The Life of George M. Troup.* Savannah, 1859.

Hunt, Gaillard (ed.), *The Writings of James Madison.* 7 vols. New York, 1900-1910.

King, Charles R. (ed.), *The Life and Correspondence of Rufus King.* 6 vols. New York, 1894-1899.

(Madison, James), *Letters and Other Writings of James Madison.* Published by Order of Congress, 4 vols. New York, 1865.

Marshall, Thomas M., *The Life and Papers of Frederick Bates.* 2 vols. St Louis, 1926. One or two letters are helpful regarding the state of mind in the West in the prewar period.

Michigan Pioneer and Historical Collections. 40 vols. Lansing, Michigan, 1877-1929. This series contains a mass of material, much of it from the Public Archives of Canada, though there is also some from American sources.

Morse, Edward Lind (ed.), *Samuel F. B. Morse; His Letters and Journals.* 2 vols. Boston, 1914. This famous inventor and painter was in England in the prewar period. His letters contain many comments on British conditions.

Pinkney, Rev. William, *The Life of William Pinkney.* New York, 1853.

Pitkin, Timothy, *A Statistical View of the Commerce of the United States of America.* New Haven, 1835.

Ravenel, Harriott Horry (Rutledge), *Life and Times of William Lowndes of South Carolina, 1782-1822.* Boston, 1901. Containing letters from Lowndes to his wife, some from the years before 1812.

Richardson, James D., *A Compilation of the Messages and Papers of the Presidents, 1789-1897.* 10 vols. Washington, 1896-1899. Volume I is relevant.

(d) PRIVATE PAPERS, MEMOIRS, ETC. BRITISH

Earl of Bessborough and Arthur Aspinall (ed.), *Lady Bessborough and her Family Circle.* London, 1940.

Bickley, Francis (ed.), *Report on the Manuscripts of Earl Bathurst preserved at Cirencester Park.* Historical Manuscripts Commission, London, 1923.

Blunden, Edmund C. (ed.), *Autobiography of Benjamin Robert Haydon.* London, 1927.

Brougham, Henry, *Memoirs of the Life and Times of Henry Brougham.* 3 vols. Edinburgh, 1871-1872.

Duke of Buckingham and Chandos, *Memoirs of the Court and Cabinets of George III.* 4 vols. London, 1853-1855. These volumes contain valuable Grenville correspondence.

Duke of Buckingham and Chandos, *Memoirs of the Court of England, during the Regency, 1811-1820.* 2 vols. London, 1856.

Cartwright, J. J. (ed.), *The Manuscripts of the Earl of Lonsdale.* Historical Manuscripts Commission, London, 1893.

Charles Abbot, Lord Colchester (ed.), *The Diary and Correspondence of Charles Abbot, Lord Colchester, Speaker of the House of Commons, 1802-1817.* 3 vols. London, 1861. Abbot was a constant commentator on political events.

Cruikshank, Ernest A. (ed.), *The Correspondence of Lieut. Governor John Graves Simcoe.* 5 vols. Toronto, 1923-1931.

Cruikshank, Ernest A. (ed.), *Documents Relating to the Invasion of Canada and the Surrender of Detroit, 1812.* Ottawa, 1912.

Robert J. Eden, Lord Auckland, Bishop of Bath and Wells (ed.), *The Journal and Correspondence of William, Lord Auckland*. 4 vols. London, 1861-1862.

Lady Edgar (ed.), *Ten Years of Upper Canada in Peace and War, 1805-1815; being the Ridout Letters*. Toronto, 1890. Apart from the information on Upper Canada, there are valuable letters on the state of England in 1811 and 1812.

Fitzpatrick, Walter (ed.), *Report on the Manuscripts in Various Collections*, vol. VI, Historical Manuscripts Commission, London, 1909. The manuscripts of Captain Howard, Vicente Knox, and Cornwallis Wykeham-Martin are relevant.

Fitzpatrick, Walter (ed.), *Report on the Manuscripts of J. B. Fortescue, Esq., preserved at Dropmore*. 10 vols. Historical Manuscripts Commission, London, 1892-1927.

Foster, Sir Augustus John, *Jeffersonian America. Notes on the United States of America, Collected in the Years 1805-6-7 and 11-12*. Edited with an introduction by Richard Beale Davis. The Huntington Library, San Marino, California, 1954.

Foster, Vere (ed.), *The Two Duchesses*, London, 1898. Hidden under this unlikely title is the fascinating correspondence between Augustus John Foster and his mother during his service in America.

Fraser, Alexander (ed.), "Proceedings of the Loyalist Commissioners Montreal, 1787 , vol. 20," *Second Report of the Bureau of Archives for the Province of Ontario, 1904*, pt. 2. Toronto, 1905. This contains a deposition of Matthew Elliott.

Gore, John (ed.), *Creevey's Life and Times*. London, 1934. This volume supplements the selection of Creevey's correspondence published in 1905 by Sir Herbert Maxwell.

Castalia, Countess Granville (ed.), *Lord Granville Leveson Gower (first Earl Granville): Private Correspondence, 1781-1821*. 2 vols. London, 1916. While Granville was away on a mission in Russia from 1804 to 1806, Lady Bessborough kept him informed of English political events.

Hall, Captain Basil, *Fragments of Voyages and Travels*. New ed. London, 1842.

Harcourt, Rev. Leveson Vernon (ed.), *The Diaries and Correspondence of the Right Hon. George Rose.* 2 vols. London, 1859-1860.

Henry Edward, Lord Holland (ed.), *Memoirs of the Whig Party during my Time, by Henry Richard Vassall Fox, third Baron Holland.* 2 vols. London, 1852-1854.

(Horne, David Milne), *Report on the Manuscripts of Colonel David Milne Horne of Weddeburn Castle, N. B.* Historical Manuscripts Commission, London, 1902.

Earl of Ilchester (ed.), *The Journal of Elizabeth, Lady Holland.* 2 vols. London, 1909.

Laughton, Sir John Knox (ed.), *Letters and Papers of Charles, Lord Barham, Admiral of the Red Squadron, 1758-1813.* 3 vols. Printed for the Navy Records Society, London, 1907-1911.

Markham, Sir Clements (ed.), *Selections from the Correspondence of Admiral John Markham during the Years 1801-1804 and 1806-1807.* Printed for the Navy Records Society, London, 1904.

Maxwell, Sir Herbert (ed.), *The Creevey Papers.* 3rd ed. London, 1905.

Countess of Minto (ed.), *Life and Letters of Sir Gilbert Elliott, First Earl of Minto, from 1751-1806.* 3 vols. London, 1874.

Pellew, George, *The Life and Correspondence of the Right Hon. Henry Addington, First Viscount Sidmouth.* 3 vols. London, 1847.

Paton, Henry (ed.), *Report on the Laing Manuscripts Preserved in the University of Edinburgh,* vol. II. Historical Manuscripts Commission, London, 1925.

Phipps, Edmund (ed.), *Memoirs of the Political and Literary Life of Robert Plumer Ward.* 2 vols. London, 1850.

Read, David B., *Life and Times of Major-General Sir Isaac Brock, K.B.* Toronto, 1894.

Rives, George L. (ed.), *Selections from the Correspondence of Thomas Barclay.* New York, 1894.

Earl of Roseberry (ed.), *The Windham Papers.* 2 vols. London, 1913.

Smith, David B. (ed.), *Letters of Admiral of the Fleet, the Earl of St. Vincent whilst First Lord of the Admiralty, 1801-1804.* 2 vols. Printed for the Navy Records Society, London, 1922-1927.

Lord Stavordale (ed.), *Further Memoirs of the Whig Party, 1807-1812, with some Miscellaneous Reminiscences, by Henry Richard Vassall, third Lord Holland.* London, 1905.

Stuart, Dorothy M., *Dearest Bess : The Life and Times of Lady Elizabeth Foster.* London, 1955. This consists largely of her journals and correspondence. She was the mother of Augustus John Foster, the British minister in America from 1811 to 1812.

Tupper, Ferdinand B., *The Life and Correspondence of Major General Sir Isaac Brock, K.B.* 2d ed. London, 1847. This work contains important selections from Brock's correspondence.

Vane, Charles W., third Marquess of Londonderry (ed.), *Correspondence, Despatches, and other Papers of Viscount Castlereagh, Second Marquess of Londonderry.* 12 vols. London, 1848-1853.

Wallace, William S. (ed.), *Documents Relating to the Northwest Company.* Champlain Society Publication, Toronto, 1934. This has a good historical introduction and an appendix containing a biographical dictionary of members of the company.

Walpole, Spencer, *The Life of the Right Hon. Spencer Perceval.* 2 vols. London, 1874. Useful for Perceval's connection with the Orders in Council, though the work is very biased in his favor.

Weld, Isaac, *Travels Through the States of North America and the Provinces of Upper and Lower Canada During the Years 1795, 1796, and 1797.* London, 1799. Weld's work contains an excellent description of Matthew Elliott's farm at Amherstburg.

Wilberforce, A. M. (ed.), *Private Papers of William Wilberforce.* London, 1897.

Wilberforce, Robert Isaac and Samuel. *The Life of William Wilberforce.* 5 vols. London, 1838. A great reformer, Wilberforce was intimate with many of the prominent figures of the period.

Wood, William H. (ed.), *Select British Documents of the Canadian War of 1812*. Champlain Society Publications, 4 vols. Toronto, 1920-1928.

Yonge, Charles D., *The Life and Administration of Robert Banks, second Earl of Liverpool, late First Lord of the Treasury*. 3 vols. London, 1868.

(e) PAMPHLETS

Alley, Jerome, *A Vindication of the Principles and Statements advanced in the Strictures of the Right Hon. Lord Sheffield on the Necessity of Inviolably Maintaining the Navigation and Colonial System of Great Britain*. London, 1806.

Atcheson, Nathaniel, *American Encroachments on British Rights; or, Observations on the Importance of the British North American Colonies and on the Late Treaties with the United States. ....* London, 1808. Atcheson was the Secretary of the Society of Shipowners of Great Britain, and of the British North American Mercantile Committee during this period.

Baring, Alexander, *An Inquiry into the Causes and Consequences of the Orders in Council; and an Examination of the Conduct of Great Britain towards the Neutral Commerce of America*. London, 1808.

The Case of the Owners of the British Ships. London, 1803.

Cock, S., *An Answer to Lord Sheffield's Pamphlet on the Subject of the Navigation System. ....* London, 1804.

Collection of Interesting and Important Reports and Papers on the Navigation and Trade of Great Britain, Ireland, and the British Colonies in the West Indies and America. Printed by Order of "The Society of Shipowners of Great Britain," London, 1807. A long and important work which contains extracts from the minutes of the meetings of the Society of Shipowners, and various papers on commerce and navigation.

Concessions to America the Bane of Britain; or the Cause of the Present Distressed Situation of the British Colonial and Shipping Interests Explained, and the Proper Remedy Suggested. London, 1807.

(John Wilson Croker), *A Key to the Orders in Council.* London, 1812.

Coxe, Tench (Juriscola), *An Examination of the Conduct of Great Britain, Respecting Neutrals.* Philadelphia, 1807.

An Examination of the Alleged Expediency of the American Intercourse Bill. ... London, 1806.

Gray, Hugh, *Letters from Canada, written during a Residence there in the Years 1806, 1807, and 1808.* ... London, 1809.

Holroyd, John Baker, first Earl of Sheffield, *Observations on the Commerce of the American States.* London, 1783.

The Orders in Council and the American Embargo Beneficial to the Political and Commercial Interests of Great Britain. London, 1809.

Strictures on the Necessity of Inviolably Maintaining the Navigation and Colonial System of Great Britain. London, 1804; enlarged edition, 1806.

Jordan, Gibbes W., *The Claims of the West India Colonists to the Right of Obtaining Necessary Supplies from America.* ... London, 1804.

Lowe, Joseph, *An Inquiry into the State of the British West Indies.* London, 1807.

Lowell, John, *Analysis of the Late Correspondence between our Administration and Great Britain and France.* ... Boston, 1808.

An Appeal to the People on the Causes and Consequences of a War with Great Britain. Boston, 1811.

Madison, James, *An Examination of the British Doctrine, which Subjects to Capture a Neutral Trade, not Open in Time of Peace.* Philadelphia, 1806.

Medford, Macall, *Oil without Vinegar, and Dignity without Pride; or British, American, and West India Interests Considered.* London, 1807.

Mercator (pseud.), *Third Letter on the Abolition of the Slave Trade, and Other West Indian Affairs.* London, 1807.

Observations on the American Intercourse Bill, and the Necessity of Adhering Strictly to the Navigation Laws of Great Britain. London, 1806.

Observations on the Importance of a Strict Adherence to the Navigation Laws of Great Britain. London, 1801.

Phillimore, Joseph, *A Letter Addressed to a Member of the House of Commons on the Subject of the Notice given by Mr. Brougham for a Motion Respecting the Orders in Council and the Licence Trade.* London, 1812.

Reflections on the Nature and Extent of the Licence Trade. London, 1811.

Stephen, James (Introduction), *The Speech of the Hon. J. Randolph, Representative for the State of Virginia, in the General Congress of America; on a motion for the Non-Importation of British Merchandize, pending the Present Disputes between Great Britain and America.* London, 1806.

War in Disguise; or, The Frauds of the Neutral Flags. London, 1805.

Vindex (pseud.), *On the Maritime Rights of Great Britain.* London, 1807.

(f) NEWSPAPERS AND PERIODICALS—AMERICAN. (These were consulted at the Library of Congress and in the Indiana University Library.)

Annapolis, Maryland, *Maryland Gazette*, 1803-1805.

Baltimore, Maryland, *Niles' Weekly Register*, 1811-1812.

Chillicothe, Ohio, *Scioto Gazette*, 1803-1812.

Vincennes, Indiana. *Western Sun*, 1807-1809.

Washington, D.C., *National Intelligencer, and Washington Advertiser*, 1803-1812.

Worthington, Ohio, *Western Intelligencer*, 1812.

(g) NEWSPAPERS AND PERIODICALS—BRITISH. (These were consulted in the British Museum [and its collection of newspapers at Colindale], and in the Birmingham and Leicester Reference Libraries.)

Birmingham, *Aris' Birmingham Gazette*, 1808-1812.

Edinburgh, *Edinburgh Review*, 1803-1812.

Leicester, *Leicester Chronicle*, 1812.

Leicester Journal, 1808-1812.

London, *Annual Register*, 1803-1812.
Cobbett's Political Register, 1803-1812.
Courier, 1808-1812.
European Magazine, and London Review, 1803-1812.
Examiner, 1808-1812.
Gentleman's Magazine, 1803-1812.
Monthly Review; or Literary Journal, 1808-1812.
Morning Chronicle, 1803-1812.
Quarterly Review, 1809-1812.
Times, 1803-1812.

II. SECONDARY WORKS

A. *Books*

Adams, Henry, *History of the United States during the Administrations of Jefferson and Madison*. 9 vols. New York 1889-1891. This is still the best general account of the period, though Adams is anti-Jefferson.

Armytage, Frances, *The Free Port System in the British West Indies: A Study in Commercial Policy, 1766-1822*. London, 1953.

Aspinall, Arthur, *Lord Brougham and the Whig Party*. Manchester, 1927.

Bemis, Samuel F. (ed.), *The American Secretaries of State and their Diplomacy*. 10 vols. New York, 1927-1929. Volume III is relevant to this study.
A Diplomatic History of the United States. 3rd. edition, New York, 1953.
Jay's Treaty: A Study in Commerce and Diplomacy. New York, 1923.

Brant, Irving, *James Madison, Secretary of State, 1801-1809*. Indianapolis, 1953.
James Madison, The President, 1809-1812. Indianapolis, 1956.

Briggs, Herbert W., *The Doctrine of Continuous Voyage*. Johns Hopkins University Studies in Historical and Political Science, Series XLIV, No. 2, Baltimore, 1926.

Brightfield, Myron F., *John Wilson Croker*. London, 1940.

Brooks, Philip C., *Diplomacy and the Borderlands. The Adams-Onis Treaty of 1819.* Berkeley, California, 1939.

Brougham, Henry, *Historical Sketches of Statesmen who flourished in the Time of George III.* 3 vols. London, 1839-1843.

Bryant, Arthur, *The Years of Endurance, 1793-1802.* London, 1942.

Years of Victory, 1803-1812. London, 1944. These works present a colorful account of this period in British history, though American relations are practically ignored.

Buck, Norman S., *The Development of the Organization of Anglo-American Trade, 1800-1850.* New Haven, 1925. Buck is primarily interested in the more technical aspects of trade relations, but he has an excellent grasp of his subject.

Burt, Alfred L., *The United States, Great Britain, and British North America from the Revolution to the Establishment of Peace after the War of 1812.* New Haven, 1940. Professor Burt has an extensive knowledge of these years.

Chittenden, Hiram M., *The American Fur Trade of the Far West.* 3 vols. New York, 1902.

Clauder, Anna C., *American Commerce as Affected by the Wars of the French Revolution and Napoleon, 1793-1812.* Philadelphia, 1932.

Cole, Arthur H., *Wholesale Commodity Prices in the United States, 1700-1861.* 2 vols. Cambridge, Mass., 1938. The second volume is a statistical supplement.

Cox, Isaac J., *The West Florida Controversy, 1798-1813; A Study in American Diplomacy.* Baltimore, 1918.

Creighton, Donald G., *The Commercial Empire of the St. Lawrence, 1760-1850.* Toronto, 1937.

Cruikshank, Ernest A., *The Political Adventures of John Henry; the Record of an International Imbroglio.* Toronto, 1936.

Darvall, Frank O., *Popular Disturbances and Public Order in Regency England.* London, 1934.

Davidson, Gordon C., *The North West Company.* Berkeley, California, 1918.

Davis, H. W. Carless, *The Age of Grey and Peel.* Oxford, 1929. An excellent collection of essays.

Dawson, Moses, *A Historical Narrative of the Civil and Military Services of Major-General William Henry Harrison.* Cincinnati, 1824. This contains documentary material, but it needs to be used with caution.

Downes, Randolph C., *Council Fires on the Upper Ohio; a Narrative of Indian Affairs in the Upper Ohio Valley until 1795.* Pittsburgh, 1940. Downes is very sympathetic towards the Indian point of view.

Drake, Benjamin, *Life of Tecumseh, and of his Brother the Prophet.* Cincinnati, 1852. This is still in many ways the best biography of Tecumseh, and one on which many later writers have based their accounts.

Lady Edgar, *General Brock.* London, 1926.

Feiling, Keith G., *The Second Tory Party, 1714-1832.* London, 1938.

Fremantle, Alan F., *England in the Nineteenth Century, 1801-1805.* London, 1929.
   England in the Nineteenth Century, 1806-1810. London, 1930.

Galpin, William F., *The Grain Supply of England during the Napoleonic Period.* Philadelphia, 1925. Galpin maintains that the desire to check the American carrying trade to Europe was a more potent cause of the November, 1807, British Orders in Council than the idea of combating French decrees.

Garratt, Geoffrey T., *Lord Brougham.* London, 1935.

Goebel, Dorothy B., *William Henry Harrison: A Political Biography.* Indianapolis, 1926.

Goodman, Warren H., The Origins of the War of 1812: A Critical Examination of Historical Interpretations. Unpublished M.A. thesis, Duke University Library. A good study which contains more detail than the author's later article on the same theme.

Graham, Gerald S., *Sea Power and British North America, 1783-1820.* Cambridge, Mass., 1941.

Griffin, Charles C., *The United States and the Disruption of the Spanish Empire, 1810-1822.* New York, 1937.

Harrison, James L. (ed.), *Biographical Directory of the American Congress: 1774-1949.* Washington, 1950.

284   BIBLIOGRAPHY

Hecksher, Eli F., *The Continental System: An Economic Interpretation.* Oxford, 1922.

Hidy, Ralph W., *The House of Baring in American Trade and
Finance: English Merchant Bankers at Work, 1763-1861.*
Cambridge, Mass., 1949.

Jennings, Walter W., *The American Embargo, 1807-1809,
with Particular Reference to its Effect on Industry.* Iowa
City, 1921. Less valuable than the volume by Louis M.
Sears on the same subject.

Kellogg, Louise P., *The British Regime in Wisconsin and the
Northwest.* Madison, 1935.

McAfee, Robert B., *A History of the Late War in the Western
Country.* Lexington, 1816 ; reprinted Bowling Green, Ohio,
1919.

Lyon, Elijah W., *Louisiana in French Diplomacy, 1759-1804.*
Norman, Oklahoma, 1934.

Maccoby, Simon, *English Radicalism, 1786-1832.* London,
1955. The second volume in a series by Maccoby on English
radicalism. He quotes extensively from source material.

Mahan, Alfred T., *The Influence of Sea Power upon the French
Revolution and Empire, 1793-1812.* 2 vols. Boston, 1892.
Sea Power in its Relations to the War of 1812. 2 vols.
Boston, 1905. Mahan's works are a valuable contribution to
the maritime history of this period.

Matheson, Cyril, *The Life of Henry Dundas: First Viscount
Melville, 1742-1811.* London, 1933.

Mayo, Bernard, *Henry Clay: Spokesman of the New West.*
Boston, 1937. An entertaining style and an extensive historical knowledge combine to produce a fascinating biography of Clay in the pre-1812 period.

Melvin, Frank E., *Napoleon's Navigation System: A Study
of Trade Control During the Continental Blockade.* New
York, 1919. Contains an extensive bibliography.

Meyer, Leland W., *The Life and Times of Colonel Richard
M. Johnson of Kentucky.* New York, 1932.

Mooney, James, *The Ghost Dance Religion and the Sioux
Outbreak of 1890.* Fourteenth Annual Report of the American Bureau of Ethnology, 1892-1893, pt. 2, Washington,
1896.

Morison, Samuel E., *The Life and Letters of Harrison Gray Otis, Federalist, 1765-1848.* 2 vols. Boston, 1913.

The Maritime History of Massachusetts, 1783-1860. Boston, 1941. Useful on the attitude of the maritime interest, and delightfully written.

Munroe, John A., *Federalist Delaware, 1775-1815.* New Brunswick, N.J., 1954.

Parkinson, C. Northcote (ed.), *The Trade Winds: A Study of British Overseas Trade during the French Wars.* London, 1948. The excellent chapter on the American trade was written by Professor Herbert Heaton.

Parks, Joseph H., *Felix Grundy: Champion of Democracy.* Louisiana State University Press, 1940.

Paullin, Charles O. and John K. Wright, *Atlas of the Historical Geography of the United States.* Washington, 1932.

Peake, Ora B., *A History of the United States Indian Factory System, 1795-1822.* Denver, 1954.

Perkins, Bradford, *The First Rapprochement: England and the United States, 1795-1805.* Philadelphia, 1955. A scholarly, well-written account, perhaps tending to overemphasize the extent of agreement between the two countries.

Phillips, Walter Alison and Arthur H. Reede, *Neutrality: Its History, Economics, and Law,* vol. II, *The Napoleonic Period.* New York, 1936.

Porter, George R., *The Progress of the Nation in its Various Social and Economical Relations from 1800 to the Present Time.* 3 vols. London, 1836; rev. edition, 1912.

Porter, Kenneth W., *John Jacob Astor, Business Man.* 2 vols. Cambridge, Mass., 1931.

Pratt, Julius W., *Expansionists of 1812.* New York, 1925. This stimulating work has proved the most influential of this century on the origins of the War of 1812. It has encountered increasing opposition in recent years.

Prentiss, Harvey P., *Timothy Pickering as the Leader of New England Federalism, 1800-1815.* Salem, Mass., 1934. Chapters from the author's dissertation.

Ragatz, Lowell J., *The Fall of the Planter Class in the British Caribbean, 1763-1833.* New York, 1928. Valuable on all aspects of policy in regard to the West Indies.

Roberts, Michael, *The Whig Party, 1807-1812.* London, 1939.
A detailed study of the groups that comprised the Whig
party. There is no discussion of their attitude towards the
United States.

Schuyler, Robert L., *The Fall of the Old Colonial System:
A Study in British Free Trade.* New York, 1945.

Sears, Louis M., *Jefferson and the Embargo.* Durham, N.C.,
1927. The best available account.

Smart, William, *Economic Annals of the Nineteenth Century.*
2 vols. London, 1910-1917. Volume I covers the period from
1801 to 1820.

Stevens, Wayne E., *The Northwest Fur Trade, 1763-1800.*
Urbana, Ill., 1928.

Swearingen, Mark, *The Early Life of George Poindexter:
A Story of the First Southwest.* New Orleans, 1934.

Tooke, Thomas, *A History of Prices and the State of Circulation, 1793-1837.* London, 1838. Contains useful statis-
tics on the state of trade.

Tucker, Glenn, *Tecumseh: Vision of Glory.* Indianapolis,
1956. Colorfully written, but disappointing. There is a mix-
ture of historical fact and legend.

Van Deusen, Glyndon G., *The Life of Henry Clay.* Boston,
1937. An excellent biography.

Whitaker, Arthur P., *The Mississippi Question, 1795-1803:
A Study in Trade, Politics, and Finance.* New York, 1934.
A standard work by a notable historian of the Southwest.

Zimmerman, James F., *Impressment of American Seamen.*
New York, 1925. This is still the standard work, though it
is not by any means a definitive treatment of the subject.

B. *Articles*

Anderson, Dice R., "The Insurgents of 1811." American Historical Association, *Annual Report,* 1911, I (Washington,
1913), 165-176. A very early statement of the importance
of western factors in the origin of the conflict. It emphasized
the West's belief that the Indian problem could be solved
only by the expulsion of the British from Canada.

Aspinall, Arthur, "The Canningite Party." *Transactions* of
the Royal Historical Society, IV Series, XVII (1934), 117-
226.

Barce, Elmore, "Tecumseh's Confederacy." *Indiana Magazine of History* (Bloomington, Ind., 1905-   ), XII (1916), 161-174.

Baty, Thomas, "The Portland Ministry and the History of the Continuous Voyage." *Law Quarterly Review* (London, 1885-   ), 38 (1922), 25-57.

Burt, Alfred L., "A New Approach to the Problem of the Western Posts." Canadian Historical Assocation, *Annual Report, 1931* (Ottawa, 1931), 61-75.

Byrd, Cecil K., "The Northwest Indians and the British Preceding the War of 1812." *Indiana Magazine of History,* XXXVIII (1942), 31-50.

Cady, John F., "Western Opinion and the War of 1812." *Ohio Archaeological and Historical Quarterly* (Columbus, Ohio, 1887-   ), XXXIII (1924), 427-476. This article contributed little that was new.

Coleman, Christopher B., "The Ohio Valley in the Preliminaries of the War of 1812." *Mississippi Valley Historical Review* (Cedar Rapids, Iowa, 1914-   ), VII (1920-21), 39-50. This suggests the conquest of Canada as the impelling cause of the war.

Cruikshank, Ernest A., "The Employment of Indians in the War of 1812." American Historical Association, *Annual Report, 1895* (Washington, 1896), 319-335.

"The Military Career and Character of Major-General Sir Isaac Brock." New York State Historical Association *Proceedings* (Albany, 1901-   ), VIII (1909), 67-90.

"Robert Dickson, the Indian Trader." *Collections of the State Historical Society of Wisconsin,* XII (1892), 133-153.

"The *Chesapeake* Crisis as it Affected Upper Canada." Ontario Historical Society, *Papers and Records* (Toronto, 1899-   ), XXIV (1927), 281-322. Here, as in many of his other articles, Cruikshank quotes extensively from the sources.

Daniels, George W., "The American Cotton Trade with Liverpool under the Embargo and Non-Intercourse Acts." *American Historical Review* (New York, 1895-   ), XXI (1915-16), 276-287.

Fisher, Josephine, "Francis James Jackson and Newspaper Propaganda in the United States, 1809-1810." *Maryland Magazine of History* (Baltimore, 1906-   ), XXX (1935), 93-113.

Fisher, Robert L., "The Western Prologue to the War of 1812." *Missouri Historical Review* (Columbia, Mo., 1906-   ), 30 (1936), 267-281.

Galpin, William F., "The American Grain Trade under the Embargo of 1808." *Journal of Economic and Business History* (4 vols., Cambridge, Mass., 1928-1932), II (1929), 71-100.

"The American Grain Trade to the Spanish Peninsula, 1810-1814." *American Historical Review*, XXVII (1921-22), 24-44.

Gates, Charles M., "The West in American Diplomacy, 1812-1815." *Mississippi Valley Historical Review*, XXVI (1939-40), 499-510.

Goodman, Warren H., "The Origins of the War of 1812: A Survey of Changing Interpretations." *Mississippi Valley Historical Review*, XXVIII (1941-42), 171-186. Based on the author's M.A. thesis, this is an excellent historiographical study of the origins of the War of 1812. Goodman cast doubt on the validity of some of Julius W. Pratt's conclusions.

Gregg, Kate L., "The War of 1812 on the Missouri Frontier." *Missouri Historical Review*, XXXIII (1938), 3-22.

Hacker, Louis M., "Western Land Hunger and the War of 1812: A Conjecture." *Mississippi Valley Historical Review*, X (1923-24), 365-395. Hacker here argues that the West brought on war because of a desire for Canadian land. The article received perceptive and convincing criticism in an article by Julius Pratt in the same journal for 1925. See below.

Hall, Ellery L., "Canadian Annexation Sentiment in Kentucky Prior to the War of 1812." *Register of the Kentucky State Historical Society* (Frankfort, Ky., 1903-   ), XXVII (1930), 372-380.

Heaton, Herbert, "Yorkshire Cloth Traders in the United States, 1770-1840." *Thoresby Miscellany* (Leeds, 1891-   ), XXXVIII (1944), 225-287.

Henderson, W. O., "The American Chamber of Commerce for the Port of Liverpool, 1801-1908." *Transactions* of the Historic Society of Lancashire and Cheshire, 85 (1933), 1-61.

Horsman, Reginald, "British Indian Policy in the Northwest, 1807-1812." *Mississippi Valley Historical Review,* XLV (1958-59), 51-66.

———— "Western War Aims, 1811-1812." *Indiana Magazine of History,* LIII (1957), 1-18.

Hunt, Gaillard, "Joseph Gales on the War Manifesto of 1812." *American Historical Review,* XIII (1907-08), 303-310.

Kaplan, Lawrence S., "Jefferson, the Napoleonic War, and the Balance of Power." *William and Mary Quarterly* (Williamsburg, Va., 1892-), 3rd Series, XIV (1957), 196-217.

Keith, Alice B., "Relaxations in the British Restrictions on the American Trade with the British West Indies, 1783-1802." *Journal of Modern History* (Chicago, 1929-), XX (1948), 1-18.

Latimer, Margaret Kinnard, "South Carolina—A Protagonist of the War of 1812." *American Historical Review,* LXI (1955-56), 914-929. In this well-written article Miss Latimer contends that South Carolina supported the war against England because of the depressed state of her export trade in cotton. She also suggests that the West saw in war the solution of its commercial difficulties.

Lewis, Howard T., "A Re-Analysis of the Causes of the War of 1812." *Americana* (New York, 1906-), VI (1911), 506-516, 577-585. A very early presentation of the view that the war was fought mainly because the West coveted the agricultural lands of Canada.

Lingelbach, William E., "England and Neutral Trade." *Military Historian and Economist* (3 vols., Cambridge, Mass., 1916-1918), II (1917), 153-178.

Morison, Samuel E., "The Henry-Crillon Affair of 1812." in Morison, *By Land and Sea* (New York, 1953), 265-286. Shows in sparkling fashion how Madison was duped by Henry and Crillon in 1812.

Penson, Lillian M., "The London West India Interest in the Eighteenth Century." *English Historical Review* (London, 1886-), 36 (1921), 373-392.

Perkins, Bradford, "George Canning, Great Britain, and the
    United States, 1807-1809." *American Historical Review,*
    LXIII (1957-58), 1-22. An attempt to present a more
    favorable view of Canning's American policy than has often
    been given. Though a useful study, it tends to ignore some
    of Canning's more unfortunate acts of this period.
Pratt, Julius W., "Fur Trade Strategy and the American Left
    Flank in the War of 1812." *American Historical Review,*
    XL (1934-35), 246-273.
        Review of Alfred L. Burt's *United States, Great Bri-
    tain,* in *American Historical Review,* XLVII (1941-42),
    87-89. Pratt here restates his views regarding the import-
    ance of western demands in the prewar period.
        "Western Aims in the War of 1812." *Mississippi Valley
    Historical Review,* XII (1925-26), 36-50. Pratt here effec-
    tively refutes Louis M. Hacker's theories of western land
    hunger as a factor of prime importance in the origins of
    the War of 1812.
Randall, Emilius O., "Tecumseh, the Shawnee Chief." *Ohio
    Archaeological and Historical Quarterly,* XV (1906), 418-
    498.
Reinhochl, John H., "Post Embargo Trade and Merchant
    Prosperity: Experiences of the Crowinshield Family, 1809-
    1812." *Mississippi Valley Historical Review,* XLII (1955-
    56), 229-249.
Robinson, Doane, "South Dakota and the War of 1812."
    South Dakota Historical Collections (Pierre, S.D., 1902-
    ), XII (1924), 85-98.
Rose, J. Holland, "British West India Commerce as a Factor
    in the Napoleonic War." *Cambridge Historical Journal*
    (Cambridge, 1923-   ), III (1929), 34-46.
Sears, Louis M., "British Industry and the Embargo." *Quar-
    terly Journal of Economics* (Cambridge, Mass., 1886-   ),
    XXXIV (1919-20), 88-113.
Smith, Theodore C., "War Guilt in 1812." Massachusetts
    Historical Society *Proceedings* (Boston, Mass., 1886-),
    3rd Series, LXIV (1931), 319-345.
Smith, W. B., "Wholesale Commodity Prices in the United
    States, 1795-1824." *Review of Economic Statistics* (Cam-
    bridge, Mass., 1919-   ), IX (1927), 171-183.

Stanley, George F. G., "The Indians in the War of 1812." *Canadian Historical Review*, 31 (1950), 145-165.

Steel, Anthony, "Anthony Merry and the Anglo-American Dispute about Impressment, 1803-1806." *Cambridge Historical Journal*, IX (1949), 331-351.
"Impressment in the Monroe-Pinkney Negotiation, 1806-1807." *American Historical Review*, LVII (1951-52), 352-369.

Stevens, Frank E., "Illinois in the War of 1812." *Transactions of the State Historical Society of Illinois*, 1904 (Springfield, 1904), 62-197.

Stevens, Wayne E., "Fur Trading Companies in the Northwest, 1760-1816." *Mississippi Valley Historical Association Proceedings*, IX (1918), 283-291.

Talmadge, John E., "Georgia's Federalist Press and the War of 1812." *Journal of Southern History* (Baton Rouge, La., 1935-   ), XIX (1953), 488-500.

Taylor, George Rogers, "Agrarian Discontent in the Mississippi Valley Preceding the War of 1812." *Journal of Political Economy* (Chicago, 1892-   ), XXXIX (1931), 471-505.
"Prices in the Mississippi Valley Preceding the War of 1812." *Journal of Economic and Business History*, III (1930), 148-163. Taylor was the first historian to draw a clear connection between the western commercial depression and the demand for war in 1812. The excellence of these articles has become increasingly apparent in recent years.

Tohill, Louis A., "Robert Dickson, British Fur Trader on the Upper Mississippi." *North Dakota Historical Quarterly* (Bismarck, N.D., 1926-   ), I-III (1928-29), 5-49, 83-128, 182-203.
"Robert Dickson, the Fur Trade, and the Minnesota Boundary." *Minnesota History* (St. Paul, 1915-   ), VI (1925), 330-342.

Van der Zee, Jacob, "Fur Trade Operations in the Eastern Iowa Country from 1800 to 1803." *Iowa Journal of History and Politics* (Iowa City, 1903-   ), XII (1914), 479-567.

Van Tyne, Claude H., "Why Did We Fight in 1812? The Causes and Significance of our Last War with Great Britain." *Independent* (121 vols., New York and Boston, 1848-1928), LXXIV (1913), 1327-1331.

Wiltse, Charles M., "The Authorship of the War Report of 1812." *American Historical Review,* XLIX (1943-44), 253-259.

Appendix

VOTE FOR WAR, JUNE 4, 1812,
HOUSE OF REPRESENTATIVES

	Yes	*No*	*Not Voting*	*Total*
Connecticut	—	7	—	7
Delaware	—	1	—	1
Georgia	3	—	1	4
Kentucky	5	—	1	6
Louisiana	—	—	1	1
Maryland	6	3	—	9
Massachusetts	6	8	3	17
New Hampshire	3	2	—	5
New Jersey	2	4	—	6
New York	3	11	3	17
North Carolina	6	3	3	12
Ohio	1	—	—	1
Pennsylvania	16	2	—	18
Rhode Island	—	2	—	2
South Carolina	8	—	—	8
Tennessee	3	—	—	3
Vermont	3	1	—	4
Virginia	14	5	3	22
	79	49	15	143

(Taken from Paullin and Wright, *Atlas of Historical Geography*, 109. The vote is in *Annals of Congress*, 12th Congress, 1st Session, 1637-1638).

Notes

CHAPTER 1 : BACKGROUND OF CONFLICT

[1] August 7, 1812 ; see also *Courier* (London), July 21, 30, 1812.

[2] *Courier*, March 4, 7, 9, 10, June 29, 1812 ; *Examiner* (London), March 29, 1812 ; *Aris' Birmingham Gazette*, March 16, July 6, 1812 ; *Leicester Journal*, March 20, July 25, 1812.

[3] Clay to Caesar A. Rodney, August 6, 1810, Rodney Papers, Library of Congress, Box 2.

[4] *Monthly Review* ; *or, Literary Journal Enlarged* (London), March, 1808, p. 310.

[5] The most scholarly work on the interaction of the British, American, and Indians in the Northwest in this period is Alfred L. Burt, *The United States, Great Britain, and British North America from the Revolution to the Establishment of Peace after the War of* 1812 (New Haven, 1940).

[6] See Lowell J. Ragatz, *The Fall of the Planter Class in the British Caribbean, 1763-1833* (New York, 1928), 173-182 ; also Samuel F. Bemis, *Jay's Treaty : A Study in Commerce and Diplomacy* (New York, 1923), 26-32.

[7] Ragatz, *Fall of the Planter Class*, 205 ff. ; also Bradford Perkins, *The First Rapprochement : England and the United States, 1795-1805* (Philadelphia, 1955), 86-89.

[8] Ragatz, *Fall of the Planter Class*, 229-230.

[9] The general question of neutral rights is discussed in Walter Alison Phillips and Arthur H. Reede, *Neutrality : Its History, Economics, and Law*, vol. II, *The Napoleonic Period* (New York, 1936). The standard work on impressment is still James F. Zimmerman, *Impressment of American Seamen* (New York, 1925).

[10] See Perkins, *The First Rapprochement*, 129-149. Professor Perkins gives a scholarly account of the measure of accord attained by Britain and the United States at this time.

CHAPTER 2 : THE THREAT OF INVASION

[1] Charles Abbot, Lord Colchester (ed.), *The Diary and Correspondence of Charles Abbot, Lord Colchester* (3 vols., London, 1861), I, 461, 469-472 ; also Lord Grenville to the Marquis of Buckingham, April 12, 1803, Duke of Buckingham and Chandos, *Memoirs of the Court and Cabinets of George III* (4 vols., London, 1853-1855), III (1855), 277-278 ; Lady Malmesbury

to Lady Minto, July, 1803, and Lord to Lady Minto, July 16, 1803, Countess of Minto (ed.), *Life and Letters of Sir Gilbert Elliot, First Earl of Minto, from* 1751 *to* 1806 (3 vols., London, 1874), III, 292-293, and 292 n. 1 ; William Windham to William Wilberforce, August 18, 1803, A. M. Wilberforce (ed.), *Private Papers of William Wilberforce* (London, 1897), 134-136.

[2] Maury to Madison, May 4, July 21, 1804, Consular Letters 2, Liverpool, Department of State, National Archives ; also Lord to Lady Minto, March 10, 1804, *Life and Letters of Minto*, III, 312-313.

[3] Colchester, *Diary and Correspondence*, II, 6, June 7. Memorandum : For the King and Cabinet, January 11, 1806, Sir John Knox Laughton (ed.), *Letters and Papers of Charles, Lord Barham, Admiral of the Red Squadron*, 1758-1813 (3 vols., London, 1907-1911), III, 108.

[4] Creevey to Dr. Currie, May 14, 1803, Sir Herbert Maxwell (ed.), *The Creevey Papers* (3rd. ed., London, 1905), 13-14.

[5] Thomas Barclay to Vice-Admiral Sir Thomas Mitchell, November 22, 1803, George L. Rives (ed.), *Selections from the Correspondence of Thomas Barclay* (New York, 1894), 154. Barclay was consul-general for Great Britain at New York from 1799 to 1812.

[6] Vincent to Hawkesbury, May 10, 1803, David B. Smith (ed.), *Letters of Admiral of the Fleet the Earl of St. Vincent whilst the First Lord of the Admiralty*, 1801-1804 (2 vols., London, 1922-1927), II, 291-292.

[7] Zimmerman, *Impressment of American Seamen*. Pages 260-263 give the figure 2,410 for the entire period before 1803, and the figure of 2,798 for the period 1803 to 1806. It is unlikely that these figures are entirely accurate, but at least they show the general trend. See also Arthur Bryant, *Years of Victory*, 1802-1812 (London, 1944), 24-25, and Perkins, *The First Rapprochement*, 65.

[8] Foster to Lady Elizabeth Foster, March 25, 1806, Vere Foster (ed.), *The Two Duchesses* (London, 1898), 276-278. Augustus John Foster was Secretary of Legation at Washington from 1804 to 1808, and Minister there from July, 1811, to June, 1812.

[9] For details of the various transactions in April and May, 1804, see Rev. Leveson Vernon Harcourt (ed.), *The Diaries and Correspondence of the Right Hon. George Rose* (2 vols., London, 1860), II, 113 ; Colchester, *Diary and Correspondence*, I, 496-515 ; William Wilberforce to Lord Muncaster, May 10, 1804, Robert I. and Samuel Wilberforce, *The Life of William Wilberforce* (5 vols., London, 1838), III, 159-161 ; Erich Eyck, *Pitt versus Fox : Father and Son*, 1735-1806 (London, 1950), 353-355. For position of Sidmouth see Colchester, *Diary and Correspondence*, I, 531-540, II, 15.

[10] Creevey to Dr. Currie, May 11, 1805, Maxwell, *Creevey Papers*, 36 ; Cyril Matheson, *The Life of Henry Dundas : First Viscount Melville*, 1742-1811 (London, 1933), 335-337.

[11] Captain Basil Hall, *Fragments of Voyages and Travels* (new ed., London, 1842), 46-49 ; also Rives, *Barclay Correspondence*, 162-188 ; Henry Adams, *History of the United States of America during the Administrations of Jefferson and Madison* (9 vols., New York, 1889-1891), III, 91-94.

[12] Harrowby to Merry, November 7, 1804, Bernard Mayo (ed.), *Instructions to the British Ministers to the United States, 1791-1812* (American Historical Association, *Annual Report*, 1936, III, Washington, 1941), 209 ; *Quarterly Review* (London), March, 1812, 29.

[13] Monroe to Madison, July 1, 1804, Stanislaus M. Hamilton, *The Writings of James Monroe* (7 vols., New York, 1898-1903), IV (1900), 218 ; Samuel F. Bemis, *A Diplomatic History of the United States* (3rd. ed., New York, 1953), 140. Figures taken from Alfred T. Mahan, *The Influence of Sea Power upon the French Revolution and Empire*, 1793-1812 (2 vols., Boston, 1892), II, 267. See also Anna C. Clauder, *American Commerce as Affected by the Wars of the French Revolution and Napoleon*, 1793-1812 (Philadelphia, 1932), 67-79.

[14] Ragatz, *Fall of the Planter Class*, 229-230.

[15] *Journals of the House of Commons*, LXI (1806), 363.

[16] Ragatz, *Fall of the Planter Class*, 286-301.

[17] (London, 1801), 14-15.

[18] *Collection of Interesting and Important Reports and Papers on the Navigation and Trade of Great Britain, Ireland, and the British Colonies in the West Indies and America* (Printed by Order of the Society of Shipowners of Great Britain, London, 1807), lvii ; xcviii, March 24, 1804.

[19] *Ibid.*, lxiv-lxxviii.

[20] *The Case of the Owners of the British Ships* (London, 1803).

[21] Sheffield, *Strictures on the Necessity of Inviolably Maintaining the Navigation and Colonial System of Great Britain* (London, 1804 ; enlarged ed., 1806).

[22] *Ibid.*, 12-19, 29, 36.

[23] *Collection of Interesting and Important Reports*, xxv ; Perkins, *The First Rapprochement*, 176.

[24] Gibbes W. Jordan, *The Claim of the West India Colonists to the Right of Obtaining Necessary Supplies in America* (London, 1804). Jordan was the colonial agent for Barbados from 1805 to 1823 ; S. Cock, *An Answer to Lord Sheffield's Pamphlet on the Subject of the Navigation System* (London, 1804). Cock was the commercial and public agent for the port of Liverpool.

[25] *Annuel Register*, XLVIII (London, 1806), 81.

[26] *Ibid.*, 81-82, for address to the King of December 18, 1804 ; Mayo, *Instructions to British Ministers*, 215 n. 10.

[27] Anthony Merry to Harrowby, January 25, 1805, Foreign Office Records, Public Records Office, London, transcripts in the Library of Congress, F.O. 5 : 45 ; Mulgrave to Merry, March 8, 1805, Mayo, *Instructions to British Ministers*, 214-215 ; *Annual Register*, XLVIII (1806), 82.

298   NOTES

[28] Good brief discussion in Perkins, *The First Rapprochement*, 177-180.

[29] Monroe to Mulgrave, August 12, 1805, Consular Letters 9, London, Department of State, National Archives ; Monroe to Madison, February 2, 1806, James Monroe Papers, Library of Congress, vol. XII ; also Adams, *History of the United States*, III, 96-97.

[30] Perkins, *The First Rapprochement*, 180 ; Monroe to Jefferson, November 1, 1805, Thomas Jefferson Papers, Library of Congress, vol. CLIII. Monroe told Jefferson that the pamphlet was said to have been written under the auspices of the government.

[31] Stephen, *War in Disguise*, 16-32, 34-57, 90, 92-95, 114, 123.

[32] *Ibid.*, 155, 163.

[33] *Ibid.*, 166, 172-176, 202-204.

[34] Lady Bessborough to Granville Leveson-Gower, January 23, 1806, Castalia Countess Granville (ed.), *Lord Granville Leveson-Gower (first earl Granville) : Private Correspondence*, 1781-1821 (2 vols., London, 1916), II, 162-163 ; Bryant, *Years of Victory*, 188-190.

CHAPTER 3 : AMERICAN INDECISION

[1] Jefferson to Livingston, April 18, 1802, Paul L. Ford (ed.), *The Writings of Thomas Jefferson* (10 vols., New York, 1892-1899), VIII (1897), 145 ; Charles E. Hill, " James Madison," in Samuel F. Bemis (ed.), *The American Secretaries of State and their Diplomacy* (10 vols., New York, 1927-1929), III (1927), 9-11.

[2] Madison to Livingston and Monroe, April 18, 1803, *American State Papers. Class I. Foreign Relations*, II (Washington, 1832), 555-556; Adams, *History of the United States*, II, 2-3, 349.

[3] Perkins, *The First Rapprochement*, 138-143 ; Burt, *United States, Great Britain*, 185-197.

[4] Professor Burt stresses this point in his excellent study of this period, *ibid.*, 225.

[5] Madison to Monroe, February 14, 1804, *American State Papers, Foreign Relations*, III, 89-90 ; Burt, *United States, Great Britain*, 197.

[6] Mrs. Samuel Smith to Mrs. Kirkpatrick, January, 1804, Margaret Bayard Smith, *The First Forty Years of Washington Society. Portrayed by the Family Letters of Mrs. Samuel Harrison Smith (Margaret Bayard) from the Collection of her grandson, J. Henley Smith*. Edited by Gaillard Hunt (New York, 1906), 46 ; Merry to Hawkesbury, December 6, 31, 1803, F.O. 5 : 41 ; also Merry to George Hammond, *ibid.*, December 7, 1803 ; Adams, *History of the United States*, II, 360-381.

[7] Augustus Foster to Lady Elizabeth Foster, December 1, 1805, Foster, *Two Duchesses*, 255 ; Madison to Monroe, February 16, 1804, Gaillard Hunt (ed.), *The Writings of James Madison* (9 vols., New York, 1900-1910), VII (1908), 120 ; Jefferson to Monroe, January 8, 1804, Ford, *Writings of Jefferson*, VIII, 291.

[8] Foster to Lady Foster, December 30, 1804, February 8, June 2, November, 1805, Foster, *Two Duchesses*, 197, 204-205, 226, 247.

[9] Burt, *United States, Great Britain*, 226-227 ; Perkins, *The First Rapprochement*, 155-156.

[10] Madison to Monroe, December 26, 1803, *Letters and Other Writings of James Madison* (Published by Order of Congress, 4 vols., New York, 1865), II, 189-191 ; Madison to Monroe, January 5, 1804, *American State Papers, Foreign Relations*, III, 81-89.

[11] *Annals of Congress*, 8th Congress, 1st Session, 232, 264 ; also Zimmerman, *Impressment of American Seamen*, 101 ff.

[12] Harrowby to Merry, November 7, 1804, Mayo, *Instructions to British Ministers*, 211-212 ; *American State Papers, Foreign Relations*, III, 88-89.

[13] Madison to Monroe, March 8, 1804, *Letters and Other Writings of Madison*, II, 200-201.

[14] See above pp. 29-30.

[15] Jefferson to Levi Lincoln, September 16, 1804, Ford, *Writings of Jefferson*, VIII, 321-322.

[16] Madison to Monroe, March 6, 1805, Hunt, *Writings of Madison*, VII, 168-176.

[17] This is discussed in Zimmerman, *Impressment of American Seamen*, 104.

[18] Adams, *History of the United States*, II, 245 ff., 422, III, 22-53 ; Madison to Monroe, April 15, 1804, Hunt, *Writings of Madison*, VII, 141-153.

[19] Madison to Livingston, July 5, 1805, James Madison Papers, Library of Congress, vol. XXIX.

[20] Jacob Wagner to Jefferson, July 29, 1805, Jefferson Papers, vol. CLI.

[21] *Ibid.*, Jefferson to Madison, August 4, 1805 ; also Jefferson to Madison, and to the Secretary of the Navy, August 7, 1805.

[22] Jefferson to Madison, August 17, 1805, Jefferson Papers, vol. CLII ; Jefferson to Madison, August 25, 1805, Madison Papers, vol. XXIX.

[23] Madison to Jefferson, September 1, 1805, Jefferson to Madison, August 27, 1805, Jefferson Papers, vol. CLII.

[24] *Ibid.*, Jefferson to Madison, September 16, 18, 1805, Gallatin to Jefferson, September 12, 1805 ; also *ibid.*, vol. CLIII, Jefferson to Madison, October 11, 1805, Madison to Jefferson, September 30, 1805.

[25] *Ibid.*, vol. CLII, Crowinshield to Jefferson, September 11, 1805 ; Madison to Monroe, September 24, 1805, Madison Papers, vol. XXIX ; Madison to Jefferson, October 5, 1805, Jefferson Papers, vol. CLIII ; Merry to Mulgrave, September 30, 1805, F.O. 5 : 45.

[26] Madison to Jefferson, September 30, 1805, Jefferson Papers, vol. CLIII.

[27] *Ibid.*, Madison to Jefferson, October 16, 1805.

[28] *Ibid.*, Jefferson to Madison, and to Gallatin, October 23, 1805, to

the Secretary of the Navy, October 24, 1805, to General Samuel Smith, November 1, 1805.

[29] *Ibid.*, Jefferson to W. C. Nicholas, October 25, 1805.

[30] Adams, *History of the United States*, III, 106 ff.

[31] Merry to Mulgrave, November 3, December 2, 1805, F.O. 5 : 45 ; Foster to Lady Foster, December 1, 1805, Foster, *Two Duchesses*, 253.

[32] Message of December 3, 1805, James D. Richardson, *A Compilation of the Messages and Papers of the Presidents* (10 vols., Washington, 1896-1899), I, 382-388; Merry to Mulgrave, December 3, 1805, F.O. 5 : 45.

[33] Monroe to Jefferson, November 1, 1805, Jefferson Papers, vol. CLIII ; Monroe to Madison, January 10, 1806, Monroe Papers, vol. XII.

[34] *Annals of Congress*, 9th Congress, 1st Session, 412-413 ; also Thomas Barclay to Sir Andrew Mitchell, February 1, 1806, Rives, *Barclay Correspondence*, 227 ; Merry to Mulgrave, February 2, 1806, F.O. 5 : 48.

[35] Madison, *An Examination of the British Doctrine, which Subjects to Capture a Neutral Trade, not Open in Time of Peace* (Philadelphia, 1806) ; Irving Brant, *James Madison : Secretary of State*, 1800-1809 (Indianapolis, 1953), 293-299.

[36] Merry to Mulgrave, February 2, 1806, F.O. 5 : 48. A direct answer to Stephen's work was given by Gouverneur Morris, *An Answer to War in Disguise* (New York, 1806).

[37] *Annals of Congress*, 9th Congress, 1st Session, 55-67, 449-451 (February 10, 1806), 458-460 ; Zimmerman, *Impressment of American Seamen*, 110-111, 160.

[38] Jefferson to Livingston, September 9, 1801, Ford, *Writings of Jefferson*, VIII, 91. Adams, *History of the United States*, I, 212-215, has a good summary of Jefferson's earlier statements on this question.

[39] Madison to Jefferson, September 14, 1805, Jefferson Papers, vol. CLII ; Monroe to Jefferson, November 1, 1805, *ibid.*, vol. CLIII.

[40] Charles F. Adams (ed.), *Memoirs of John Quincy Adams* (12 vols., Philadelphia, 1874-1877), I, 408 (February 13), 415 (February 25).

[41] *Annals of Congress*, 9th Congress, 1st Session, 537 ff.

[42] *Ibid.*, 552-553.

[43] *Ibid.*, 559.

[44] *Ibid.*, 537-778, 801 ff., 240. See also Hill, "James Madison," in Bemis (ed.), *American Secretaries of State*, III, 60 ff. The list consisted of articles composed of leather, silk, hemp, tin or brass, expensive woolens, glass, paper, silverware, men's hats, millinery, beer, and ale.

[45] Breckenridge to Henry Clay, March 22, 1806, Henry Clay Papers, Library of Congress, vol. I.

[46] Jefferson to Thomas Paine, March 25, 1806, Ford, *Writings of Jefferson*, VIII, 438.

Chapter 4 : A Whig Interlude

[1] For the various maneuvers at this time see Harcourt, *Diaries and Correspondence of Rose*, II, 222-253 ; Colchester, *Diary and Correspondence*, II, 37-38 ; Alan F. Fremantle, *England in the Nineteenth Century*, 1806-1810 (London, 1930), 147-150 ; H. W. Carless Davis, *The Age of Grey and Peel* (Oxford, 1929), 115-116.

[2] Lady Bessborough to Lord Granville Leveson-Gower, February 24, 1806, *Granville Private Correspondence*, II, 180.

[3] Adams, *History of the United States*, III, 415-440.

[4] William Wilberforce to Lord Muncaster, May 10, 1804, Wilberforce, *Life of Wilberforce*, III, 161.

[5] Quoted in Marjorie Villiers, *The Grand Whiggery* (London, 1939), 201.

[6] From manuscript material in the possession of Lord Dormer, quoted in Dorothy M. Stuart, *Dearest Bess : The Life and Times of Lady Elizabeth Foster* (London, 1955), 138.

[7] For the illness of Fox see Colchester, *Diary and Correspondence*, II, 48, 50, 53, 71, 73-76.

[8] Lady Bessborough to Lord Granville Leveson-Gower, June 29, 1806, *Granville Private Correspondence*, II, 205.

[9] Mayo, *Instructions to British Ministers*, 223 n. 16, 223-225 ; Creevey to Dr. Currie, March 22, 1804, Maxwell, *Creevey Papers*, 25.

[10] Auckland to Lord Grenville, April 7, 1806, Walter Fitzpatrick (ed.), *Report on the Manuscripts of J. B. Fortescue Esq., preserved at Dropmore* (10 vols., Historical Manuscripts Commission, London, 1892-1927), VIII (1912), 85. Hereafter cited as *Dropmore Papers*.

[11] Colchester, *Diary and Correspondence*, II, 51, April 20, 1806.

[12] Stuart, *Dearest Bess*, 135.

[13] Fox to Merry, March 7, 1806, Mayo, *Instructions to British Ministers*, 220 and n. 3.

[14] Merry to Fox, June 1, 1806, F.O. 5 : 49.

[15] Lord Erskine to Lord Grenville, May 20, 1806, *Dropmore Papers*, VIII, 152. David M. Erskine (1776-1855) was minister in the United States from November, 1806, to October, 1809.

[16] Madison to Monroe, May 25, 1807, Madison Papers, vol. XXXII.

[17] Thomas Barclay to Vice-Admiral Berkeley, November 17, 1806, Rives, *Barclay Correspondence*, 249.

[18] Thomas C. Hansard (ed.), *The Parliamentary Debates from the Year* 1803 *to the Present Time*, vols. I-XXIII, 1803-1812 (London, 1812), V, 732-733, July 4, 1805. Hereafter cited as *Hansard*.

[19] Grenville to Auckland, March 4, 1806, *Dropmore Papers*, VIII, 47-48.

[20] *Annual Register*, XLVIII (1806), 83.

[21] Auckland to Grenville, March 4, 16, 1806, *Dropmore Papers*, VIII, 47, 59.

302

[22] *Hansard*, VI, 592-597 ; Auckland to Grenville, April 17, 1806, *Dropmore Papers*, VIII, 102.

[23] *Journals of the House of Lords*, XLV (1805-1806), 565 ; *Journals of the House of Commons*, LXI (1806), 560 ; *Annual Register*, XLIII (1806), 84-85 ; Ragatz, *Fall of the Planter Class*, 301-302.

[24] *Annual Register*, XLVIII (1806), 85.

[25] Among the pamphlets supporting the shipping interest issued in 1806 were Jerome Alley, *A Vindication of the Principles and Statements Advanced in the Strictures of the Right Hon. Lord Sheffield* (London, 1806) ; Anonymous, *An Examination of the Alleged Expediency of the American Intercourse Bill* (London, 1806) ; Anonymous, *Observations on the American Intercourse Bill and the Necessity of Adhering Strictly to the Navigation Laws of Great Britain* (London, 1806) ; Lord Sheffield, *Strictures on the Necessity of Inviolably Maintaining the Navigation and Colonial System of Great Britain* (enlarged ed., London, 1806).

[26] *Observations on the American Intercourse Bill*, 7.

[27] Sheffield, *Strictures*, 252.

[28] Alley, *A Vindication*, 29, 82.

[29] *Ibid.*, 74-75 ; *Observations on the American Intercourse Bill*, 4-5 ; Sheffield, *Strictures*, 140-215, 251, 271-292.

[30] *Observations on the American Intercourse Bill*, 12-15 ; Sheffield, *Strictures*, 134-138, 251, 254-256, 305-308.

[31] Alley, *A Vindication*, 27-28.

[32] Sheffield, *Strictures*, 202.

[33] *Ibid.*, 196-198 ; Alley, *A Vindication*, 76-77.

[34] Alley, *A Vindication*, 74.

[35] *Collection of Interesting and Important Reports*, cxxi-cxxii.

[36] *Journals of the House of Commons*, LXI (1806), 311, 358-359, 362-363, 375, 409, 415.

[37] See above pp. 36-39.

[38] Rose to Viscount Lowther, June 15, 1806, J. J. Cartwright (ed.), *The Manuscripts of the Earl of Lonsdale* (Historical Manuscripts Commission, London, 1893), 193.

[39] *Hansard*, VII, 336-347, 349, 508, 689-690, 696, 716-717.

[40] Auckland to Grenville, May 17, 1806, *Dropmore Papers*, VIII, 141-142.

[41] *Collection of Interesting and Important Reports*, clviii, clx-clxi.

[42] *Granville Private Correspondence*, I, 345, quoted in Bryant, *Years of Victory*, 31.

[43] *Hansard*, VI, 595-596, 835-836, VII, 96, 116-117, 341, 346-347, 691-692, 696, 969, 983-984, 999-1000.

[44] *Ibid.*, VII, 697-712.

[45] *Ibid.*, 345.

[46] *Ibid.*, 725-726, June 17, 1806.

[47] *Ibid.*, 969, also 346, 696.

⁴⁸ *Ibid.*, 970, 971.

⁴⁹ *Ibid.*, 974-984.

⁵⁰ *Ibid.*, 344.

⁵¹ See above p. 68.

⁵² *Hansard*, VI, 594.

⁵³ *Ibid.*, VII, 1009.

⁵⁴ Grenville to Auckland, February 18, 1806, *Dropmore Papers*, VIII, 36-37.

⁵⁵ Phillips and Reede, *Neutrality*, II, 130-131.

⁵⁶ See Tench Coxe to Madison, June 8, 1806, Madison Papers, vol. XXX.

⁵⁷ James Stephen (Introduction), *The Speech of the Hon. John Randolph . . . on a Motion for the Non-Importation of British Merchandize* (London, 1806), xxx.

CHAPTER 5 : THE MONROE-PINKNEY TREATY

¹ Jefferson to Monroe, May 4, 1806, Monroe Papers, vol. XIII.

² Thomas Barclay to Anthony Merry, April 26, 27, May 13, 1806, Rives, *Barclay Correspondence*, 230-233, 240-241.

³ Madison to Monroe, March 11, 1806, Private, Madison Papers, vol. XXX.

⁴ Jefferson to Monroe, March 16, 1806, Monroe Papers, vol. XIII.

⁵ *Ibid.*, Madison to Monroe and Pinkney, May 17, 1806 ; Madison to Monroe, May 17, 1806, Private, Madison Papers, vol. XXX.

⁶ Monroe to Madison, April 3, 18, 1806, *American State Papers, Foreign Relations*, III, 115-116 ; Fox to Merry, April 7, 1806, Mayo, *Instructions to British Ministers*, 221 ; Madison to Monroe, June 4, 1806, Private, Madison Papers, vol. XXX.

⁷ Note in Monroe's hand, July, 1806, Monroe Papers, vol. XIII.

⁸ *Ibid.*, Pinkney to Monroe, June 19, 1806, Sir Francis Vincent to Monroe, June 27, 1806, Monroe to Pinkney, July 5, 25, 1806 ; Grenville to Auckland, August 8, 1806, *Dropmore Papers*, VIII, 263.

⁹ Holland to Monroe, October 14, 1807, Monroe Papers, vol. XVI ; also *ibid.*, vol. XV, March, 1807.

¹⁰ Merry to Fox, May 4, 1806, F.O. 5 : 49 ; Foster to Lady Elizabeth Foster, November 7, 1806, Foster, *Two Duchesses*, 297.

¹¹ Henry Edward, Lord Holland (ed.), *Memoirs of the Whig Party during my Time, by Henry Richard Vassall Fox, third Baron Holland* (2 vols., London, 1852-1854), II, 103.

¹² Auckland to Grenville, August 21, 1806, *Dropmore Papers*, VIII, 289-290.

¹³ Earl of Ilchester (ed.), *The Journal of Elizabeth, Lady Holland* (2 vols., London, 1909), II, 191, December 12, 1806.

[14] Lady Bessborough to Lord Granville Leveson-Gower, September 10, 1806, *Granville Private Correspondence*, II, 208.

[15] Randolph to Monroe, December 5, 1806, Monroe Papers, vol. XIII.

[16] *Ibid.*, William Wirt to Monroe, June 10, 1806.

[17] Memorandum : for the King and Cabinet, January 11, 1806, Laughton, *Letters and Papers of Lord Barham*, III, 118.

[18] Zimmerman, *Impressment of American Seaman*, 120-122.

[19] Holland and Auckland to Lord Howick, October 20, 1806, quoted in Anthony Steel, " Impressment in the Monroe-Pinkney Negotiation, 1806-1807," *American Historical Review*, LVII (1951-1952), 357 ; also Steel, " Anthony Merry and the Anglo-American Dispute About Impressment, 1803-1806," *Cambridge Historical Journal*, IX (1947-1949), 331-351.

[20] *Monthly Review*, May, 1812, p. 66. For additional Whig opinions on impressment see *ibid.*, August, 1812, pp. 375-376 ; *Edinburgh Review*, October, 1807, pp. 9-24.

[21] Adams, *History of the United States*, III, 407-408 ; Monroe and Pinkney to Madison, September 11, 1806, and enclosure, *American State Papers, Foreign Relations*, III, 133-134, 137.

[22] Jefferson to Monroe, October 26, 1806, Monroe Papers, vol. XIII ; also Madison to Governor Williams, November 9, 1806, Madison Papers, vol. XXXI.

[23] Auckland to Charles Abbot, January 1, 1807, Colchester, *Diary and Correspondence*, II, 87.

[24] Ilchester, *Journal of Lady Holland*, II, 194, January 4, 1807 ; draft copy of the treaty is in the Monroe Papers, vol. XIV ; see also *American State Papers, Foreign Relations*, III, 147-151.

[25] *Ibid.*, 149 ; also Hill, " James Madison," in Bemis (ed.), *American Secretaries of State*, III, 114.

[26] Eli Hecksher, *The Continental System* (London, 1922), 88-97 ; Frank E. Melvin, *Napoleon's Navigation System* (New York, 1919), 6-14.

[27] *American State Papers, Foreign Relations*, III, 151-152 ; Auckland to Grenville, December 27, 1806, *Dropmore Papers*, VIII, 484-485.

[28] Monroe and Pinkney to Madison, January 3, 1807, Monroe Papers, vol. XIV.

[29] *Ibid.*, Madison to Monroe and Pinkney, February 3, 1807.

[30] Erskine to Lord Howick, March 6, 10, 1807, F.O. 5 : 52.

[31] Madison to Monroe, March 20, 1807, Madison Papers, vol. XXXI.

[32] Jefferson to Monroe, March 21, 1807, Monroe Papers, vol. XV.

[33] *Ibid.*, Nicholson to Monroe, April 12, 1807.

[34] Madison to George Joy, May 22, 1807, Madison Papers, vol. XXXII.

[35] Auckland to Grenville, December 18, 1806, *Dropmore Papers*, VIII, 473 ; Melvin, *Napoleon's Navigation System*, 41.

[36] Order is printed in *Hansard*, X, 126-128 ; Adams, *History of the United States*, III, 416.

[37] *Hansard*, VIII, 627.

[38] *Ibid.*, 641-643.

[39] *Ibid.*, 647.

[40] *Ibid.*, 620-633.

[41] *Ibid.*, 635-636.

[42] *Ibid.*, 646-647 ; Hecksher, *Continental System*, 245, gives the real value of exports of British produce to America in 1807 as £11,850,000.

[43] *Ibid.*, 324.

[44] Michael Roberts, *The Whig Party*, 1807-1812 (London, 1939), 336 n. I.

[45] Edmund C. Blunden, *Autobiography of Benjamin Robert Haydon* (London, 1927), 68, quoted in Bryant, *Years of Victory*, 213.

CHAPTER 6 : EMBARGO AND ORDERS IN COUNCIL

[1] Madison to Erskine, March 29, 1807, F.O. 5 : 52.

[2] Jefferson to Madison, April 25, 1807, Madison Papers, vol. XXXII.

[3] Madison to Monroe and Pinkney, May 20, 1807, Monroe Papers, vol. XV.

[4] Madison to Monroe, May 25, 1807, Private, Madison Papers, vol. XXXII ; Adams, *History of the United States*, III, 438.

[5] This order, dated June 1, 1807, is in F.O. 5 : 52.

[6] For a discussion of the details of the whole incident see Adams, *History of the United States*, IV, 1-26, and Burt, *United States, Great Britain*, 241-243.

[7] Richard B. Davis (ed.), *Jeffersonian America : Notes on the United States of America Collected in the Years 1805-6-7 and 11-12 by Sir Augustus John Foster, Bart.* (San Marino, California, 1954), 293.

[8] Erskine to Canning, July 2, 4, 17, 1807, F.O. 5 : 52 ; John Dawson to Madison, June 28, 1807, Madison Papers, vol. XXXII ; Adams, *History of the United States*, IV, 27-29.

[9] Barclay to Canning, July 2, 1807, Rives, *Barclay Correspondence*, 264.

[10] Gerry to Madison, July 5, 1807, Madison Papers, vol. XXXII.

[11] Erskine to Canning, July 31, 1807, F.O. 5 : 52.

[12] Richardson, *Messages and Papers of the Presidents*, I, 422-424.

[13] Jefferson to the Governor of Virginia, June 29, 1807, Ford, *Writings of Jefferson*, IX, 87-88.

[14] Jefferson to Thomas Cooper, July 9, 1807, *ibid.*, 102-103.

[15] Jefferson to John W. Eppes, July 12, 1807, *ibid.*, 107-108 ; also Jefferson to James Bowdoin, and to John Page, July 10, 17, 1807, *ibid.*, 117-119.

[16] Jefferson to General Samuel Smith, July 30, 1807, War of 1812 MSS, Indiana University Library ; Adams, *History of the United States*, IV, 30-31.

[17] Madison to Monroe, July 6, 1807, Hunt, *Writings of Madison*, VII 454-460.

[18] Canning to Monroe, July 25, August 3, 1807, *American State Papers, Foreign Relations*, III, 187-188.

[19] Madison to Monroe, July 25, 1807, Private, Madison Papers, vol. XXXII.

[20] *Ibid.*, Crowinshield to Madison, August 18, 1807 ; also *ibid.*, J. G. Jackson to Madison, August 2, 1807.

[21] *Ibid.*, Gallatin to Madison, August 15, 1807 ; Raymond Walters, Jr., *Albert Gallatin : Jeffersonian Financier and Diplomat* (New York, 1957), 195-196.

[22] Barclay to Canning, August 5, 1807, to Vice-Admiral Berkeley, August, 1807, Rives, *Barclay Correspondence*, 264-268.

[23] Vice-Admiral Berkeley to Earl Bathurst, August 13, 1807, and *ibid.*, August 17, 1807, Francis Bickley (ed.), *Report on the MSS of Earl Bathurst, preserved at Cirencester Park* (Historical Manuscripts Commission, London, 1923), 63-65.

[24] Jefferson to Thomas Leiper, August 21, 1807, Jefferson Papers, vol. CLXX.

[25] *Ibid.*, Jefferson to Thomas Paine, September 6, 1807 ; also *ibid.*, vol. CLXXI, Jefferson to J. W. Eppes, and to the Attorney General, October 8, 1807.

[26] *Ibid.*, Jefferson to Paine, October 9, 1807. Jefferson was placing hope in the fact that the alliance of Napoleon and Alexander of Russia, which had been consummated by the Treaty of Tilsit in July, 1807, would force England to recognize the rights of neutrals.

[27] *Ibid.*, vol. CLXXII, Gallatin to Jefferson, October 21, 1807.

[28] *Ibid.*, Jefferson to Randolph, October 26, November 30, 1807, to Governor Cabell, November 1, 1807 ; Monroe to Madison, October 10, 1807, *American State Papers, Foreign Relations*, III, 191.

[29] *Ibid.*, 25-26 ; Adams, *History of the United States*, IV, 166.

[30] Erskine to Canning, December 21, 1807, F.O. 5 : 52 ; Adams, *History of the United States*, IV, 166-167 ; Brant, *James Madison : Secretary of State*, 394.

[31] Jefferson to the Senate and the House, December 17, 1807, Jefferson Papers, vol. CLXXIII ; Adams, *History of the United States*, IV, 168-171 ; Walters, *Albert Gallatin*, 198; Brant, *James Madison : Secretary of State*, 394-395.

[32] *Annals of Congress*, 10th Congress, 1st Session, 50-51, 1217-1223.

[33] Erskine to Canning, December 23, 1807, F.O. 5 : 52.

[34] See for example, Anonymous, *Concessions to America the Bane of Britain* (London, 1807) ; Joseph Lowe, *An Inquiry into the State of the British West Indies* (London, 1807) ; Mercator (pseud.), *Third Letter on the Abolition of the Slave Trade, and Other West Indian Affairs* (London, 1807); Vindex (pseud.), *On the Maritime Rights of Great Britain* (London, 1807). For Stephen's arguments see above pp. 39-42.

[35] *Concessions to America*, 23.

[36] *Ibid.*, 44, 50.

[37] *Ibid.*, 47-50.

[38] *Collection of Interesting Reports and Papers on the Navigation and Trade of Great Britain, Ireland, and the British Colonies in the West Indies and America* (Printed by Order of the Society of Shipowners of Great Britain, London, 1807), xxii.

[39] Macall Medford, *Oil without Vinegar, and Dignity without Pride; or British, American, and West India Interests Considered* (London, 1807), 12-13. Medford was an American who had spent considerable time in England. He sent a copy of his pamphlet to Jefferson, Medford to Jefferson, September 14, 1807, Jefferson Papers, vol. CLXXI.

[40] Medford, *Oil without Vinegar*, 30.

[41] *Ibid.*, 79-80, 84.

[42] *Edinburgh Review*, October, 1807, p. 9.

[43] *Ibid.*, 30.

[44] William F. Galpin, *The Grain Supply of England during the Napoleonic Period* (Philadelphia, 1925), 45-48.

[45] *Journals of the House of Commons*, LXII (1807), 188.

[46] *Hansard*, IX, 85-101, 140-141 (March 17, 1807) ; *Journals of the House of Commons*, LXII (1807), 281-282, March 24, 1807. There were also petitions by the West India merchants to the Board of Trade, Galpin, *Grain Supply of England*, 51.

[47] *Hansard*, X, lxxx-lxxxvi, Appendix to the Parliamentary Debates, *Report of the Committee of the House of Commons on the Commercial State of the West India Colonies.*

[48] See Nathaniel Atcheson, *American Encroachments on British Rights ; or, Observations on the Importance of the British North American Colonies and on the Late Treaties with the United States* (London, 1808), *Appendix, Minutes of the Evidence Taken Before the Committee of the House of Commons on the Commercial State of the West India Islands*, 119-238.

[49] *Hansard*, IX, Appendix, lxxx-lxxxiii.

[50] *Ibid.*, lxxxiv.

[51] *Ibid.*, lxxxiv-lxxxvi.

[52] See above pp. 96-97.

[53] Castlereagh to Perceval, October 1, 1807, Charles Vane, third Marquis of Londonderry (ed.), *Memoirs and Correspondence of Viscount Castlereagh, Second Marquis of Londonderry* (London, 1848-1853), VIII (1851), 87-88.

[54] See Spencer Walpole, *The Life of the Right Hon. Spencer Perceval* (2 vols., London, 1874), I, 264-269 ; also Adams, *History of the United States*, IV, 79-104.

[55] Fremantle, *England in the Nineteenth Century*, 1806-1810, p. 227.

[56] Walpole, *Spencer Perceval*, I, 267-268.

[57] Brougham to Lord Howick, September 13, 1807, Henry Brougham, *Memoirs of the Life and Times of Henry Brougham* (3 vols., Edinburgh, 1871-1872), I, 383-384.

[58] Henry Lord Brougham, *Historical Sketches of Statesmen who Flourished in the Time of George III* (3 vols., London, 1839-1843), I, 251.

[59] Diary of William Wilberforce, January 9, 1808, Wilberforce, *Life of Wilberforce*, III, 358.

[60] Lord Stavordale (ed.), *Further Memoirs of the Whig Party, 1807-1821, with some Miscellaneous Reminiscences, by Henry Richard Vassall, third Lord Holland* (London, 1905), 159.

[61] Colchester, *Diary and Correspondence*, II, 134-135.

[62] For the text of these Orders, and the various supplementary Orders issued during November, see *Hansard*, X, 131-148 ; for an interpretation of the meaning of the Orders see Report of the Committee of American Merchants, November 21, 1807, F.O. 115 : 16. Fremantle, *England in the Nineteenth Century*, 1806-1810, p. 226, gives a reasonable simplification of these measures. The whole system of the free ports is treated in Frances Armytage, *The Free Port System in the British West Indies*, 1766-1822 (London, 1953).

[63] *American State Papers, Foreign Relations*, III, 290-291.

[64] Augustus Foster to Lady Foster, March 31, 1807, Foster, *Two Duchesses*, 309.

[65] Canning to Erskine, December 1, 1807, Mayo, *Instructions to British Ministers*, 245.

CHAPTER 7 : THE FAILURE OF THE EMBARGO

[1] The standard works are Louis M. Sears, *Jefferson and the Embargo* (Durham, North Carolina, 1927), and Walter W. Jennings, *The American Embargo, 1807-1809* (Iowa City, 1921). There is also considerable information in Adams, *History of the United States*, IV, 200-289, 339-383, 408-453.

[2] Auckland to Grenville, November 7, 1807, *Dropmore Papers*, IX, 143.

[3] Grenville to the Marquis of Buckingham, November 23, 1807, Duke of Buckingham and Chandos, *Memoirs of the Court and Cabinets of George III*, vol. IV, 210 ; also *ibid.*, 224-225, W. H. Fremantle to Buckingham, December 31, 1807.

[4] Auckland to Grenville, January 18, 24, 1808, *Dropmore Papers*, IX 173-174 ; see also a letter of February 12, 1808, *ibid.*, 177-178, in which Auckland discussed the possibility of drawing the public attention to the state of affairs by action in regard to the Orders in Council.

[5] *Hansard*, X, 126-128. The papers laid before the House included the Whig Order of January 7, 1807, with the explanatory Orders of February 4, 18, and August 19, in addition to the main Orders of November 11,

18, and 25. In all, on these three dates in November, 1807, ten Orders were issued.

⁶ *Ibid.*, 153, 314, 320, 465-469, 477-483, 735-736, 929-971.

⁷ *Ibid.*, 317-318, 465-469, 665-666, 676-678, 780-783, 929-971.

⁸ Lady Bessborough to Lord Granville Leveson-Gower, February 6, 1807, *Granville Private Correspondence*, II, 236-237.

⁹ *Hansard*, X, 485.

¹⁰ See especially *Six Letters of A.B. on the Differences between Great Britain and the United States of America. Preface by the Editor of the Morning Chronicle* (London, 1807). These were originally published in the *Morning Chronicle* (London) in November and December, 1807 ; *Edinburgh Review*, October, 1807, pp. 1-30, January, 1808, pp. 484-498, April, 1808, pp. 225-246.

¹¹ Baring, *An Inquiry into the Causes and Consequences of the Orders in Council ; and an Examination of the Conduct of Great Britain towards the Neutral Commerce of America* (London, 1808). Another pamphlet presenting the Whig point of view was the anonymous *Orders in Council, or an Examination of the Justice, Legality, and Policy of the New System of Commercial Regulations* (London, 1808).

¹² Ralph W. Hidy, *The House of Baring in American Trade and Finance. English Merchant Bankers at Work*, 1763-1861 (Cambridge, Mass., 1949), 32-34.

¹³ Sir Francis Baring to Rufus King, March 1, 1804, Charles R. King (ed.), *The Life and Correspondence of Rufus King* (6 vols., New York, 1894-1900), IV (1897), 386.

¹⁴ Herbert Heaton, "The American Trade," in C. Northcote Parkinson (ed.), *The Trade Winds* (London, 1948), 201-202. This position was clearly stated in the evidence given before Parliament by opponents of the Orders in Council in the spring of 1808, see *Minutes of Evidence upon Taking into Consideration several Petitions, Presented to the House of Commons, Respecting the Orders in Council* (London, 1808), *passim*.

¹⁵ The pamphlet was given an enthusiastic reception by the *Edinburgh Review*, April, 1808, pp. 225-246, and by the *Monthly Review*, March, 1808, pp. 306-318.

¹⁶ Pinkney to Madison, February 22, 1808, Madison Papers, vol. XXXIII.

¹⁷ *Hansard*, X, 483.

¹⁸ Baring, *Inquiry*, 12.

¹⁹ *Ibid.*, 136, also 1-10, 72-82.

²⁰ *Ibid.*, 170.

²¹ *Ibid.*, 129.

²² *Ibid.*, 146, also 4-6, 138-153.

²³ See the *Examiner*, January, 17, 24, 31, 1808, for rumors and definite news of the Embargo.

²⁴ Pinkney to Madison, November 23, 1807, *American State Papers, Foreign Relations*, III, 203 ; Auckland to Grenville, February 12, 20, May 23, 1808, *Dropmore Papers*, IX, 177-179, 200-201.

²⁵ For accounts of this meeting see *Aris' Birmingham Gazette*, March 7, 1808, and the *Leicester Journal*, March 11, 1808.

²⁶ *Aris' Birmingham Gazette*, March 14, 1808.

²⁷ *Courier*, March 11, 1808 ; *Cobbett's Political Register* (London), March 19, 1808 ; *Hansard*, X, 1058-1059.

²⁸ *Hansard*, X, 889-895, 1056-1065 ; *Journals of the House of Commons*, LXIII (1808), 163, 168, 194, 203. Petitions were received in March from Liverpool, London, Manchester, Hull, and Cork.

²⁹ *Hansard*, X, 1182-1183.

³⁰ Creevey to Mrs. Creevey, October 17, 1812, Maxwell, *Creevey Papers*, 171.

³¹ For Brougham's contributions to the *Edinburgh Review* see Arthur Aspinall, *Lord Brougham and the Whig Party* (Manchester, 1927), appendix, 256-261. Brougham's " Randolph and Others on the Neutral Questions," *Edinburgh Review*, October, 1807, pp. 1-30, advocated friendship with the United States. He commented on this article in a letter to Lord Howick, November 7, 1807, Brougham, *Memoirs*, I, 387-388.

³² *Minutes of Evidence upon Taking into Consideration several Petitions, Presented to the House of Commons, Respecting the Orders in Council* (London, 1808).

³³ *Ibid.*, 23-38, 65-71.

³⁴ Abraham Mann was typical when he stated that he presumed the Embargo was adopted in consequence of the Orders, and if the Orders were removed the Embargo would also disappear, *ibid.*, 59.

³⁵ *Hansard*, X, 1235-1239.

³⁶ *Ibid.*, 1272.

³⁷ *Ibid.*, 1304. The speech was published as a pamphlet entitled *The Speech of Henry Brougham, Esq., before the House of Commons, Friday April 1, 1808, in Support of the Petitions from London, Liverpool, and Manchester, against the Orders in Council* (London, 1808).

³⁸ *Minutes of Evidence, Orders in Council*, 1808, pp. 107-171.

³⁹ *Dropmore Papers*, IX, 198 ; also Auckland to Grenville, May 18, 23, 1808, *ibid.*, 200-201.

⁴⁰ Taken from the table of exports of United Kingdom produce (real values) in Hecksher, *Continental System*, 245.

⁴¹ *European Magazine, and London Review*, January, 1808, pp. 77-78, February, 1808, p. 158, March, 1808, p. 237.

⁴² *Hansard*, X, 321-333, 469-471, 474-476, 485, 666-676.

⁴³ *Ibid.*, 683.

⁴⁴ *Ibid.*, 312-313.

⁴⁵ Quoted in Adams, *History of the United States*, IV, 326.

⁴⁶ Pinkney to Madison, August 2, 1808, Madison Papers, vol. XXXIV. Pinkney did think, however, that the Embargo was hurting England, Pinkney to Madison, September 21, 1808, *American State Papers, Foreign Relations*, III, 229.

⁴⁷ Pinkney to Canning, August 23, 1808, Canning to Pinkney, September 23, 1808, *ibid.*, 228, 231-232.

⁴⁸ Barclay to Sir John B. Warren, September 3, 1808, Rives, *Barclay Correspondence*, 283-284.

⁴⁹ Thomas Grenville to the Marquis of Buckingham, January 14, 1809, Duke of Buckingham and Chandos, *Memoirs of the Court and Cabinets of George III*, vol. IV, 299.

⁵⁰ Jefferson to Monroe, February 18, 1808, Monroe Papers, vol. XVI.

⁵¹ Canning to Rose, October 24, 1807, and Draft of Convention, October 25, 1807, Mayo, *Instructions to British Ministers*, 235-242.

⁵² Rives, *Barclay Correspondence*, 272, 275 ; Madison to Monroe, March 18, 1808, Madison Papers, vol. XXXIV. There is a good account of Rose's mission in Adams, *History of the United States*, IV, 178 ff., and in Brant, *James Madison : Secretary of State*, 404-418.

⁵³ Jefferson to Madison, March 11, 1808, to General Benjamin Smith, May 20, 1808, to Doctor Thomas Leib, June 23, 1808, Ford, *Writings of Jefferson*, IX, 179-180, 194-197.

⁵⁴ Jefferson to Madison, September 6, 1808, Madison Papers, vol. XXXV.

⁵⁵ Jefferson to Monroe, January 28, 1809, Monroe Papers, vol. XVII.

⁵⁶ Phillips and Reade, *Neutrality*, II, 175, 180 ; Adams, *History of the United States*, IV, 195, 303-304.

⁵⁷ *Annals of Congress*, 10th Congress, 2nd Session, 1203-1421, 1432.

⁵⁸ *Ibid.*, 911-912, 1437-1536, 1539-1541.

⁵⁹ Canning to Bathurst, March 24, 1809, Bickley, *Report on the MSS of Earl Bathurst*, 86-87.

⁶⁰ Robert Ferguson to Lieutenant General Alexander Ross, April 22, 1810, War of 1812 MSS, Indiana University Library.

CHAPTER 8 : THE ERSKINE AGREEMENT

¹ Adams, *History of the United States*, IV, 386-395 ; Canning to Erskine, January 23, 1809, Mayo, *Instructions to British Ministers*, 261.

² *Ibid.*, 261-266.

³ For these notes see *American State Papers, Foreign Relations*, III, 295-297.

⁴ The proclamation was issued on April 19, Richardson, *Messages and Papers of the Presidents*, I, 472.

⁵ Jefferson to Madison, March 17, 1809, Madison Papers, vol. XXXVI.

⁶ *Ibid.*, vol. XXXVII, Madison to Jefferson, April 9, 1809.

⁷ *Ibid.*, Rodney to Madison, April 17, 1809.

⁸ *Ibid.*, Jefferson to Madison, April 19, 1809.

⁹ *Ibid.*, Madison to Jefferson, April 24, May I, 1809.

¹⁰ Hamilton to Porter, May 23, 1809, War of 1812 MSS, Indiana University Library.

¹¹ *Ibid.*, Colonel Troup to Colonel John Ferguson, June 2, 1809.

¹² The most recent expression of this point of view is in Bradford Perkins, "George Canning, Great Britain, and the United States, 1807-1809." *American Historical Review*, LXIII (1957-1958), 1-22.

¹³ Bickley, *Report on the MSS of Earl Bathurst*, 87-89, April 12, 1809 ; Canning to Bathurst, March 24, 1809, *ibid.*, 86-87.

¹⁴ *Ibid.*, 89, *American State Papers, Foreign Relations*, III, 241.

¹⁵ Canning to Francis James Jackson, July 1, 1809, Mayo, *Instructions to British Ministers*, 285-286.

¹⁶ Canning to Bathurst, April 28, 1809, Bickley, *Report on the MSS of Earl Bathurst*, 91.

¹⁷ Pinkney to Madison, May 3, 1809, Reverend William Pinkney, *The Life of William Pinkney* (New York, 1853), 238.

¹⁸ Baring to King, May 2, 1809, King, *Correspondence of Rufus King*, V (1898), 155.

¹⁹ Canning to Erskine, May 2, 1809, F.O. 5 : 63 ; Canning to Francis James Jackson, July 1, 1809, Mayo, *Instructions to British Ministers*, 286.

²⁰ Madison to Jefferson, June 12, 1809, Madison Papers, vol. XXXVIII.

²¹ *Ibid.*, Jefferson to Madison, June 16, 1809.

²² *Ibid.*, Madison to Jefferson, June 20, 1809.

²³ *American State Papers, Foreign Relations*, III, 303 ; see also F.O. 5 : 63 *passim* for this whole question of the Erskine agreement and its disavowal ; Adams, *History of the United States*, VI, 108.

²⁴ Canning to Erskine, January 23, May 22, 23, 1809, Mayo, *Instructions to British Ministers*, 261-266, 270-276.

²⁵ Hamilton to Madison, July 24, 1809, Madison Papers, vol. XXXVIII ; *ibid.*, July 25.

²⁶ Canning to Erskine, May 30, 1809, Mayo, *Instructions to British Ministers*, 276.

²⁷ Canning to Jackson, July 1, 1809, *ibid.*, 277-287.

²⁸ Madison to Jefferson, August 3, 1809, Madison Papers, vol. XXXVIII.

²⁹ Richardson, *Messages and Papers of the Presidents*, I, 473 ; Madison to Jefferson, August 16, 1809, Madison Papers, vol. XXXVIII.

³⁰ *Ibid.*, Rodney to Jefferson, September 6, 1809.

³¹ *American State Papers, Foreign Relations*, III, 308-319 ; Wellesley to Jackson, April 14, 1810, Mayo, *Instructions to British Ministers*, 302-303.

³² Quoted in Bernard Mayo, *Henry Clay : Spokesman of the New West* (Boston, 1937), 325.

[33] Roberts, *The Whig Party, 1807-1812*, pp. 347-348 ; Fremantle, *England in the Nineteenth Century, 1806-1810*, pp. 289-297 ; Duke of Buckingham and Chandos, *Memoirs of the Court and Cabinets of George III*, vol. IV, 374-376 ; Earl of Roseberry (introd.), *The Windham Papers* (2 vols., London, 1913), II, 361-365.

[34] *American State Papers, Foreign Relations*, III, 349-364 ; Adams, *History of the United States*, V, 262-288.

[35] Julius W. Pratt, *Expansionists of 1812* (New York, 1925), 12-13.

CHAPTER 9 : THE PROBLEM OF THE WEST

[1] The population figures are taken from Frederick L. Paxson, *History of the American Frontier* (Boston, 1924), 73, 191.

[2] Francis Gore to Sir James Craig, April 2, 1808, *Michigan Pioneer and Historical Collections* (40 vols., Lansing, Michigan, 1877-1929), XXV (1896), 240 ; Burt, *United States, Great Britain*, 246.

[3] McKee to Prideaux Selby, August 12, 1804, *Michigan Pioneer and Historical Collections*, XXIII (1895), 31.

[4] The best treatment of this effect is Ernest A. Cruikshank, "The Chesapeake Crisis as It Affected Upper Canada," *Ontario Historical Society Papers and Records* (Toronto, 1899-   ), XXIV (1927), 281-322. There is very little analysis, but considerable source material. See also Isaac Brock to Thomas Dunn, July 17, 23, 1807, and Brock to Castlereagh, July 25, 1807, Ferdinand B. Tupper, *Life and Correspondence of Major General Sir Isaac Brock* (London, 1847), 60-63.

[5] Pratt, *Expansionists of 1812*, pp. 12, 42.

[6] William Claus to Gore, April 20, 1808, *Michigan Pioneer and Historical Collections*, XV (1889), 47-48 ; Cruikshank, "The *Chesapeake* Crisis," *Ontario Historical Society Papers and Records*, XXIV, 286-287.

[7] Craig to Gore, December 6, 1807, Douglas Brymner (ed.), *Report on the Canadian Archives, 1896* (Ottawa, 1897), Note B, 31.

[8] *Ibid.*, 32.

[9] Craig to Gore, December 28, 1807, *Michigan Pioneer and Historical Collections*, XXV, 232-233.

[10] Gore to Craig, January 5, 1808, *Report on Canadian Archives, 1896*, Note B, 36.

[11] Gore to William Claus, January 29, 1808, enclosing "Secret Instructions," RG 10, vol. 11 (Indian Affairs), Public Archives of Canada, Ottawa.

[12] Craig to David M. Erskine, May 13, 1808 ; Craig to Edward Cooke, July 15, 1808, *Report on Canadian Archives, 1893*, pp. 10, 13.

[13] Craig to Gore, May 11, 1808, RG 10, vol. 2 ; see also Burt, *United States, Great Britain*, 251-252.

[14] Gore to Craig, June 5, 1808, RG 10, vol. 486.

[15] *Ibid.*, and Gore to Craig, January 5, 1808, *Report on Canadian Archives* 1896, *Note B*, 36.

[16] Ernest A. Cruikshank (ed.), *Documents Relating to the Invasion of Canada and the Surrender of Detroit*, 1812 (Ottawa, 1912), 142 n. ; Gore to Craig, January 5, 1808, *Report on Canadian Archives*, 1896, Note B, 36 ; Gore to Craig, January 8, April 2, 1808, *Michigan Pioneer and Historical Collections*, XXV, 238-239, 240 ; Claus to Gore, April 20, 1808, *ibid.*, XV, 48 ; Craig to Gore, February 10, 1808, Miscellaneous Documents, vol. 8, Public Archives of Canada ; Claus to Selby, February 15, 1808, Craig to Gore, March 10, 1808, Cruikshank, " The *Chesapeake* Crisis," *Ontario Historical Society Papers and Records*, XXIV, 300-301.

[17] For a brief account of Elliott's early life see Alexander Fraser (ed.), " Proceedings of the Loyalist Commissioners, Montreal, 1787, Vol. 20," *Second Report of the Bureau of Archives for the Province of Ontario*, 1904 (Toronto, 1905), Part 2, pp. 985-987. See also Reuben G. Thwaites and Louise P. Kellogg (eds.), *Frontier Defense on the Upper Ohio*, 1777-1778 (Madison, 1912), 249-250 n. For the correspondence concerning Elliott's dismissal and his efforts to regain his position, see *Michigan Pioneer and Historical Collections*, XII (1888), 268-270, 300-301 ; XX (1892), 519-669 *passim* ; XXV, 155-216 *passim*.

[18] An excellent description of Elliott's house and farm is in Isaac Weld, *Travels through the States of North America and the Provinces of Upper and Lower Canada during the Years* 1795, 1796, *and* 1797 (London, 1799), 349 ; also Hector McLean to James Green, September 14, 1797, *Michigan Pioneer and Historical Collections*, XX, 538.

[19] *Ibid.*, XXXVI (1908), 181-189, 201-205 ; XV, 42. See also McKee to Selby, December 4, 1807, *ibid.*, XXIII, 42-43.

[20] Claus to Gore, February 14, 1808, *ibid.*, XXIII, 45 ; also Claus to Gore, February 27, 1808, *ibid.*, XV, 44-45.

[21] There is still no good modern biography of Tecumseh. Glenn Tucker, *Tecumseh : Vision of Glory* (Indianapolis, 1956), is colorful, but also over-imaginative and at times inaccurate. Benjamin Drake, *Life of Tecumseh, and of his Brother the Prophet* (Cincinnati, 1852), though an old study, is still in many ways the most valuable.

[22] Claus to Selby, March 25, 1808, Claus Papers, vol. 9, Public Archives of Canada ; " Proceedings of a Private Meeting with the Shawenoes," *Michigan Pioneer and Historical Collections*, XXV, 242-245 ; Gore to Craig, April 8, 1808, *ibid.*, XXV, 245.

[23] Account of John Johnston, Draper MSS, State Historical Society of Wisconsin, 11YY17 ; also *ibid.*, 1YY24, and 3YY60. The Bonner was reputed to have been first in General Arthur St. Clair's camp, along with Tecumseh and Blackfish, in 1791, see Account of Thomas Forsyth, *ibid.*, 8YY54. See also Hector McLean to James Green, August 8, 1799, *Michigan Pioneer and Historical Collections*, XX, 656, and Thomas Ridout's

narrative of his captivity by the Shawnee, in Lady Edgar (ed.), *Ten Years of Upper Canada in Peace and War*, 1805-1815 ; *Being the Ridout Letters* (Toronto, 1890), 370.

²⁴ Gore to Craig, January 5, 1808, *Report on Canadian Archives*, 1896, Note B, 37.

²⁵ Claus to Selby, May 3, 1808, *Michigan Pioneer and Historical Collections*, XV, 49 ; also Claus to Gore, May 22, 1808, *ibid.*, XXIII, 62.

²⁶ Craig to Gore, May 11, 1808, *ibid.*, XXV, 246.

²⁷ Claus to Gore, May 22, 1808, *ibid.*, XXIII, 62 ; also Diary of Claus, May 16, June 11, 13, 14, July 1, 1808, *ibid.*, 50, 53-57.

²⁸ Claus to Gore, April 20, *ibid.*, XV, 48.

²⁹ Claus to Selby, January 18, 1809, Military, Series C, vol. 256, Public Archives of Canada.

³⁰ Gore to Craig, February 20, 1809, *Michigan Pioneer and Historical Collections*, XV, 53.

³¹ See Castlereagh to the Earl of Chatham, December 31, 1807, Vane, *Castlereagh Correspondence*, VIII, 104-107.

³² Castlereagh to Craig, April 8, 1809, *Michigan Pioneer and Historical Collections*, XXIII, 69.

³³ Pratt, *Expansionists of 1812*, pp. 25-32, maintains this point of view.

³⁴ Resolutions of the Kentucky House of Representatives, December 16, 1808, Madison Papers, vol. XXXIX.

³⁵ Clay to John Breckenridge, January 5, 1806, quoted in Mayo, *Henry Clay*, 287.

³⁶ Arthur Campbell to Madison, August, 1807, Madison Papers, vol. XXXII.

³⁷ Worthington to Jefferson, August 23, 1807, Jefferson Papers, vol. CLXX.

³⁸ Pratt, *Expansionists of 1812*, p. 12. This was questioned by Burt, *United States, Great Britain*, 310.

³⁹ Quoted in Adams, *History of the United States*, IV, 36.

⁴⁰ Lafayette to Jefferson, September 10, 1807, Jefferson Papers, vol. CLXXI.

⁴¹ *Ibid.*, Campbell to Jefferson, October 10, 1807 ; see also John Nicholas to Madison, August 2, 1807, Madison Papers, vol. XXXII ; *ibid.*, Campbell to Madison, July 11, 1807.

⁴² Erastus Granger to Henry Dearborn, September 14, 1807, Jefferson Papers, vol. CLXXI.

⁴³ Gallatin to Jefferson, October 21, 1807, *ibid.*, CLXXII ; Walters, *Albert Gallatin*, 196-197.

⁴⁴ Warren H. Goodman, " The Origins of the War of 1812 : A Survey of Changing Interpretations," *Mississippi Valley Historical Review*, XXVIII (1941-1942), 177.

316 NOTESNOTES

[45] Castlereagh to the Earl of Chatham, December 31, 1807, Vane *Castlereagh Correspondence*, VIII, 106.

[46] Pratt, *Expansionists of 1812*, pp. 12, 120-125.

[47] Madison to Livingston and Monroe, March 2, 1803, *American State Papers, Foreign Relations*, II, 540-544.

[48] Adams, *History of the United States*, II, 68.

[49] Hill, "James Madison," in Bemis (ed.), *American Secretaries of State*, III, 43.

[50] See above pp. 51-56.

[51] Jefferson to Madison, September 1, 1807, Jefferson Papers, vol. CLXX.

[52] *Ibid.*, August 16, 1807.

[53] Canning to Jackson, July 1, 1809, Mayo, *Instructions to British Ministers*, 292.

[54] Richardson, *Messages and Papers of the Presidents*, I, 480-481 ; Isaac J. Cox, *The West Florida Controversy, 1798-1813 : A Study in American Diplomacy* (Baltimore, 1918), 312-436.

[55] Morier to Robert Smith, December 15, 1810, *American State Papers, Foreign Relations*, III, 399.

[56] Pratt, *Expansionists of 1812*, pp. 76-119 ; Cox, *West Florida Controversy*, 487 ff.

[57] Several historians have questioned the importance of the demand for Florida in producing a war with England. See Burt, *United States, Great Britain*, 306 ; Goodman, "The Origins of the War of 1812," *Mississippi Valley Historical Review*, XXVIII, 181 ; Margaret Kinnard Latimer, "South Carolina—A Protagonist of the War of 1812," *American Historical Review*, LXI (1955-1956), 927-928.

[58] See Charles O. Paullin and John K. Wright, *Atlas of the Historical Geography of the United States* (Washington, 1932), 109.

[59] Samuel E. Morison, *The Maritime History of Massachusetts* (Boston, 1941), 191.

[60] These factors are discussed in Latimer, "South Carolina—A Protagonist of the War of 1812," *American Historical Review*, LXI, 914-929.

[61] See Louis M. Hacker, "Western Land Hunger and the War of 1812: A Conjecture," *Mississippi Valley Historical Review*, X (1923-1924), 366.

[62] George Rogers Taylor, "Prices in the Mississippi Valley Preceding the War of 1812," *Journal of Economic and Business History*, III (1930), 148.

[63] Figures taken from *ibid.*, 154-163. See also Arthur H. Cole (ed.), *Wholesale Commodity Prices in the United States, 1700-1861* (2 vols., Cambridge, Mass., 1938), I, 65-76, II (Statistical Supplement), 131-164.

[64] See George Rogers Taylor, "Agrarian Discontent in the Mississippi Valley Preceding the War of 1812," *Journal of Political Economy*, XXXIX (1931), 471-505.

CHAPTER 10 : THE TURN OF THE TIDE

¹ Jefferson to Madison, August 17, 1809, Madison Papers, vol. XXXVIII.

² *Ibid.*

³ Resolutions from Washington County, Kentucky, August 28, 1809 ; Charleston and Columbia, South Carolina, September 5 and 20, 1809 ; City and County of New York, September 16, 1809 ; McIntosh County, Georgia, September 25, 1809, *ibid.*, and vol. XXXIX.

⁴ See David Ramsey to Madison, September 5, 1809 ; Caesar A. Rodney to Madison, October 17, 1809 ; Jefferson to Madison, November 26, 1809, *ibid.*, vols. XXXVIII and XXXIX.

⁵ See above pp. 153-155

⁶ Madison to George Joy, January 17, 1810, Madison Papers, vol. XL.

⁷ *Ibid.*, Resolutions of the First Congressional District of Pennsylvania (at Philadelphia), February 14, 1810.

⁸ *Ibid.*, Resolutions of the General Assembly of Ohio, February 22, 1810.

⁹ The material relating to Clay in this paragraph is taken from Mayo, *Henry Clay*.

¹⁰ *Annals of Congress*, 11th Congress, 2nd Session, *passim.*

¹¹ *Ibid.*, 579-582, February 22.

¹² See above pp. 168-171.

¹³ James L. Harrison (comp.), *Biographical Directory of the American Congress*, 1774-1949 (Washington, 1950), 94-98.

¹⁴ *Annals of Congress*, 12 Congress, 2nd Session, 498, January 2, 1813. Matthew Clay (1754-1815) was a representative from Virginia from 1797 to 1813, and again for a brief period in 1815. He was a supporter of Jefferson.

¹⁵ *Ibid.*, 676, January 8, 1813. Both Matthew and Henry Clay were speaking in favor of a bill to raise an additional military force.

¹⁶ A group of these men and their speeches are cited in Mayo, *Henry Clay*, 349 n. 5.

¹⁷ *Annals of Congress*, 11th Congress, 2nd Session, 2051-2052, 2582-2583.

¹⁸ Madison to Jefferson, May 7, 1810, Madison Papers, vol. XLI.

¹⁹ See Hecksher, *Continental System*, 140.

²⁰ Hamilton to Caesar A. Rodney, May 23, 1810, War of 1812 MSS, Indiana University Library.

²¹ *Ibid.*, July 27, 1810. Hamilton was doubtful that his orders would have any effect. He accused all his naval officers of being Federalists.

²² Clay to Rodney, August 6, 1810, Rodney Papers, Box 2.

²³ See Harrison, *Biographical Directory of the American Congress* (1950), 94-103 ; also Mayo, *Henry Clay*, 360.

²⁴ *American State Papers, Foreign Relations*, III, 386-387.

[25] Madison to Rodney, September 30, 1810, Rodney Papers, Box 2.

[26] Richardson, *Messages and Papers of the Presidents*, I, 481-482.

CHAPTER 11 : THE GROWTH OF OPPOSITION

[1] *Courier*, June 9, 1810.

[2] Wellesley to Foster, April 10, 1811, Mayo, *Instructions to British Ministers*, 317-319.

[3] *Courier*, June 21, 1810.

[4] *Leicester Journal*, March 30, 1810.

[5] Morse to his parents, August 6, 1812, Edward Lind Morse (ed.), *Samuel F. B. Morse, His Letters and Journals* (2 vols., Boston, 1914), I, 81-82.

[6] Pinkney to Madison, October 10, 1807, January 7, 1808, December 10, 1809, Pinkney, *Life of Pinkney*, 190-191, 193-194, 241 ; also Pinkney to Madison, April 25, 1808, Madison Papers, vol. XXXIV.

[7] *Leicester Journal*, May 6, 1808.

[8] *Courier*, August 5, 6, 13, 1808.

[9] *Leicester Journal*, October 21, 1808.

[10] *Ibid.*, November 11, 1808.

[11] *Quarterly Review*, March, 1812, p. 7.

[12] *Gentleman's Magazine* (London), January, 1808, p. 75.

[13] *Cobbett's Political Register*, July 2, 1808, p. 6.

[14] *Courier*, August 22, 1811, also *ibid.*, July 25, 27, August 10, 1811 ; *Leicester Journal*, August 9, 1811.

[15] Baring, *Inquiry into the Causes and Consequences of the Orders in Council*, 19-20.

[16] *Leicester Chronicle*, March 14, 1812.

[17] *Examiner*, November 13, 1808. See also the *Quarterly Review*, November, 1809, pp. 319-337, for an article which attacked every facet of American life. Examples of some of the extreme abuse hurled at the Americans are to be found in *Cobbett's Political Register* for the first half of 1808, *passim.*

[18] James Maury to William Pinkney, July 5, 1809, Consular Letters 2, Liverpool.

[19] Canning to Pinkney, September 23, 1808, *American State Papers, Foreign Relations*, III, 231-232.

[20] *Courier*, November 23, 1808.

[21] Richardson, *Messages and Papers of the Presidents*, I, 481-482.

[22] Hecksher, *Continental System*, 238-247 ; Thomas Tooke, *A History of Prices and the State of Circulation*, 1793-1837 (London, 1838), 303 ff. ; William Smart, *Economic Annals of the Nineteenth Century* (2 vols., London, 1910-1917), I, 227, 254-304 ; Frank O. Darvall, *Popular Disturbances and Public Order in Regency England* (London, 1934), 7-20.

[23] *Annals of Congress*, 11th Congress, 3rd Session, 1338-1339.

[24] See tables in Hecksher, *Continental System*, 245.

[25] Maury to Robert Smith, January 30, 1811, Consular Letters 2, Liverpool ; also *ibid.*, Maury to the Secretary of State, July 15, September 26, 1811 ; Maury to Madison, April 11, 1811, Madison Papers, vol. XLIV.

[26] *Annual Register*, LI (1809), 597 ; *ibid.*, LII (1810), 427 ; *ibid.*, LIII (1811), 271.

[27] See petition from Paisley, May 8, 1811, *Hansard*, XIX, 1017-1018 ; also *ibid.*, 1018-1019, for petition from Lanark, Ayr, and Renfrewshire of the same day.

[28] Petition from Manchester, May 30, 1811, *ibid.*, XX, 339-341 ; see also petition from Bolton on the same day, *ibid.*, 341.

[29] *Ibid.*, 431-437, 608-610, 715, 744-745.

[30] *Examiner*, July 28, 1811.

[31] Thomas Ridout to his father, September 26, November 8, 1811, Lady Edgar, *Ten Years of Upper Canada in Peace and War*, 58-59, 65 ; also *ibid.*, 62-63, October 10, 1811.

[32] Morse to his parents, November 25, December 1, 1811, Morse, *Letters and Journals of Morse*, I, 56.

[33] *Hansard*, XX, 435, June 5.

[34] For the license system see Phillips and Reade, *Neutrality*, II, 158-166 ; Hecksher, *Continental System*, 205-213.

[35] Phillips and Reade, *Neutrality*, II, 159.

[36] (London, 1811) ; *Dropmore Papers*, X, 115-116. Phillimore (1775-1855) had been appointed Regius Professor of Civil Law at Oxford in 1809.

[37] Phillimore, *Reflections on the Licence Trade*, xi.

[38] Wellesley to Jackson, April 14, 1810, Mayo, *Instructions to British Ministers*, 302-303.

[39] Wellesley to John Philip Morier, June 26, 1810, *ibid.*, 303-305.

[40] For the Pinkney-Wellesley correspondence see *American State Papers, Foreign Relations*, III, 365-379, 408-412.

[41] Pinkney to Wellesley, January 14, February 13, 1811, *ibid.*, 411, 413.

[42] Edmund Phipps (ed.), *Memoirs of the Political and Literary Life of Robert Plumer Ward, Esq.* (2 vols., London, 1850), I, 373, February 2, 1811.

[43] Jefferson to Madison, March 8, 1811, Madison to Jefferson, March 18, 1811, Madison Papers, vol. XLIV.

[44] Rodney Papers, Box 2.

[45] For events at the end of 1810 and the beginning of 1811 see Roberts, *The Whig Party*, 1807-1812, 359-371 ; Fremantle, *England in the Nineteenth Century*, 1806-1810, 279 ff.

[46] Wellesley to Pinkney, February 15, 1811, *American State Papers, Foreign Relations*, III, 413.

[47] Adams, *History of the United States*, VI, 18-19.

[48] See above p. 49.

[49] Foster to Lady Elizabeth Foster, September 22, 1805, Foster, *Two Duchesses*, 239-240.

[50] Elizabeth, Duchess of Devonshire to Augustus Foster, February 15, 1811, the Prince Regent to Elizabeth, Duchess of Devonshire, February 14, 1811, *ibid.*, 347-349.

CHAPTER 12 : CRISIS IN THE NORTHWEST

[1] See above pp. 158-167.

[2] Elliott to Claus, October 16, November 16, 1810, and Speech of Tecumseh, November 15, 1810, Transcripts of Colonial Office Records, Series *Q*, vol. 114, Public Archives of Canada.

[3] See Augustus Foster to James Monroe, December 28, 1811, William R. Manning (ed.), *Diplomatic Correspondence of the United States : Canadian Relations*, 1784-1860 (4 vols., Washington, 1940-1945), I, 608-609. See also Foster to Monroe, June 7, 1812, *ibid.*, 612-613.

[4] Craig to Gore, February 2, 1811, Q 114.

[5] See Craig to David M. Erskine, June 2, 1808, Dispatches to the British Minister at Washington, vol. I. From the Governor-in-chief of Canada, 1798-1816, Public Archives of Canada, transcripts in the Library of Congress.

[6] Craig replied to Gore on February 2, 1811, Q 114, and Gore wrote to Claus on February 26, *ibid.*

[7] Elliott to Claus, November 16, 1810, *ibid.*

[8] Brock to Craig, February 27, 1811, Tupper, *Life and Correspondence of Brock*, 94-96. Brock, who had been in Canada since 1802, became a major-general in June, 1811, and in October, after the departure of Francis Gore for England, he was given complete command in Upper Canada.

[9] McLean to Green, August 27, 1799, *Michigan Pioneer and Historical Collections*, XII, 305.

[10] McLean to Green, September 14, October 9, 1797, *ibid.*, XX, 535-539, 554-555 ; also " Remarks Submitted to the Commander in Chief relating to the Indian Department," November 10, 1797, *ibid.*, 571-574.

[11] Craig to Brock, February 4, 1811, David B. Read, *Life and Times of Major-General Sir Isaac Brock, K.B.* (Toronto, 1894), 69-70.

[12] Brock to Taylor, March 4, 1811, Tupper, *Life and Correspondence of Brock*, 96-98.

[13] See Draper MSS, 4YY *passim*, for Tecumseh's visit to the southern tribes ; also Drake, *The Life of Tecumseh*, 144.

[14] Craig resigned his position on November 23, 1810, because of ill-health, Craig to Liverpool, November 23, 1810, *Report on Canadian*

Archives, 1893, p. 44, but he did not actually leave for England until June, 1811, Dunn to Liverpool, June 20, 1811, *ibid.*, 48.

[15] See *Michigan Pioneer and Historical Collections*, XV, 54-61, 63-66, 68-83, 85-87. See also Tupper, *Life and Correspondence of Brock*, 147-178, for information on Brock's energetic preparations for war.

[16] Brock to Prevost, December 2, 1811, Tupper, *Life and Correspondence of Brock*, 123-130.

[17] Prevost to Brock, December 24, 1811, *ibid.*, 133-135 ; cf. Craig to Gore, December 6, 1807, *Report on Canadian Archives*, 1896, Note B, 30-32.

[18] Ernest A. Cruikshank, " The Employment of Indians in the War of 1812," American Historical Association, *Annual Report*, 1895 (Washington, 1896), 324.

[19] See Wayne E. Stevens, *The Northwest Fur Trade*, 1763-1800 (Urbana, 1928), 109 ; Clarence W. Alvord, *The Illinois Country*, 1673-1818 (Springfield, Illinois, 1920), 400-401. The best account of the American pressure after 1803 is to be found in Louise P. Kellogg, *The British Regime in Wisconsin and the Northwest* (Madison, 1935), 248 ff. A dispute over the application of Jay's Treaty to the Louisiana territory caused a delay in the signing of the unratified Monroe-Pinkney treaty in 1806, see Manning, *Diplomatic Correspondence of the United States : Canadian Relations*, I, 585-587.

[20] Manning, *Diplomatic Correspondence of the United States : Canadian Relations*, I, 574, August 26, 1805 ; also Louis A. Tohill, " Robert Dickson, British Fur Trader on the Upper Mississippi," *North Dakota Historical Quarterly*, III (1928-1929), 33-34.

[21] Mayo, *Instructions to British Ministers*, 229 n. 4, 253-254 ; Manning, *Diplomatic Correspondence of the United States : Canadian Relations*, I, 571-579, 581, 601-605 ; *Michigan Pioneer and Historical Collections*, XV, 50, XXV, 241, 250-257.

[22] Hiram M. Chittenden, *The American Fur Trade of the Far West* (3 vols., New York, 1902), I, 113-127, 140, 159 ; Kenneth W. Porter, *John Jacob Astor* (2 vols., Cambridge, Mass., 1931), I, 251.

[23] Ora B. Peake, *A History of the United States Indian Factory System*, 1795-1822 (Denver, 1954). 19.

[24] Kellogg, *The British Regime in Wisconsin*, 255-256, 259 ; Wayne E. Stevens, "Fur Trading Companies in the Northwest, 1760-1816," Mississippi Valley Historical Association, *Proceedings*, IX (1918), 287-288, 290 ; William S. Wallace (ed.), *Documents Relating to the Northwest Company* (Toronto, 1934), 224-229 ; Donald G. Creighton, *The Commercial Empire of the St. Lawrence* (Toronto, 1937), 167-168 ; Porter, *John Jacob Astor*, I, 253-255, II, 461-469.

[25] Ernest A. Cruikshank, " Robert Dickson, the Indian Trader," *Collections of the State Historical Society of Wisconsin* (31 vols., Madison, 1854-1931), XII (1892), 136-137 ; Tohill, "Robert Dickson," *North Dakota Historical Quarterly*, III, 37 ff.

[26] Doane Robinson, " South Dakota and the War of 1812," *South Dakota Historical Collections*, XII (1924), 85.

[27] Josiah Dunham to William Clark, August 20, 1807, Clarence E. Carter (ed.), *The Territorial Papers of the United States*, vol. X, *The Territory of Michigan*, 1805-1820 (Washington, 1942), 127. See also Nicholas Boilvin to William Eustis, February 2, 1811, *Wisconsin Historical Collections*, XIX (1910), 247-251.

[28] For attempts of the Canadian traders to check the first efforts of the St. Louis traders to enter the upper Louisiana country see Tohill, "Robert Dickson," *North Dakota Historical Quarterly*, III, 20.

[29] "Some account of the Fur trade Carried on by the Northwest Company (1809)," in *Report on Canadian Archives*, 1928, Appendix E, 56-73.

[30] *Ibid.*, 58, 62, 64, 69.

[31] Gray to Prevost, January 13, 1812, *Michigan Pioneer and Historical Collections*, XV, 70-72.

[32] Memoranda from the North West and Michilimackinac Companies, January 13, 31, 1812, *ibid.*, 68-69.

[33] Brock to Edward Baynes, February 12, 1812, Read, *Life and Times of Brock*, 93.

[34] Ernest A. Cruikshank, "The Military Career and Character of Major-General Sir Isaac Brock," New York State Historical Association, *Proceedings*, VIII (1909), 73.

[35] Statement of Robert Dickson, December 3, 1812, William H. Wood (ed.), *Select British Documents of the Canadian War of* 1812 (4 vols., Toronto, 1920-1928), I, 426-427.

[36] Confidential Letter to Dickson, February 27, 1812, *ibid.*, 423.

[37] *Ibid.*, 424 ; John B. Glegg to Baynes, November 11, 1812, *ibid.*, 421.

[38] Prevost to Lord Liverpool, January 13, 1812, *Michigan Pioneer and Historical Collections*, XXV, 291 ; see also Manning, *Diplomatic Correspondence of the United States : Canadian Relations*, I, 613 n.

[39] Brock to Prevost, February 25, 1812, Wood, *Select British Documents*, I, 169-171.

[40] Baynes to Brock, March 19, 1812, Tupper, *Life and Correspondence of Brock*, 159-161.

[41] Prevost to Brock, April 30, 1812, *ibid.*, 171-172 ; Prevost to Brock, March 31, 1812, *Report on Canadian Archives*, 1896, Note B, 67-68 ; Brock to Prevost, May 15, 1812, *Michigan Pioneer and Historical Collections*, XV, 85-86 ; Brock to Liverpool, May 25, 1812, Bickley, *Report on the MSS of Earl Bathurst*, 174-175.

[42] Thomas G. Ridout to his father, May 23, 1812, Lady Edgar, *Ten Years of Upper Canada in Peace and War*, 114.

[43] B. F. Stickney to the Secretary of War, June 7, 1812, Letter Book of the Fort Wayne Indian Agency, William L. Clements Library, University of Michigan, 91.

CHAPTER 13 : THE WAR HAWKS

[1] Adams, *History of the United States*, V, 317.

[2] *Annals of Congress*, 11th Congress, 3rd Session, 55-64, December 28, 1810. The effect of this speech on the country is discussed in Mayo, *Henry Clay*, 365-369.

[3] *Annals of Congress*, 11th Congress, 3rd Session, 1094-1096.

[4] *Ibid.*, 1035.

[5] *Ibid.*, 1034. Joseph Desha of Kentucky also voted for this measure, *ibid.*, 1035.

[6] *Ibid.*, 884.

[7] *Ibid.*, 358. It passed the Senate on March 1.

[8] Madison to Jefferson, April 19, 1811, Madison Papers, vol. XLIV.

[9] Adams, *History of the United States*, VI, 25-26.

[10] *Ibid.*, 26-37, for a discussion of the incident, and of the dispute that arose as to who fired the first shot.

[11] *Courier*, July 17, 1811.

[12] Wellesley to Foster, April 10, 1811, Mayo, *Instructions to British Ministers*, 318-319.

[13] "Part of a Journal in the United States of America, 1811-1812," Augustus John Foster Papers, Library of Congress, 18.

[14] For these somewhat tedious negotiations see *American State Papers, Foreign Relations*, III, 435-462, 468-470.

[15] Julius W. Pratt, "James Monroe," in Bemis (ed.), *American Secretaries of State*, III, 219-221.

[16] Lyon to Monroe, September 26, 1811, Monroe Papers, vol. XVIII.

[17] A. Butler to Andrew Jackson, October 12, 1811, Andrew Jackson Papers, Library of Congress, vol. IX. The *Guerrière* was one of the British ships interfering with American shipping off the American coast in 1811.

[18] See Pratt, *Expansionists of 1812*, *passim*, for the best statement of the importance of the Indian problem in producing the war. See Burt, *United States, Great Britain*, 305-310, for an opposing viewpoint.

[19] See debates of the Twelfth Congress *passim*, especially those of December, 1811 ; also Carter, *The Territorial Papers of the United States*, VIII, *The Territory of Indiana*, 1810-1816 (Washington, 1939) ; X, *The Territory of Michigan*, 1805-1820 ; XIV, *The Territory of Louisiana-Missouri*, 1806-1814 (Washington, 1949).

[20] Logan Esarey (ed.), *Messages and Letters of William Henry Harrison* (2 vols., Indianapolis, 1922) ; this is Volume VII and IX of the Indiana Historical *Collections*.

[21] *Ibid.*, I, 541.

[22] *Kentucky Gazette*, August 27, 1811, quoted in Ellery L. Hall, "Canadian Annexation Sentiment in Kentucky Prior to the War of 1812," *Register of the Kentucky State Historical Society*, XXVIII (1930), 375.

[23] *Annals of Congress*, 12th Congress, 1st Session, 425-426 ; Jackson to William Henry Harrison, November 30, 1811, John Spencer Bassett (ed.), *The Correspondence of Andrew Jackson* (6 vols., Washington, 1926-1933), I, 210.

[24] See *Annals of Congress*, 12th Congress, 1st Session, 1637, for list of voters. There is an analysis of the vote for war in Paullin and Wright, *Atlas of the Historical Geography of the United States*, 109.

[25] Ages of some of the War Hawks when Congress met : William Lowndes, 29 ; John C. Calhoun, 29 ; George M. Troup, 31 ; Israel Pickens, 31 ; Henry Clay, 34 ; Felix Grundy, 34 ; Langdon Cheves, 36. See Harrison, *Biographical Directory of the American Congress*.

[26] *Annals of Congress*, 12th Congress, 1st Session, 330, November 4.

[27] Richardson, *Messages and Papers of the Presidents*, I, 494.

[28] Madison to John Quincy Adams, November 15, 1811, Madison Papers, vol. XLVI ; see also *ibid.*, Madison to Joel Barlow, November 17, 1811.

[29] *Annals of Congress*, 12th Congress, 1st Session, 333 ; Mayo, *Henry Clay*, 410 ; Glyndon Van Deusen, *The Life of Henry Clay* (Boston, 1937), 79.

[30] *Annals of Congress*, 12th Congress, 1st Session, 342-343.

[31] Grundy to Jackson, November 28, 1811, Jackson Papers, vol. IX.

[32] *Annals of Congress*, 12th Congress, 1st Session, 373-377.

[33] *Ibid.*, 414.

[34] *Ibid.*, 415-417.

[35] *Ibid.*, 599-601.

[36] *Ibid.*, 11th Congress, 2nd Session, 1869.

[37] *Ibid.*, 12th Congress, 1st Session, 457.

[38] *Ibid.*, 424.

[39] *Ibid.*, 483-490.

[40] *Iibid.*, 637.

[41] *Ibid.*, 470, December 11, 1811.

[42] *Ibid.*, 807. For a discussion of the opposition to this enlarged naval force see below pp. 240-241.

[43] *Ibid.*, 482, December 12, 1811.

[44] *Ibid.*, 533, December 16, 1811. See Pratt, *Expansionists of 1812*, 143 ; Hacker, "Western Land Hunger," *Mississippi Valley Historical Review*, X, 376.

[45] *Annals of Congress*, 12th Congress, 1st Session, 521.

[46] *Ibid.*, 623.

[47] Mayo, *Henry Clay*, 382-383.

[48] *Reporter* (Lexington, Kentucky), December 10, 1811, quoted in Taylor, "Agrarian Discontent in the Mississippi Valley," *Journal of Political Economy*, XXXIX, 500.

[49] Carter, *The Territorial Papers of the United States*, VI, *The Territory of Mississippi*, 1809-1817 (Washington, 1938), 226-227, 238-240, 241-242.

⁵⁰ *Ibid.*, 239.
⁵¹ Resolution of the General Assembly of the State of Ohio, December 26, 1811, transmitted in R. J. Meigs to Madison, January 1, 1812, Madison Papers, vol. XLVI.
⁵² Bassett, *Correspondence of Andrew Jackson*, I, 221-222.
⁵³ *Annals of Congress*, 12th Congress, 1st Session, 481.
⁵⁴ *Ibid.*, 519.
⁵⁵ *Ibid.*, 646, January 4, 1812.
⁵⁶ *Ibid.*, 663, January 4, 1812.

CHAPTER 14 : AMERICA GOES TO WAR

¹ *Annals of Congress*, 12th Congress, 1st Session, 377, 545-548, 565-566 ; see also Adams, *History of the United States*, VI, 146.
² *Annals of Congress*, 12th Congress, 1st Session, 29-30, 35-54, 84.
³ Grundy to Jackson, December 24, 1811, Jackson Papers, vol. IX.
⁴ *Ibid.*
⁵ *Ibid.*, George Washington Campbell to Jackson, December 24, 1811.
⁶ *Annals of Congress*, 12th Congress, 1st Session, 596-602.
⁷ *Ibid.*, 691 ; the bill passed by a vote of 94 to 34.
⁸ *Ibid.*, 96.
⁹ *Ibid.*, 97, 717-718, 2229-2234.
¹⁰ *Ibid.*, 583.
¹¹ *Ibid.*, 782-800.
¹² *Ibid.*, 800-801.
¹³ Madison Papers, vol. XLVI.
¹⁴ Grundy to Jackson, February 12, 1812, Jackson Papers, vol. IX.
¹⁵ *Annals of Congress*, 12th Congress, 1st Session, 803-823.
¹⁶ *Ibid.*, 910-928.
¹⁷ *Ibid.*, 999.
¹⁸ Grundy to Jackson, February 12, 1812, Jackson Papers, vol. IX.
¹⁹ *Annals of Congress*, 12th Congress, 1st Session, 1050-1056.
²⁰ *Ibid.*, 1092-1155.
²¹ Madison to Jefferson, March, 1812, Madison Papers, vol. XLVII.
²² Hamilton to Caesar A. Rodney, March 8, 1812, War of 1812 MSS, Indiana University Library. Irving Brant, *James Madison : The President, 1809-1812* (Indianapolis, 1956), stresses the importance of Madison in the coming of the war.
²³ A discussion of Henry's activities, heavily documented, is found in Ernest A. Cruikshank, *Political Adventures of John Henry* (Toronto, 1936).
²⁴ Richardson, *Messages and Papers of the Presidents*, I, 498.
²⁵ Clay to Monroe, March 15, 1812, Monroe Papers, vol. XVIII.
²⁶ Jefferson to Madison, March 26, 1812, Madison Papers, vol. XLVII.
²⁷ Foster Journal, 1811-1812, p. 34, Foster Papers.

[28] Richardson, *Messages and Papers of the Presidents*, I, 499 ; Mayo, *Henry Clay*, 498-499.

[29] Foster Journal, 1811-1812, p. 37, April 1, Foster Papers.

[30] *Annals of Congress*, 12th Congress, 1st Session, 1587-1589, 1598.

[31] *Ibid.*, 187-190, 1614, 2262-2264.

[32] Madison Papers, vol. XLVII.

[33] Jackson Papers, vol. IX.

[34] Foster Journal, 1811-1812, pp. 43-44, Foster Papers. Two days later Foster added, " Calhoun very violent—just from College," *ibid.*, 46, April 17.

[35] Madison Papers, vol. XLVII.

[36] Brougham, *Memoirs*, II, 8.

[37] Brougham to Joseph Walker, March 6, 1812, *ibid.*, 8-11.

[38] *Hansard*, XXI, 685-686, 762-801, 825-826, 1041-1074.

[39] See Phipps, *Memoirs of Plumer Ward*, I, 439-441 ; also Walpole, *Spencer Perceval*, II, 293.

[40] *Hansard*, XXI, 1163.

[41] Phipps, *Memoirs of Plumer Ward*, I, 450-451. The vote is in *Hansard*, XXI, 1163-1164.

[42] Brougham to Thorneley, March 4, 1812, Brougham, *Memoirs*, II, 13.

[43] *Minutes of Evidence Taken before the Committee of the Whole House, to whom it was referred to consider of the several Petitions which had been Presented to the House, in this Session of Parliament, Relating to the Orders in Council* (London, 1812), 152-156. Ebeneezer Rhodes of Sheffield gave details about a duplicated copy of a letter from Brougham to Thomas Attwood, High Bailiff of Birmingham, which had been read at a meeting called in Sheffield to petition against the Orders in Council.

[44] See *Edinburgh Review*, February, 1812, pp. 291 ff. ; also *Morning Chronicle*, January-June, 1812, *passim*.

[45] Joseph Phillimore, *A Letter Addressed to a Member of the Commons on the Subject of the Notice given by Mr. Brougham for a Motion Respecting the Orders in Council and the Licence Trade* (London, 1812), 50 ; see also Anonymous, *Conciliation with America the true Policy of Great Britain* (London, 1812), which discussed the great importance of the American market.

[46] Petition from Birmingham, April 17, from Walsall, April 27, *Journals of the House of Commons*, LXVII (1812), 285, 321.

[47] Petitions from the manufacturers in the Staffordshire potteries, April 14, June 15 ; from the Journeymen-Potters, May 11, *ibid.*, 266, 427, 372.

[48] *Hansard*, XXII, 1-2, March 17.

[49] Petition from Worcester, June 5, from Shrewsbury, May 15, *Journals of the House of Commons*, LXVII (1812), 412, 381.

[50] *Ibid.*, 285, April 17, Sheffield.

[51] *Ibid.*, 266, April 14, West Riding.

[52] Petition from Blackburn, March 20, from Chorley, May 4, and from Chow Bent, May 13, *ibid.*, 216, 348, 374-375.

[53] *Ibid.*, 216, Blackburn.

[54] *Ibid.*, 320-321, April 27, 807-808, May 5, Liverpool.

[55] Petitions from Glasgow, April 24, May 21, from Dunfermline, May 20, from Paisley, May 20, *ibid.*, 317, 390, 385-386.

[56] *Hansard*, XXII, 1112.

[57] *Ibid.*, 107, 245-246, 410-418, 425-440, 500-502, 853-856, 1041-1042, 1058-1064.

[58] Thomas Ridout to his father, April 17, 1812, Lady Edgar, *Ten Years of Upper Canada in Peace and War*, 108-109 ; also James Maury to Monroe, April 22, 1812, Consular Letters 3, Liverpool ; Darvall, *Popular Disturbances and Public Order in Regency England*, 93-101, 114-118.

[59] Phipps, *Memoirs of Plumer Ward*, I, 478.

[60] *Ibid.*, 477, April 11, 1812.

[61] *Hansard*, XXII, 1104. The debate is in *ibid.*, 1092-1112.

[62] *Minutes of Evidence Taken before the Committee of the Whole House, to whom it was referred to consider of the several Petitions which had been presented to the House, in this Session of Parliament, Relating to the Orders in Council* (London, 1812).

[63] *Hansard*, XXII, 430, April 17, 1812.

[64] *Minutes of Evidence Relating to the Orders in Council*, 20-21, 28, 136, 162.

[65] *Ibid.*, 16, 24, 67, 101, 165, 235, 434, 478-479.

[66] *Ibid.*, 90, 97.

[67] Reference to the growth of American manufactures frequently appeared in British newspapers and journals, see *Aris' Birmingham Gazette*, March 11, 1811 ; *Cobbett's Political Register*, March 6, September 14, 1811 ; *Examiner*, January 6, 1811 ; *Gentleman's Magazine*, January, 1809, p. 79, August, 1810, p. 175. The general fear was increased by reports that agents were being employed by persons in the United States to persuade British artisans to emigrate to that country, and to attempt to export machinery used in British manufacturing, see *Courier*, September 29, 1809, October 22, 1811 ; *Aris' Birmingham Gazette*, November 18, 1811.

[68] *Minutes of Evidence Relating to the Orders in Council*, 1812, pp. 440-454. Various British manufacturers also expressed the fear that they would suffer from American manufacturing competition, *ibid.*, 5, 8, 25, 33, 51, 54, 58, 91, 138, 169, 284.

[69] Petitions came into Parliament from the shipowners of London, Sunderland, and North Shields, on May 14 ; from South Shields on May 20 ; and from Scarborough and the "Merchant Venturers" of Bristol on May 25, *Journals of the House of Commons*, LXVII (1812), 377-378, 386, 395-396. In addition Tory groups in some towns that had petitioned against the Orders tried to redress the balance by petitioning

in favor of them ; petitions came from Blackburn on April 7, from Glasgow on April 24 and May 15, and from Liverpool on May 13, *ibid.*, 237, 318, 375, 381. However, significant of the extent to which the importance of the United States had been impressed upon British opinion was the fact that the group in Blackburn, in spite of petitioning in favor of the Orders, asked that every effort should be made to cultivate a friendly understanding with the United States, *ibid.*, 237.

[70] *Minutes of Evidence Relating to the Orders in Council*, 1812, pp. 375-395, 396-423, 481-483.

[71] *Ibid.*, *passim*, especially 396-423, 511-514, 655-658, 663-667.

[72] *American State Papers, Foreign Relations*, III, 435 ff. ; also Adams, *History of the United States*, VI, 189 ff.

[73] See Myron F. Brightfield, *John Wilson Croker* (London, 1940), 79-80.

[74] *A Key to the Orders in Council*, 16.

[75] *Ibid.*, 17.

[76] *Ibid.*, 18.

[77] Mayo, *Instructions to British Ministers*, 368. Castlereagh became Foreign Secretary in February, 1812, after the resignation of Wellesley.

[78] Castlereagh to Foster, April 10, 21, 1812, *ibid.*, 366-367, 372 ; *American State Papers, Foreign Relations*, III, 429-432.

[79] *Leicester Journal*, May 15, 1812.

[80] *Morning Chronicle*, May 15, 1812.

[81] Thomas Ridout to his brother, June 1, 1812, Lady Edgar, *Ten Years of Upper Canada in Peace and War*, 118-119.

[82] See Roberts, *The Whig Party, 1807-1812*, 382-404.

[83] Brougham, *Memoirs*, II, 16, 19 ; Stavordale (ed.), *Further Memoirs of the Whig Party by Lord Holland*, 132.

[84] *Hansard*, XXIII, 486-522 (Brougham), 537-542, 545 (Castlereagh).

[85] Wilberforce, *Life of William Wilberforce*, IV, 35, diary for June 11, 1812 ; also Stavordale (ed.), *Further Memoirs of the Whig Party by Lord Holland*, 158-159 ; *American State Papers, Foreign Relations*, III, 433.

[86] See Castlereagh to Foster, June 17, 1812, Mayo, *Instructions to British Ministers*, 381-383.

[87] This French decree had been completely unknown until this time, see Hecksher, *Continental System*, 144-145 ; Melvin, *Napoleon's Navigation System*, 320-322 ; *American State Papers, Foreign Relations*, III, 602-603.

[88] Wilberforce, *Life of Wilberforce*, IV, 35, diary for June 24, 1812.

[89] *Leicester Chronicle*, July 4, 1812 ; also the *Courier*, June 22, 1812, and the *Times*, June 23, 1812, which gave extracts from the *Leeds Mercury*, the *Stafford Advertiser*, and the *Sheffield Mercury*, concerning rejoicing in the areas served by those papers.

[90] *Aris' Birmingham Gazette*, July 6, 1812.

[91] See *ibid.*, June 29, July 6, 13, 1812 ; *Leicester Chronicle*, July 18, 25, 1812; *Examiner*, September 13, 1812; also Brougham, *Memoirs*, II, 29-34.

[92] Foster to Elizabeth, Duchess of Devonshire, April 18, 1812, Foster, *Two Duchesses*, 360.

[93] Foster to Castlereagh, April 23, 1812, F.O. 5 : 85, quoted in Burt, *United States, Great Britain*, 298.

[94] Foster Journal, 1811-1812, p. 75, Foster Papers ; see also *ibid.*, 52 (April 22), 61 (May 1), 69 (May 13), 81-82 (May 19), 87 (May 24).

[95] Foster to Elizabeth, Duchess of Devonshire, May 26, 1812, Foster, *Two Duchesses*, 365.

[96] George M. Bibb to Henry Clay, May 24, 1812, Henry Clay Papers, Library of Congress, vol. 1 ; Foster Journal, 1811-1812, p. 85, May 22, Foster Papers ; Madison to Jefferson, May 25, 1812, Madison Papers, vol. XLVIII.

[97] Richardson, *Messages and Papers of the Presidents*, I, 499-505.

[98] *Annals of Congress*, 12th Congress, 1st Session, 1630-1633.

[99] *Ibid.*, 1637-1638.

[100] For a breakdown of the House vote see Appendix.

[101] *Annals of Congress*, 12th Congress, 1st Session, 296-298.

Index